"On My Way"

The Untold Story of Rouben Mamoulian, George Gershwin, and *Porgy and Bess*

JOSEPH HOROWITZ

W. W. NORTON & COMPANY
New York   London

Since this page cannot legibly accommodate all the copyright notices, page 257 constitutes
an exension of the copyright page.

For information about permission to reproduce selections from this book,
write to Permissions, W. W. Norton & Company, Inc.,
500 Fifth Avenue, New York, NY 10110

For information about special discounts for bulk purchases, please contact
W. W. Norton Special Sales at specialsales@wwnorton.com or 800-233-4830

Manufacturing by RR Donnelley, Harrisonburg, VA
Book design by Dana Sloan
Production manager: Anna Oler

Library of Congress Cataloging-in-Publication Data

Horowitz, Joseph, 1948–
"On my way" : the untold story of Rouben Mamoulian, George Gershwin, and Porgy and
Bess / Joseph Horowitz. — First edition.
pages cm
Includes bibliographical references and index.
ISBN 978-0-393-24013-9 (hardcover)
1. Gershwin, George, 1898–1937. Porgy and Bess. 2. Heyward, DuBose, 1885–1940.
Porgy. 3. Mamoulian, Rouben—Criticism and interpretation. I. Title.
ML410.G288H67 2013
782.1—dc23
2013013748

W. W. Norton & Company, Inc.
500 Fifth Avenue, New York, N.Y. 10110
www.wwnorton.com

W. W. Norton & Company Ltd.
Castle House, 75/76 Wells Street, London W1T 3QT

1 2 3 4 5 6 7 8 9 0

For Bernie and Maggie

CONTENTS

———— ❧ ————

What I'd seen of American burlesque, vaudeville, singing and dancing struck me so forcefully. . . . They have contributed a great deal to this country. . . . And I thought how odd it was that in America there was no indigenous theatrical form. What you had was grand opera and that [is] a European tradition. Viennese operetta is the same. You had the so-called musical comedy. . . . A girl would break into song and deliver it to the audience. Then there would be a dance specialty. It was strung together very loosely. So I thought there was a possibility here of a new style of stage production which would integrate all the elements. That would be a tremendously powerful theatrical medium.

—ROUBEN MAMOULIAN (1973)

Have you read the reviews of *Porgy and Bess*? Did you notice how patronizing the critics were to George Gershwin? They kept asking, "What is this? It's not an opera. It's not this, it's not that." It took those bastards five years to realize that [it] was the greatest single contribution to the American musical theater.

—ROUBEN MAMOULIAN (1973)

I have created a new form.

—GEORGE GERSHWIN ON *PORGY AND BESS* (1935)

PREFACE

A COUPLE OF YEARS AGO I boasted to a colleague that I could encapsulate the history of classical music in the United States in one name and a half. I proceeded to write:

$$DVOŘÁK \rightarrow GERSH/$$

The colleague—who happened to be Richard Crawford, then as now embarked on what is certain to be a landmark biography of George Gershwin—laughed not incredulously but knowingly. Rich is long familiar with my passions and idiosyncrasies as a musical scholar.

In *Classical Music in America: A History* (2005), I called American classical music a "mutant high culture." Normal musical high cultures are founded on a native canon. But American orchestras and opera companies are Eurocentric in repertoire; no native canon of sufficient consequence materialized. Instead, classical music in the United States ultimately gravitated to—my terminology—a "culture of performance."

One reason the story of classical music in America peaks before World War I is that the eventual emergence of a native canon was then taken for granted—and the compositional ferment of those *fin-de-siècle* decades produced, in the person of Charles Ives, one of the two great creative talents in the annals of American art music. The other reason is that the turn of the twentieth century was a period of phenomenal institutional growth and attendant heroic personal vision. I here refer to people like Theodore Thomas, Henry Higginson, Jeannette Thurber, Antonín Dvořák, Anton Seidl, Laura Langford, and Oscar Hammerstein, and to institutions like the Thomas Orchestra, the Boston Symphony, the Chicago Orchestra, the National Conservatory of Music, the Seidl Society, and the Manhattan Opera. Dvořák, as director of Thurber's National Conservatory, was the influential (and controversial) central embodiment of the aspiration to produce an American canon; he also—presciently, ardently—prophesied that an American "school of music" would be founded upon "negro melodies."

After World War I, the creative impulse in American music migrated to jazz. American concert composers took a back seat to Ellington and Armstrong, and to famous orchestras, conductors, and instrumentalists. Some would say that Aaron Copland was a front-seat occupant, but this is wishful thinking. The composer in the front seat was the one composer of genius who could mediate between the high culture of performance and a popular musical culture in which creativity and performance were never severed from one another. That composer—alongside Ives, the second great creative talent to buoy American art music—was of course George Gershwin.

Gershwin lived barely long enough to produce an operatic masterpiece: *Porgy and Bess*. Then, in 1937 at the age of thirty-eight, he died of a brain tumor. Had he enjoyed a normal span of years, the course of American music would have changed. More than anyone else, he commanded the talent to heal the schism between what had become (as the present book emphasizes) mutually estranged worlds of American music. Hence: Dvořák → Gersh/.

My obsession with the late Gilded Age is partly a product of my life-long obsession with Wagner—on both sides of the Atlantic, this was the time for Wagnerism. Wagner has doubtless been more written about than any other composer in Western history. It was my good fortune to discover the story of Seidl and Langford's Seidl Society as central catalysts for American Wagnerism, and so produce a Wagner book with something new to say: *Wagner Nights: An American History* (1994).

Gershwin, for decades, was little written about by scholars. That is changing now, and fast. That I would also stumble on something new to say about him was, again, a stroke of luck. But I did have the advantage of an educated guess. Everything I knew about Rouben Mamoulian, who directed the premiere of *Porgy and Bess* in 1935, told me that Mamoulian had to have been a major creative force in fashioning Gershwin's opera, not least because he had previously directed the play *Porgy* in 1927. So when the Mamoulian archive opened at the Library of Congress in 2009, I went looking for evidence. It turned up quickly. My basic discovery was that all published versions of the play *Porgy* did not represent the *Porgy* that Mamoulian directed, and that Gershwin saw and knew. The final script, never published, was full of Mamoulian touches that foretold Gershwin's opera. That became the starting point for the present book—and also for a talk, " 'Bring My Goat!'—The Untold Story of Rouben Mamoulian's Contributions to *Porgy and Bess*," delivered at the Society for American Music conference in Little Rock on March 7, 2013: my first announcement of my Mamoulian-Gershwin findings.

Jeff Magee, having read my Mamoulian chapter in *Artists in Exile* (2008), was the person who nudged me to write a Mamoulian book. Rich Crawford, as ever, informed my work and calmed me down when needed. Wayne Shirley, whose scholarly edition of *Porgy and Bess* all Gershwinites eagerly await, and who knows more about *Porgy and Bess* than any other living human being, was even more invaluable to my research than on many previous occasions. Bob Kimball and Howard Pollack helped with advice and assistance. Solomon Volkov supplied a couple of essential Russian books about Vakhtangov.

The world of Mamoulian scholarship is tiny. The sole extant biography, by Mark Spergel, is admirably acute given the paucity of information readily accessible prior to the advent of the Mamoulian archives.

Mark generously shared his knowledge and also various Mamoulian papers in his possession. Miles Kreuger, who knew Mamoulian, and André Previn, who worked with Mamoulian, shared keen memories. Seta Tchekmedyian put me in touch with Archbishop Vatché Hovsepian and Osheen Keshishian—part of Mamoulian's Armenian community in Los Angeles. Kurt Jensen, working on what will be an important Mamoulian biography, collegially advised me of discoveries I had overlooked and graciously fact-checked my manuscript.

My thanks to Maribeth Payne and Ariella Foss, at W. W. Norton, for believing in this book's potential to reach a wide audience. Fred Wiemer was an exemplary copy editor. Arielle Datz created the musical examples. As ever, my agent, Elizabeth Kaplan, my wife, Agnes, and my children, Bernie and Maggie, put up with my various writer's demands, no matter how tedious or unpredictable.

"On My Way"

MAMOULIAN, GERSHWIN, AND CULTURAL FLUIDITY

AT THE CLOSE of George Gershwin's *Porgy and Bess*, Porgy—a crippled beggar who ambulates on a cart pulled by a goat—learns that Bess, whom he loves, has left for New York. Porgy is in Charleston, South Carolina, and New York is far away—but he will somehow get there. "Bring my goat!" he says. When this request is met with stupefaction, he repeats it emphatically. The goat is brought. Porgy mounts his cart. He leads the community in an ecstatic final song:

> Oh Lawd,
> I'm on my way.
> I'm on my way
> To a Heav'nly Lan',
> I'll ride dat long, long road.
> If You are there
> To guide my han'.

Porgy's startling decision is equally a declaration of character. Stephen Sondheim has called "Bring my goat!" "one of the most moving

moments in musical theater history." Wayne Shirley, the editor of a
forthcoming critical edition of *Porgy and Bess*, thinks "Bring my goat!"
may be the "best line in the opera."[1] Until now, it was assumed that
DuBose Heyward, Gershwin's librettist, wrote these three words. In
fact, "Bring my goat!" was belatedly added to *Porgy*, the play, eight years
earlier by the director of that production—who would also direct *Porgy
and Bess*. And the same is true of "Oh Lawd, I'm On My Way." *Porgy and
Bess* as we know it would be unthinkable without the contributions of
Rouben Mamoulian.

    I discovered Mamoulian when writing a book: *Artists in Exile: How
Refugees from Twentieth-Century War and Revolution Transformed the American Performing Arts* (2008). A forgotten hero of American musical theater, he directed *Porgy and Bess, Oklahoma!* (1943), and *Carousel* (1945)—
Broadway landmarks embodying Mamoulian's signature high integration of music and drama, a feat ignited by early exposure to Russian
experimental theater. In Hollywood, Mamoulian directed the most
restlessly creative of all interwar screen musicals: *Love Me Tonight* (1932),
with Maurice Chevalier and Jeanette MacDonald, and a score by Rodgers and Hart. Absorbing the magnitude of Mamoulian's gift, and the
tenacity with which he inflicted it, I realized that his creative input into
Porgy and Bess could only be formidable—not least because he had earlier directed the phenomenally successful 1927 Broadway play *Porgy*, by
Heyward and his wife Dorothy.

    In the Mamoulian archive at the Library of Congress—a copious
depository of letters, articles, clippings, scores, scripts, photographs, diaries, and private "Jottings" only catalogued in 2009—I found a smok-
ing gun: a final revised script for *Porgy*, never published, with revisions
in Mamoulian's hand. Mamoulian's emendations included "Bring m'
goat!" It turns out that, unknown to Gershwin scholars, the Heywards'
published *Porgy* script was superseded by a later version incorporating fundamental changes initiated by Mamoulian. More than anyone
else—more than DuBose or Dorothy Heyward, more than George

or Ira Gershwin—it was Mamoulian who transformed DuBose Heyward's 1925 novella *Porgy* from a quasi-realistic regional cameo into an epic theater work, a parable of suffering and redemption. This discovery became one starting point for the present book.

My other starting point was a Gershwin discovery. Writing *Classical Music in America: A History* (2005), I absorbed with astonishment that the important classical musicians of Gershwin's generation who most admired him were typically foreign-born. A short list would include Walter Damrosch, Vernon Duke, Amelita Galli-Curci, Leopold Godowsky, Percy Grainger, Jascha Heifetz, Otto Klemperer, Fritz Kreisler, Charles Martin Loeffler, John McCormack, Sergei Rachmaninoff, Fritz Reiner, Arnold Schoenberg, and Ernst Toch in the United States, and Fyodor Chaliapin, Walter Gieseking, Riccardo Malipiero, Maurice Ravel, and Dmitri Shostakovich abroad. The United States had no composers commensurate with a Schoenberg, Ravel, or Shostakovich. But it at least had Aaron Copland—who mainly ignored Gershwin in his books and lectures about American music. Asked in 1937 to compare his own music with "Mr. Gershwin's jazz," Copland replied: "Gershwin is serious up to a point. . . . My idea was to intensify [jazz]. Not what you get in the dance hall but to use it cubistically—to make it more exciting than ordinary jazz." The view that Gershwin was not a "finished" composer was pervasive in the American musical press. For Olin Downes, in the *New York Times*, "he never passed a certain point as a 'serious' composer." And for Paul Rosenfeld, who championed modern music in intellectual circles, Gershwin was

a gifted composer of the lower, unpretentious order; yet there is some question whether his vision permits him an association with the artists. . . . A musician has to "compose" his material, to sustain and evolve and organize it to a degree sufficient to bring its essence, their relationships, their ideas, to expression. And this Gershwin has accomplished to no satisfactory degree.

As recently as 1980, an American contributor to *The New Grove Diction-ary of Music and Musicians* dismissed Gershwin in fewer than two pages; the tone of the entry is Copland's, Rosenfeld's, or Virgil Thomson's: "limited experience in developing musical material," "serious works are structurally defective," etc.[2]

Copland and various American colleagues were intent upon fos-tering a modernist school of composition aligned with the lean aes-thetics of Igor Stravinsky and Nadia Boulanger. But Gershwin's most distinguished, most prestigious admirers—Schoenberg, Ravel, Shostakovich—were not known to admire Copland or Thomson or Roy Harris. And Gershwin was popular and famous, surrounded by adoring family members and friends, maddeningly endowed with an ego immune to jealousy. He was also a millionaire. Europe, having given birth to a ripe musical high culture, could comfortably esteem an out-sider of genius: Gershwin was a refreshment. America's nascent musical modernists, being parentless pioneers, circled their wagons: Gershwin was an interloper.

The larger context of this Gershwin threat was the interwar "jazz threat" I adduce in *Classical Music in America*. Antonín Dvořák had in 1893 predicted a "noble school" of American music founded upon "negro melodies." Some Americans thought Dvořák's prediction naïve or obnoxious. Downes echoed this reaction when thirty-six years later he saw fit to warn the visiting Arthur Honegger to steer clear of jazz, "which too many European musicians have striven to imitate."[3] Jazz sig-nified blacks and brothels. Like Gershwin, it was acclaimed abroad by musicians of consequence and prestige. And Gershwin had not "steered clear"; rather, he had enthusiastically practiced jazz; he had invoked it.

With the passing of modernism, a new musical topography is today under way—and the notion that Gershwin is not a real composer is no longer credible. American music historians are flocking to Gershwin studies. David Schiff's *Rhapsody in Blue* handbook (1997) sets a new standard for acute Gershwin discourse. Howard Pollack's 800-page

Gershwin biography (2006) is a sprawling information compendium. Larry Starr's *George Gershwin* (2010) constitutes a succinct manifesto for the "new Gershwin"; his essential theme is that Gershwin's music is not only timeless and affecting, but subtle and sophisticated. If the old Gershwin was an inspired dilettante, the new Gershwin is versatile, protean, universal. The old Gershwin was impure, in limbo, betwixt and between; the new Gershwin is wholesome, ecumenical.

· · ·

My own *Porgy and Bess* history parallels a larger history of Gershwin reception. As a child, in the 1950s, I knew *Porgy and Bess* through an LP of "highlights" with Risë Stevens, Robert Merrill, and Marian Anderson. I can vaguely remember Cab Calloway as Sporting Life in the touring Robert Breen production when it visited Denver. Seeing *Porgy and Bess* as a young adult at the New York City Opera in 1965 was a disappointment: the excerpts I knew seemed stitched together; the opera appeared to lack a binding style or trajectory. When the touring Houston Grand Opera production came to New York in 1976 and 1980, I stayed away— I bought the conventional wisdom that *Porgy and Bess* was crippled. Nonetheless, I enthusiastically programmed Robert Russell Bennett's *Porgy and Bess* concert suite when as executive director of the Brooklyn Philharmonic I produced a 1995 "From Gospel to Gershwin" weekend conducted by Gunther Schuller at the Brooklyn Academy of Music.

It was not until I quite by accident attended *Porgy and Bess* at Washington's National Opera in 2005 that I discovered that Gershwin had composed a masterpiece after all. Great operas are forgiven for their flaws. Well cast, acted, and paced, *Porgy and Bess* overwhelmed my acquired reservations. When Gordon Hawkins, as Porgy, launched "Oh Bess, Oh Where's My Bess?" the work's largesse, musical and dramatic, simply took over. My strongest impression, however, was of the culminating sequence beginning with "Bring m' goat!"

My Washington *Porgy* epiphany was clinched by a Wagnerian discovery that for me sealed the work's personal impact and world stature via the high craftsmanship of its signature tunes, or "leitmotifs." In *Götterdämmerung*, punctuating the death of Siegfried, Wagner achieves closure with the famous Funeral Music. The weighted drumbeat of his megadirge stirs the blood—but does not account for the eloquence of this interlude. Superimposed on the thundering threnody are lyric reminiscences of the music we associate with Siegfried's hapless parents Siegmund and Sieglinde, with their love and death. Once these aching strains come into play, the sadness and world-weariness of Siegfried's fate—of a doomed family history so gloriously begun—attains an epic resonance.

Is it preposterous to compare Gershwin to Wagner? I would have thought so. And yet, when at the outset of "O Lawd, I'm On My Way" Gershwin's violins twirl a snatch of "I Got Plenty O' Nuttin'," we subliminally grasp that this tune and Porgy's theme are musically kindred; what consciously or unconsciously registers is a final, conclusive reminder that Porgy, who spurns affluence and understands the value of nuttin', is the moral compass of the community, and of the opera. Then a blaring solo trumpet recalls "What You Want Wid Bess?"—and unexpectedly, unsuspectingly, we remember the helplessness of Porgy's woman, the futility of her pathetic attempt to escape the carnal savagery of her previous lover, Crown:

> What you want wid Bess?
> She gettin' ole now;
> Take a fine young gal
> For to satisfy Crown. . . .
> These five years I been yo' woman,
> You could kick me in the street,
> And when you wanted me back,
> You could whistle, an' there I was

Back again, lickin' yo' hand.

There's plenty better lookin' gal than Bess.

At a stroke, we grasp the magnitude of Porgy's journey to manhood, the heartache and courage of it all.*

The genius of Wagner's leitmotifs is complex. The themes are more than markers; they are explainers, weighted with psychological implication. And their musical relationships, one to another, are again equally narrative and psychological. In *Porgy and Bess*, Porgy's theme signifies strength and suffering:

The primal interval of a fifth—B down to E—girds a blue minor third crippled by a mashed grace note. "I Got Plenty O' Nuttin'"—with its rising fifth and major third—is cousin to Porgy's theme; it conveys the wholeness of Porgy's nature, the core of optimism and empathy that is at first more latent—more crippled—than not. With the opera's final cadence, its pervasive E major/E minor tonality—encapsulated in Porgy's theme—drives to E major closure. In *Tristan und Isolde*, Wagner ultimately directs his harmonically ambiguous *Tristan* chord to a healing B major. At the end of *Porgy and Bess*, Porgy's theme finally acquires a healing destination of its own.

In Washington, I mistrusted my response to these humbling final moments of Gershwin's opera. Were they serendipitous or planned? Conventional wisdom dies hard.

· · ·

---

*A full list of the leitmotifs in the orchestra at this juncture would also include "Bess, You Is My Woman Now," Porgy's theme, and the Prelude's opening flourish.

Adumbrating the new Gershwin in his recent book, Larry Starr launches a climactic peroration about Gershwin "blurring, perhaps even collapsing, the distinction between American 'art music' and American 'popular music.'" Starr crucially adds:

> As a composer, he never seriously evinced a divided allegiance. For this reason it is ultimately erroneous to speak of a rapprochement between cultivated and vernacular in Gershwin's art; his music tells us in the clearest possible way that, while the schism might be our perception, it is not his aesthetic reality. . . . The efforts of [Leonard] Bernstein and others to bridge the gap—or the abyss—that separates "classical" and "popular" in American culture must command our admiration. Yet Gershwin set a singular benchmark in this area, and it is simply because he never believed in the validity of the schism to begin with. His oeuvre . . . proceeds from no fundamental position of illness or imbalance whatsoever. There is a terrific feeling of healthiness to Gershwin's art—a healthiness in relation to aesthetic, cultural, racial and any number of other perplexing matters—that may strike us as naïve. But this is our problem.[4]

It was partly through "healthiness"—his personal immunity to chronic American insecurities of cultural status—that Gershwin blithely transcended the schisms of his day. Ira put it in a nutshell when he observed that after composing *Porgy and Bess* George wrote some of his "best hits"[5] for the movies. For Gershwin, the road to the concert hall and opera house was no Stairway to Paradise; a model of sanity, he traversed level ground when moving serendipitously from Hollywood to Carnegie Hall and back. Revisited today, the instabilities of style and genre cited by his detractors may be read as strengths. For Gershwin, "high" and "popular" were not hierarchized strata of artistic experience. He splendidly embodies what I will call "cultural fluidity."

And so it is, as well, with Mamoulian, who all his life railed against distinctions between "art" and "entertainment." Gershwin's Piano Concerto in F subverts genre: it misbehaves; and so, compared to the Hollywood film operetta template of Ernst Lubitsch, does Mamoulian's *Love Me Tonight*. That the Broadway folk opera *Porgy and Bess* is *sui generis*, that it does not subscribe to Old World categories of artistic production, is crucial to what Gershwin and Mamoulian were about. It is part of what makes them, and it, "American."

From this New World perspective, Gershwin and Mamoulian were intended for one another. With their mixed origins and bold intentions, they were inspired exemplars of cultural exchange, beneficiaries of the rubbing action of widely intermingled influences. Born in Brooklyn to Russian parents, Gershwin embraced Tin Pan Alley and Hollywood, Broadway and Yiddish theater, Paris and Vienna (who else among his American contemporaries so esteemed Alban Berg?). Mamoulian was an Armenian born in Tiflis (now Tbilisi). English was his seventh language, after Armenian, Russian, Georgian, French, German, and Latin. As a youth, he lived in Paris, studied experimental theater in Moscow, and debuted as a professional stage director in London at the age of twenty-five. Both Gershwin and Mamoulian achieved controversial early fame and influence. They concurrently brought a layered aesthetic complexity both to Hollywood and to Broadway. They moved up and down the cultural ladder with clairvoyant assurance.

That Gershwin, in his short lifetime, was misunderstood and undervalued, and that Mamoulian, in his long lifetime, was ultimately undervalued and forgotten, have something to do with cultural fluidity as they purveyed it, with precocious experiments truncated by Gershwin's early death, and unsustained during Mamoulian's long decline.

· · ·

If Gershwin's roots are tangled but tangible, Mamoulian's tangled roots are elusive—not least because he wanted it that way. Though some sources show his year of birth as 1898, he was actually born on Octo-

ber 8, 1897[6]—about a year before George Gershwin. His Tiflis home
was affluent: his father, Zachary, was a bank president, his mother,
Virginia, a leading figure in the local Armenian theater. Virginia was
a fervent actress, whether amateur or professional. She was twenty-one
when Rouben was born. A daughter, Svetlana, followed two years later.
Virginia's relationship to her husband was at all times remote; her dedication to her son, and to his career, was lifelong. The family moved to
Paris and back to Tiflis while Rouben was a boy. He went to Moscow to
study law (his parents' choice) but wound up attending classes taught by
Yevgeny Vakhtangov at Constantin Stanislavski's Moscow Art Theatre.
He also met Stanislavski. His Moscow years were 1915 or 1916 until
early 1918.

Back in Tiflis, Mamoulian staged and reviewed plays. His relationship to the Russian Revolution and civil war is a murky topic: perhaps he
was an eyewitness to warfare in Moscow or Tiflis, perhaps not. In any
event, he wound up in London directing a play—*The Beating at the Door*
by Austin Page—in 1922. This was his first and last exercise in Stanis-
lavskian naturalism: the theater replicated life; chopping wood meant
really chopping real wood. A telegram from George Eastman brought
him to the United States in 1923; he lived there ever after. Svetlana having died in Scotland in 1925, Mamoulian's parents moved into his Los
Angeles home in 1931 and remained there until he married in 1945.[7]

No episode of Mamoulian's early life is more tantalizing than his
studies with Vakhtangov in Moscow, which reportedly lasted anywhere
from three months to a year. Though in America Mamoulian invested
in minimizing Vakhtangov's influence, this exposure to Russian experimental theater, contradicting Stanislavski's aesthetic, could not have
been irrelevant to his later espousal of radically integrated musical theater
imposed by a singular directorial vision. In fact, an abundance of stray
evidence—needles in a dense haystack of diaries and memorabilia—
shows that Stanislavski and Vakhtangov both mattered to Mamoulian.

In 1973, Mamoulian recalled how his parents' home was a meeting place of actors, writers, and directors—and that when Stanislavski's Moscow Art Theatre came to Georgia, the company gravitated to the Mamoulian house. Stanislavski's company, he added, "was subconsciously ingrained in me." In 1958 he recalled his student days in Moscow as "intellectually alive and brewing. It was like a new wine—restless, inquisitive." Though Mamoulian soon rejected Stanislavski's realism, Stanislavski's masterful handling of crowds, and his commensurate treatment of every actor as an individual, foretold a Mamoulian trademark. Stanislavski's way of breaking down a script into beats also forecast the Mamoulian style. "Stanislavski was the greatest man in the theater," Mamoulian said in 1973; his method "was tortured to death [in America] and twisted out of shape completely."[8]

Also suggestive of the Mamoulian touch is Vakhtangov's "fantastic realism." During the period that Mamoulian participated in exercises and classwork at Vakhtangov's studio, a production of Maeterlinck's *The Miracle of St. Anthony* was in rehearsal; within a decade, Mamoulian's Rochester production of Maeterlinck's *Sister Beatrice* was his most ambitious creation. In Moscow, Vakhtangov meticulously attended to every aspect of production. Mamoulian, too, was consumed (or overly consumed) with detail. Mamoulian's papers include an English-language excerpt from Vakhtangov's diary, as well as an article, "Evgenii Vakhtangov: Our Man in Moscow," from the Spring 1969 issue of the journal *Ararat*.[9] Vakhtangov, in his diary, rejects the polarities of Stanislavski and the iconoclastic constructivist Vsevolod Meyerhold. Stanislavski, he writes, forgets "that the actor's emotions must be communicated to the audience by means of theatrical methods." Meyerhold has arrived at "real theater," but "absorbed in theatrical truth [he] has lost track of feeling."

Not everything contemporary is eternal, but that which is eternal is always contemporary. Meyerhold has never felt "today," but he has felt "tomorrow." Stanislavsky has never felt "tomorrow"; he has felt only "today." But "today" must be felt in tomorrow, and "tomorrow" in today.

In the *Aratat* article, Vakhtangov is extolled as an exhaustive exponent of "total theater." Considered by Stanislavski "the future leader of the Russian theater," he creates new artistic principles. He is quoted arguing: "The theater has a realism of its own, its own theatrical truth." While an actor's feelings must be true, the truth must be projected "in a theatrical manner." A review of Vakhtangov's 1914–1915 Moscow production of Henning Berger's *The Deluge*—which Mamoulian would doubtless have seen—observed: "Vakhtangov developed rhythm and tempo for each of the characters' behavior. For instance, to establish a frenzied American tempo, Vakhtangov had a minor character do the following in the background: rush into the saloon; order and gulp down in rapid succession soup, a whole chicken, and dessert; pay the bill and leave, all in one swift action." Such signature Vakhtangov productions as *The Miracle of St. Anthony*, *The Deluge*, and *The Dybbuk* (which Mamoulian would have seen on tour in the United States as presented by the Habima Theatre) were distinguished by the wizardry with which he choreographed sound and music, by his gift for pantomime, and by the communality of his company of actors. But Vakhtangov's work was also criticized, by some Moscow critics, for elaborate artifice, a surfeit of detail, and a failure to project interior feeling.[10]

All this is more than Mamoulian ever chose to talk about. And yet the connections to Mamoulian, and to his self-described aesthetic of "stylization," are obvious. A formative memory from Mamoulian's childhood was driving in a carriage with his mother and hearing "the sound of horse hooves on the dirt road and crossing of a wooden ridge"—it was "sheer music," especially at night. Mamoulian the director was obsessed with sound; to an exceptional degree, music and "noise" were one and the same to him. Another formative childhood memory: a teacher said, "When a regiment of soldiers crosses a stone bridge, it is always ordered to break step, because if it walked in step, the power of its rhythmic vibration would destroy the bridge." Mamoulian commented, "It stuck in my mind that rhythm can have a great power: if it can destroy, it can also build." Mamoulian the director was obsessed with rhythm, with tempo and meter; that he directed with metronome and baton was a singular accoutrement. As a youth, he played the violin; as an adult, he revised and abridged musical scores as vigorously as he did scripts.[11]

Mamoulian's fixation on sound and rhythm girded his aesthetic: stage action should be "stylized," never realistic, in order to maximize emotional truth. At the same time, Mamoulian had no use for aestheticism; he insisted that art be constructive, uplifting. Though not a churchgoer, he believed in Christianity and the power of love. His credo became "art for life's sake."

• • •

Mamoulian's public memories of Moscow were scant and highly selective. Never, in public discourse, was he nostalgic about Tiflis or Moscow; nor did he return to either city. Rather, he said: "The minute I stepped on [American] soil and took my first walk in New York, I felt completely and utterly at home. I had a much closer rapport with Americans than I ever found . . . in Europe, even though Paris is my second home."[12] The nub is not that Mamoulian regarded himself as patriotic,* but that he regarded himself as self-invented as an artist, the originator of a personal theatrical vision.

The American Opera Company he found himself shaping in Rochester was itself experimental and self-invented, a lavishly subsidized adventure in opera in English. Rochester became Mamoulian's ticket to Broadway, and his first Theatre Guild production, *Porgy* (1927), was his early ticket to fame. His subsequent Theatre Guild productions were of

---

*In wartime, however, his exhortations to the *Oklahoma!* cast were those of a grateful immigrant. See p. 176.

O'Neill's *Marco Millions* (1928), Romain Rolland's *The Game of Love and Death* (1929), Capek's *R.U.R.* (1930), Turgenev's *A Month in the Country* (with Alla Nazimova, 1930), *Porgy and Bess* (1935), *Oklahoma!* (1943), *Carousel* (1945), and *Arms and the Girl* (1950), which he cowrote with Herbert and Dorothy Fields—all short runs except *Porgy, Oklahoma!*, and *Carousel*. Mamoulian otherwise directed nine times on Broadway between 1928 and 1949, most notably Kurt Weill's *Lost in the Stars* (1949). Also, for Leopold Stokowski, he directed Arnold Schoenberg's *Die glückliche Hand* in New York and Philadelphia (1930).

Meanwhile, the advent of the sound film sent filmmakers scrambling for skilled stage directors—including Mamoulian. Hollywood in the early thirties was necessarily experimental: Mamoulian thrived. His first films—*Applause* (1929), *City Streets* (1931), *Dr. Jekyll and Mr. Hyde* (1931), and *Love Me Tonight* (1932)—bristle with technical achievement and artistic novelty. Mamoulian liked Hollywood and stayed there. But, like Broadway, Hollywood petered out as a playground for Mamoulian's originality. The twelve films he additionally directed there between 1933 and 1957—a modest number, including *Queen Christina* with Greta Garbo (1933)—ignite sporadically if at all. Following *Silk Stockings* (1957), he was fired from Samuel Goldwyn's *Porgy and Bess* in 1958, and resigned from Fox's *Cleopatra* in 1961: traumatic terminal events. He spent his many remaining years essentially unemployed. He died in 1987 at the age of ninety. Ultimately, the immigrant in Mamoulian remained displaced in America. His progeny—he and his wife Azadia had no children—were the plays and films in which he fitfully achieved a form of self-realization through art; hence, the importance he attached to self-invention; hence, his penchant for minimizing the influence of Vakhtangov and others he observed or partnered. *Porgy and Bess*—via the play, the opera, and the film debacle—was pivotal for Mamoulian both personally and professionally. To a remarkable degree, it both made and unmade him—a binding motif of my book. Commensurately, I narrate his steep rise to high celebrity and even steeper fall. I treat Mamoulian as a forgotten hero of American musical theater. The current iconography of *Porgy and Bess, Oklahoma!,* and *Carousel* fixes on the Gershwins and the Heywards, on Agnes de Mille, on Rodgers and Hammerstein.[13] Mamoulian deserves more.

• • •

Notwithstanding the vicissitudes of his career and its truncated end, Mamoulian's credo, and the anecdotes embellishing it, remained constant during his six American decades. His artistic persona emerged fully formed in Rochester in the 1920s; it remained intact during his enforced retirement of the sixties and seventies. "I am not arty or highbrow," he told the *New York Times* in 1934. A 1935 radio talk began:

> In discussing what I call, "The World's Latest Fine Art," I feel I must tell you at once that I mean the motion picture. . . . Some of you may even resent the classification of motion pictures among the arts. . . . To avoid misunderstanding, may I clarify that art in my opinion is not contrary to entertainment. I firmly believe that while all entertainment is not art, all art is entertainment.

In the aftermath of his 1961 *Cleopatra* ordeal, he told an interviewer: "I think *Cleopatra* could have been fine art and fine entertainment. It's possible—not a contradiction. Indeed, I think it's an ideal." In 1970, interviewed by the *Los Angeles Times,* he said:

> If it's not entertainment it must be very poor art. In the whole of the arts, what have been greater "box office" than Shakespeare, Michelangelo, Da Vinci, all the great composers? For me, at the age of 18 I had a sort of artistic philosophy, art for art's sake. I outlived it by the time I was 19. Art is for life's sake! . . . The goal is to add to the beauty and dignity of man. . . .
>
> All through history there has never been a high civilization or

culture that didn't have a highly diversified theater—ancient Greece, Italy, Britain, you name it. The theater is the most authentic reflection of the well-being of a nation.[14]

Beginning in Rochester, Mamoulian's vision of an integrated theatrical exercise—of music, drama, and dance unified by rhythm and gesture—was also a vision of an indigenous American theatrical experience rooted in indigenous popular art. This rejection of European roots was equally a rejection of traditional European genres: an assertion of cultural fluidity. *Sister Beatrice* in Rochester and *Porgy* on Broadway were unclassifiable musical-dramatic entertainments. The songs of *Applause* and *Love Me Tonight*, the gangsters of *City Streets* and horrors of *Dr. Jekyll* do not fit the well-known cinema genres they skirt.

No less than Gershwin's, Mamoulian's mutual pursuit of artistic ambition and popular appeal was steadfast. The question asked from all sides about *Porgy and Bess* in 1935—"What is it?"—could have equally applied to Maeterlinck's *Sister Beatrice* in Rochester and to *Porgy* on Broadway. This is one reason *Porgy and Bess* was a special collaborative opportunity for both young men, both powerfully self-created, both early celebrated and iconoclastic. That the Theatre Guild gave them equal billing did not—and does not—equalize their contributions. But Mamoulian was much more than an implementer.

Like Mamoulian, Gershwin proceeded to Los Angeles after *Porgy and Bess* began its modest New York run. Like Mamoulian, he experienced Hollywood as a suppressant of the creative energies their Broadway partnership had unleashed. Less than two years later, Gershwin was dead.

· · ·

My book is not chronological. Chapter 1 examines Mamoulian's transformative impact directing *Porgy* in 1927. Chapter 2 has two parts: it backs up to Rochester and explores Mamoulian's formative experience directing opera in English; it fast-forwards to 1932 to explore Mamoulian's integration of music in the film *Love Me Tonight*. Chapter 3 is a detailed inquiry into Mamoulian's collaboration with Gershwin. And chapter 4 follows Gershwin and Mamoulian to their early and late endings—in Mamoulian's case, his unfinished attempt to film *Porgy and Bess*, and his unfulfilled hope to turn *Carmen* into a Hollywood film that would have become his final opus. There are three appendices: the "Noise Symphony" Mamoulian created for *Porgy* (and revisited in *Porgy and Bess*); a synopsis of *Porgy and Bess*; and four versions of the story's end—from Heyward's novella; from the published *Porgy* script; from the script as amended in Mamoulian's hand; and from the opera.

Cultural fluidity, as practiced by Gershwin and Mamoulian, was both prescient and American. Partly because they were ahead of their time, partly because Gershwin died too young, partly because Mamoulian ran out of steam, they both embody great achievement and unfulfilled promise. *Porgy and Bess*, their peak moment, remains a lonely pinnacle in the quest for an American equivalent of grand opera.

CHAPTER 1

ENTER *PORGY*

Porgy lived in the Golden Age. Not the Golden Age of a remote and legendary past; nor yet the chimerical era treasured by every man past middle life, that never existed except in the heart of youth; but an age when men, not yet old, were boys in an ancient, beautiful city that time had forgotten before it destroyed.[1]

DUBOSE HEYWARD'S 1925 novella *Porgy* is two things. The first is a state-of-nature fable heightened by primal bodies and passions. The second is a realistic cameo recording an exotic subculture—the African-American Gullahs of South Carolina—resistant to the refinements and distractions of civilization.

Porgy and Bess would be neither of these. Notwithstanding his vital contributions to the opera that *Porgy* ultimately inspired, Heyward was temperamentally and intellectually remote from George Gershwin or Rouben Mamoulian. His physical frailty influenced his admiration for the robust Gullahs. His attunement to southern tradition, however tempered, supported his own resistance to modernity.

Born in 1885 in Charleston, Heyward was descended from founders of the Charleston colony; his father's great-great-grandfather was a signer of the Declaration of Independence. Charleston emerged as the genteel cultural capital of the Old South. But after the Civil War it was home to genteel poverty. Heyward's immediate family was, in the saying of the day, "too poor to paint and too proud to whitewash." He initially made a modest living selling insurance and real estate before becoming a full-time writer. The Charleston literary scene remained polite, untouched by the modernist sympathies of such writers as Sherwood Anderson, William Faulkner, and John Dos Passos. And yet *Porgy*, if stylistically mild, broke with genteel norms. A national bestseller, it was acclaimed for attempting to portray black Americans unsentimentally. Heyward's subsequent output included *Mamba's Daughters* (1929), a novel ambitiously registering the complexities of race and class in Charleston, and *Brass Ankle* (1930), a play in which a husband murders his wife and child when the infant's blackness discloses the mother's "tainted" blood. But neither repeated his *Porgy* success. He died in 1940, only fifty-four years old.

It was Heyward's mother, Janie, who led him to the Gullahs as a subject for art. At the time, Gullahs comprised nearly all of Charleston's blacks. A self-contained community, they had been imported and enslaved largely intact (on the assumption that, so maintained, they would be less prone to revolt). They spoke their own English-based creole dialect, related to Caribbean and West African speech. Their religion was a mixture of Christianity and paganism. Their social fabric vibrated with story and song. For Janie, as later for her son, the Gullahs were fortifying. They generated the subject matter for her poems and stories, and for public appearances as a popular "dialect recitalist," performing Gullah tales along the eastern seaboard.

DuBose's 1923 marriage to Dorothy Hartzell Kuhns broadened his literary horizons and social sympathies. They had met at the MacDowell Colony in New Hampshire. Dorothy was a fledgling writer, born in Ohio. She had studied drama at Columbia University, and playwriting at George Pierce Baker's famous Harvard workshop. Dorothy settled in, but DuBose was never fully at ease in the cosmopolitan literary and intellectual circles they sometimes broached. As a regional critic of southern mores, he charted a tenuous middle path between accommodation and resistance.[2]

Porgy, then, was and is distinctly a product of its time and place. Its flights of picturesque poetic elegance today retain pungency even as Porgy, Bess, and Crown recede into stereotype. The title character is a crippled beggar who ambulates in a goat cart:

> He was seated with the utmost gravity in an inverted packing-case that proclaimed with unconscious irony the virtues of a well-known toilet soap. Beneath the box two solid lop-sided wheels turned heavily. Before him, between a pair of improvised shafts, a patriarchal goat tugged with the dogged persistence of age which had been placed upon its mettle, and flaunted an intolerable stench in the face of the complaisant and virtuous soap box.[3]

Early in the novella, Crown, a hulking stevedore, kills Robbins during a craps game and flees to Kittiwar Island. Porgy falls in love with Bess, once Crown's woman. When Crown reappears to reclaim Bess, Porgy stabs him to death. Porgy is detained to identify Crown's body and is jailed for refusing to do so. He returns home to discover that Bess has left on a riverboat. He sinks into apathy and despair "in an irony of morning sunlight."[4]

Though Porgy's story ends in tragedy, though the courtyard tenement Catfish Row is home to vice and crime, his communal "Golden Age" milieu is vital. His neighbors, strong and unrestrained, are sharers of unmediated feeling and thought. Their propensities—toward superstition and magic, toward mercurial ecstasies—are natural, even childlike. The stevedores are of "great size," "possessing vast physical strength in a world of brute force," attired "in the clashing crimsons and purples that they loved." Porgy, though a cripple, retains innate gifts—even in the terrific heat of midday, he experiences "a pleasant atavistic calm," dozing lightly "as only a full-blooded negro can." Above all, "with that instant emotional release that is the great solace of the negro," Catfish Row sings. It hums and shouts, weeps and prays. On a Saturday night, a "deep baritone" raises "an air":

> Ain't it hahd tuh be a nigger;
> Ain't it hahd tuh be a nigger;
> Ain it hahd tuh be a nigger;
> 'Cause yuh can't git yo' rights w'en yuh do.

The snoring of the courtyard is rhythmic. The wind is music—it whines in a "treble key," then "drops an octave." In one of the novella's set pieces, a Gullah picnic parade "crashed through the slow, restrained rhythm of the city's life like a wild, barbaric chord."

Then the band, two score boys attired in several variations of the band master's costume, strode by. Bare, splay feet padded upon the cobbles; heads were thrown back, with lips to instruments that glittered in the sunshine, launching daring and independent excursions into the realm of sound. . . .

After the band came the men members of the lodge, stepping it out to the urge of the marshals who rode beside them, reinforcing the marching rhythm with a series of staccato grunts. . . .

Then came the carriages, and suddenly the narrow street hummed and bloomed like a tropic garden. Six to a carriage sat the sisters. The effect produced by the colors was strangely like that wrought in the music; scarlet, purple, orange, flamingo, emerald; wild, clashing, unbelievable dischords; yet, in their steady flow before the eye, possessing a strange, dominant rhythm that reconciled them to each other and made them unalterably right. . . .

For one brief moment out of the year the pageant had lasted. Out of its fetters of civilization this people had risen, suddenly, amazingly.

Exotic as the Congo, and still able to abandon themselves utterly to the wild joy of fantastic play, they had taken the reticent, old Anglo-Saxon town and stamped their mood swiftly and indelibly into it. Then they passed, leaving behind them a wistful envy among those who had watched them go;—those whom the ages had rendered old and wise.[5]

The white world is harsh and unpoetic, a world of barked speech deaf to song. When the Catfish Row courtyard would "withdraw into itself," it could only mean that "a white man had entered." Typically, it is the white law—an arbitrary authority with its arcane badges, courts, and jails—that silences the Gullahs. "That place is alive with crooks," says the coroner about Catfish Row. "I'd like to get something on it that would justify closing it up as a public nuisance, and throwing the whole lot of 'em out in the street." Investigating Robbins's death, a policeman draws a pistol—unlike Porgy's knife, a tool of civilization—and points it at an old black man he knows to be blameless. "You killed Robbins. . . . And I'm going to hang you for it."[6]

The white author of *Porgy* was as prone to "wistful envy" as the picnic parade watchers. Heyward was cadaverous and frail, condemned to watch. By the time he was twenty-one, he had endured polio, typhoid, and pleurisy. Pondering the status of black Americans in the modern world, his 1923 essay "And Once Again—the Negro" exhorts: "In an ideal civilization, a man should expend but half of his power to secure the necessities of physical existence, and devote the remainder of his time to the realization and enjoyment of life."[7]

If Catfish Row was therefore "ideal," it was also real: coexisting with the Golden Age aspect of *Porgy* is an anthropological investigation bent on verisimilitude. Catfish Row was inspired by such crowded black courtyards as Cabbage Row, in the heart of Charleston. Porgy, in real life, was a disabled beggar-vendor named Samuel Smalls, whose goat cart was on at least one occasion run down by policemen. Insofar as it was a white writer's attempt to plumb the southern black experience, exploring Gullah beliefs, values, and customs without caricature or condescension, *Porgy* elaborated a vein of social realism relatively new to southern literature. Heyward wrote of the Gullahs: "What, I wondered, was the unique characteristic . . . that endowed them with the power to stir me suddenly and inexplicably to tears or laughter, when the chaste beauty of the old city created by my own people awakened a distinctly different and more intellectual sort of delight? What was the mysterious force that for generations had resisted the pressure of our civilization and underlaid the apparently haphazard existence of the Negro with a fundamental unity?" Reading *Porgy* in manuscript, the writer John Bennett, who had mentored DuBose in Charleston, was struck by "the absolute unexampled newness of its outlook upon the southern Negro"; he judged *Porgy* a "radical . . . novel on Negro Life." James Southall Wilson, in the *Virginia Quarterly Review*, called *Porgy* "authentic." Heyward himself, while capable of waxing nostalgic for "beautiful and tender and enriching" relationships "that existed between master and servant" in antebellum times, said he aspired to produce a "new note in southern literature," "a psychologically true . . . picture of contemporary southern Negro life," "an authentic record." He dubbed *Porgy* a "folk novel."[8]

Obviously, the cultural anthropologist in Heyward, documenting a society cohabiting with modern civilization and yet apart, was not merely factual. He admired the Gullahs; he also mourned their impending extinction. As a member of Charleston's Society for the Preservation of Spirituals, he supported the perpetuation of Gullah praise songs. He assumed that (like so much of the world in which he was raised) innocent Gullah virtues would fall prey to modernity. In this context, the novella's dour ending is metaphoric—as are the "passing" of the picnic parade, the coroner's resolve to "close up" Catfish Row, and the policeman's unarguable gun.

And so *Porgy* may be read as a mirror of the author's transitional identity, of shifting allegiances in shifting times. Its florid style and Golden

Age yearnings merge paradoxically with a progressive factual bent. Its gentility and authenticity would prove equally irrelevant to its Broadway incarnations, as epic and sanguine as Heyward was local and resigned.

NOVELLA TO PLAY

In retrospect, *Porgy* was fated for the musical stage. In how many other novels are the lovers observed "singin' tuhgedduh in dey room"?[9] The picnic is far from the most notable of its "musical" episodes. Robbins's death ignites six pages of lamentation and ceremony. Heyward, who experienced the Charleston hurricane of 1911, makes the hurricane that drives Crown back to Catfish Row audibly articulate; the novella's most heroic, most inspired prose poem narrates the music of shrilling terror and cacophonous prayer, boiling cataracts and detonating timber crashes.

The transformation from novella to opera occurred in stages, with multiple versions of the scripted play coming in between. In the process, Heyward's story lost in verisimilitude and grew in scale; a book of 150 pages fostered an opera that, unabridged, lasts more than three hours.

It was Dorothy who, unbeknownst to DuBose, began redrafting *Porgy* for the stage. She was nearly done when in 1926 a letter for DuBose arrived from George Gershwin, suggesting that they collaborate on an opera based on the book. Dorothy now read to her husband what she had been writing. "He was torn between the prospect of the play and the opera," she later recalled. "We both thought of it as 'or.'" DuBose wrote to Gershwin that a play was already in process and would have to take precedence. To the delight of the Heywards, Gershwin realized that the play could actually facilitate an opera as "a good forerunner." Declining their offer to collaborate, he urged them to proceed with a nonoperatic version for the stage—which they did. The script was then offered for production. The Theatre Guild accepted.[10]

In 1926, the Guild had not yet acquired the high imprimatur secured by its premieres of Eugene O'Neill (*Strange Interlude*, *Mourning Becomes*

Electra, Ah, Wilderness! and *The Iceman Cometh*), and of Rodgers and Hammerstein (*Oklahoma!* and *Carousel*). Founded in New York City in 1918, it sought to sponsor significant new American and European works with limited commercial prospects. To date, plays by Strindberg, Molnár (including *The Guardsman* with Alfred Lunt and Lynn Fontanne), and Shaw (including Lunt and Fontanne in *Arms and the Man*) had been notable Theatre Guild productions. That the Guild's search for groundbreaking American fare should result in a play about black Americans was a startling yet (at least in retrospect) logical outcome, part of a larger quest for American roots.

In American classical music, the quest had begun with Louis Moreau Gottschalk (1829–1869), who mined the black Caribbean delicacies of his native New Orleans in such tangy piano cameos as *Bamboula* and *The Banjo*—and so became the earliest American concert composer whose music we still hear, and hear as "American." Gottschalk's great successor was, improbably, a Bohemian: Antonín Dvořák, who during his American sojourn (1892–1895) predicted that "Negro melodies" would foster a distinctive "American school" of operas, symphonies, art songs, and chamber works. For Dvořák—as for such inspired Dvořák adherents as the critic Henry Krehbiel and the music educator Jeannette Thurber—black music did not embody cultural marginalia. Rather, plantation song seemed to him America's most pregnant "folk music"—and its native practitioners seemed nothing less than Americans. Although this view alienated some—Boston regarded Dvořák as naïve—Dvořák's own *New World* Symphony (1893) swiftly became the most beloved ever composed on American soil, and its Largo, saturated with the mournful pentatonic strains of enslaved African-Americans, was duly transformed into the ersatz spiritual "Goin' Home."

In 1917, the composer-baritone Harry Burleigh, Dvořák's black assistant from 1892 to 1895, reconceived "Deep River" as a reverent concert song; remarkably, this too was an offshoot of the immortal Largo.[11] It and other instantly popular Burleigh arrangements ushered slave song into the recital hall alongside Schubert and Brahms—an initiative shaping the distinctive concert repertoire of Roland Hayes, Paul Robeson, and Marian Anderson. Meanwhile, Dvořák's New York student Rubin Goldmark composed a symphonic *Negro* Rhapsody (1922). Henry F. Gilbert, who did not study with Dvořák, composed an ephemeral hit in this style: *The Dance in Place Congo* (1922). Louis Gruenberg composed a briefly successful opera, *The Emperor Jones* (1933), after O'Neill's play about a Pullman porter who takes command of a Caribbean island. Its magnificent star, the Metropolitan Opera's Lawrence Tibbett, would two years later become the first baritone to record Porgy's songs—songs fulfilling Dvořák's stirring prophecy: "In the negro melodies of America I discover all that is needed for a great and noble school of music. They are pathetic, tender, passionate, melancholy, solemn, religious, bold, merry, gay or what you will. . . . There is nothing in the whole range of composition that cannot be supplied with themes from this source."[12]

Meanwhile, African-Americans were coursing toward *Porgy and Bess* from another point of entry. In 1903, Broadway hosted a musical created and performed by black artists that would become a long-running hit. This was *In Dahomey*, with music by Will Marion Cook (whose complex lineage included violin studies in Berlin); minstrelsy, vaudeville, ragtime, comic opera, and musical comedy were all on board. *Shuffle Along* (1921), by Eubie Blake and Noble Sissle, was a landmark post–World War I black musical with further progeny. *The Emperor Jones* (1920) launched Eugene O'Neill's career with a black protagonist. In O'Neill's *All God's Chillun Got Wings* (1924), a black attorney was victimized by his white wife; the attorney was Paul Robeson, who also starred in an *Emperor Jones* revival the same year (and would be Crown in *Porgy* four years later). In Paul Green's *In Abraham's Bosom* (1927), a black farm worker's self-improvement was stymied by segregation; it won a Pulitzer Prize. Meanwhile, black folk plays incorporating spirituals proliferated.

Notwithstanding this auspicious trajectory toward American music and drama infused with black vernacular strains, the Theatre Guild was challenged by the prospect of mounting *Porgy*. The Heywards' play, which eschewed the minstrel humor and conventions that black musicals had to some degree retained, was anticipated as a "window" on "an alien world." Robert Milton, the Theatre Guild director assigned to the play, shelved it in favor of another.

In fall 1926, the Heywards met Gershwin for the first time: "a young man of enormous physical and emotional vitality, who possessed the faculty of seeing himself impersonally and realistically," DuBose recorded.[13] But Gershwin remained in no hurry to put Catfish Row to music. With *Porgy* in suspension, Dorothy and DuBose left for England. They were on the Cornwall coast when a letter arrived informing them that *Porgy* would open the Theatre Guild season in October 1927 with a new director barely thirty years old. His name was Rouben Mamoulian.

ENTER MAMOULIAN

Mamoulian's work in Rochester had come to the attention of the Theatre Guild's Lawrence Langner—who engaged him to teach at the Theatre Guild School beginning in 1926. For the Guild School, Mamoulian had directed *Enter Madame* by Gilda Varesi Archibald and Dorothea Donn-Byrne, *Clarence* by Booth Tarkington, and *He Who Gets Slapped* by Leonid Andreyev. He "began to pester the Guild directors in a most efficiently irritating manner, to come and see the plays given by his pupils and, of course, directed by himself," Langner would recall.[14] Mamoulian had apparently been promised a full-length public matinee not in Scarborough, New York, where the school was located, but at the Garrick—a Broadway house the Guild often rented. The school "was to be a stepping stone to directing at the Theatre Guild," Mamoulian would explain.

Eight months went by and they never came around and never offered me anything, so I caught them once at a party and I really gave them hell—all six of them. So they said, "All right. If we had a Russian play, a French play, a European play of some kind, but it so happens that we only have American plays now and you couldn't do any of them. You've only been here two and a half or three years," which made me rather angry, so they said, "All right, pick a play and we'll give you the Garrick Theatre for a special matinee." So I picked George M. Cohan's *Seven Keys to Baldpate*, and I stylized it completely. It became a rhythmic stylized production.[15]

All six members of the Theatre Guild board—Langner, Theresa Helburn, Lee Simonson, Helen Westley, Philip Moeller, and Maurice Wertheim—attended the Cohan play, given May 3, 4, and 6, 1927. They had told Mamoulian they could only spare twenty minutes. Some days later, at a party, Mamoulian told them that their preperformance caveat had been "a lousy thing to say." Langner confessed that none of the board members regretted having "stayed to the unbitter end"; the shelved *Porgy* script was now proffered.[16] For Mamoulian, this was an ideal assignment. As his career would show, he required, more than opportunity, challenge: problems to be solved, experiments to be attempted, innovations to be discovered.

Three decades later, Mamoulian reminisced: "Due to the fact that the only Negro I had intimate knowledge of was the shoeblack in a Rochester hotel, I thought it might be a good idea for me to take a trip to Charleston before starting to work on the production." In Charleston that August with his set designer, Cleon Throckmorton, Mamoulian connected with DuBose Heyward's onetime mentor John Bennett. They visited with the leader of the Society for the Preservation of Spirituals and heard some of the collected songs. Bennett shared photographs from his collection of "Negro types and scenes." According to Bennett, they also navigated "the most picturesque and disreputable sections of the city." To Mamoulian's eye, the wharf's muscled black workers evoked bronze statues.[17]

Finally, Bennett introduced Mamoulian to the Jenkins Orphanage for black children (today the Jenkins Institute for Children), whose band performed up and down the East Coast. At a private performance, Mamoulian was charmed by an "infinitesimally small darkey boy who led the band" and by the "melodious discordance" of the band itself. He hatched the idea of bringing the Jenkins Orphanage Band to Broadway for the picnic scene in *Porgy*. He also catalogued local sounds—the germ of his "Symphony of Noises" to come. He told a local reporter that Charleston reminded him of his native Georgia:

> I am, after all, a Southerner. Charleston is typically southern in much the same way that Tiflis is: in its music and its hospitality. Both cities have a link with the past. I have been especially glad to visit Charleston after having spent some time in the cold of upstate New York. In Charleston one sees the tropical luxuriance of vegetation. Every house seems to have a jungle of its own. I have seen many beautiful old houses, with their wrought iron work, and I have been delighted with the museum collections of costumes and furniture.

Upon returning to New York, Mamoulian informed the *Brooklyn Daily Eagle* that "southern Negroes, like southern people everywhere, possess such vitality. Only among northern peoples do you find economy of gesture, of movement, of speech." He was convinced that, in its "sensitivity to rhythm and music," its physical "grace and freedom," its "lush richness" of feeling, "Negro life . . . would fit . . . my favorite idea of stylized, rhythmic composition" for the stage.[18]

No less than the Heywards, and Theresa Helburn of the Theatre Guild directorate, Mamoulian was excited by the prospect of assembling a black cast for *Porgy*. Others at the League were worried or dubious. The script called for twenty black roles plus a black ensemble—a slice-of-life onstage community, eschewing minstrel stereotypes. There were rumors of Porgy and Bess being enacted by Lunt and Fontanne.[19] And there was a practical problem: where to find black candidates for such a cast? Mamoulian toyed with the notion of using amateurs: actual Gullahs from South Carolina. Instead, accompanied by his assistant stage manager Cheryl Crawford, he undertook an exhaustive search of Harlem clubs and vaudeville theaters; a "dragnet method of casting," Heyward called it.[20] Mamoulian and Crawford even stopped and queried likely-looking Harlem pedestrians.

Some chosen candidates never showed up to audition. Ella Madison, cast in a supporting role (Annie), was an aged and illiterate domestic, long retired from the stage, for whom the play became a living reality; when excited, she would spontaneously interject her own commentary on the action. In other instances, Mamoulian engaged what proven black talent was available. Frank Wilson, Mamoulian's Porgy, had just starred in *In Abraham's Bosom*; he was also a postman. Evelyn Ellis, selected for Bess, came from a Harlem musical stock company. Wilson seemed too young to Heyward, Ellis too radiant to fit the gaunt Bess of his novella—but Porgy and Bess, onstage, would ever after be thought of as relatively youthful. Percy Verwayne, the Sporting Life, was a colleague of Ellis's, a popular singer and comedian who had never attempted a dramatic role. The *Abraham's Bosom* cast that supplied Wilson also supplied Rose McClendon as Maria, Richard J. Huey as Mingo, and Melville Green as Scipio. Eleanor Ball, keeping track for the *Charleston News and Courier*, wrote that the "regular agencies had little to offer," since "negro actors are rarely sought, except for musical performances." She also reported that "many in the cast, including some who appear in leading roles, have never spoken lines before, their whole professional experience consisting of singing the blues and dancing the black bottom." The eclectic cast, the novelty of the play, the inexperience of the Guild in a rapidly changing world of black theater, were all factors vesting authority in a visionary director.[21]

From the last row of the orchestra, Mamoulian, always in jacket and tie, took charge with a megaphone, a metronome, a whistle, and a baton. He propped his script on a music stand. The megaphone was for his daily call to order—"Everybody into his own house!"—sorting bodies throughout the windows and doorways of Throckmorton's detailed set. The whistle was to restore order when chaos reigned. The baton and metronome were for setting and enforcing the rhythms in which Mamoulian took justifiable pride, fixing the beats in a spoken line, the shifting tempos of a scene, the calibrated momentum of a climax. Off-stage, Crawford was additionally charged with conducting noise effects precisely punctuating the action. Mamoulian was routinely called "mad" and "crazy"; what people actually thought changed from day to day. For Heyward, there was the additional anomaly of literate black profession-als unlike any he had encountered in South Carolina. "I wonder what [my friends] in Charleston would have said if [they] could have seen me singing at the piano with the cast today, and calling them ladies and gentlemen," he wrote to his mother.*[22]

Early on, Mamoulian discovered that confidence and technique were not enough—and rode with this discovery. Leigh Whipper, who created the memorable singing vendor the Crab Man (and later founded the Negro Actors Guild), left this account:

Mamoulian didn't understand the type of Negro with which he was dealing. And I also knew that he knew very little about Negroes. . . . So

---

*On another occasion, Heyward found it "strange" and "unusual" to visit with James Weldon Johnson and his wife. "What would Grannie have said?" he asked his mother in a letter. See James M. Hutchisson, *DuBose Heyward: A Charleston Gentleman and the World of "Porgy and Bess"* (2000), p. 78.

I watched him very closely. Now Mamoulian was the youngest director I had had. . . . I saw how he was going about his work and I didn't
want to butt in and tell him he was wrong, so I thought the best thing
for me to do was to leave the company. . . .

Well, I said, you don't know these people. . . . I said, I see you trying to do the church scene, the wake for Robbins . . . do you want to
see the scene unrehearsed? He says yes. I says, all right you come to
Harlem with me and I'll show it to you. Well, he took the opportunity. Well, I wanted him to see first the type of people he was dealing
with. . . . I carried him to the club, the Association of Trade and Com-
merce, and I introduced him to a couple of lawyers and a couple of
doctors that were in there playing bridge and he didn't say anything,
but I could see his reaction. . . .

Mamoulian and Whipper proceeded to the YMCA, then to Small's Paradise, where the waiters spun their trays, then to a storefront church on
136th Street.

By the time we got to within a hundred feet of the church you could
hear clapping, and so we went on in . . . and took seats at the rear,
and we heard the singing and all the shouting, the amens and all, you
know, and we stayed there. There were some testimonies given and
then they looked for a collection and we put in our[s] . . . and came
out. Mamoulian says, "I see what you mean." I said, "Yes, you don't
know these people. . . . Now you let them be themselves and not take
up the tragic way you have of trying to put fright into Evelyn Ellis. Let
her put her fright into it and you'll have a scene."

According to Whipper, Mamoulian told the cast the next morning
to "forget everything I told you and be yourselves"—and the actors
applauded.[23]

Mamoulian's own recollections—unreliable in many small details of fact—identified other difficulties: actors arriving late, forgetting lines, ignoring instructions. He also recalled:

The first two weeks, it all seemed utterly hopeless to me. Practically everyone in the cast was trying to copy what they thought was "legiti-mate" acting—the result was rank artificiality, nothing came through emotionally. Also, they were most self-conscious, even unwilling, about singing the spirituals the passionate, religious way in which they should be sung. They were inclined to do it in a manner of a cold, formal concert. Somehow they felt that the spirituals were too primitive, old-fashioned and historically way behind them and below them. . . . So one day I addressed the cast at great length. I told them I was indignant and wrathful about their attitude; I told them that their approach was tragically wrong and unforgivable; that spirituals were probably the greatest contribution that their race has made to the music and drama of this country and the world; that they should be sung and ached [sic] the way they were conceived: with passionate dedication of heart and spirit, not merely as a vocal exercise; that in snubbing the spirituals, they were snubbing what the whole country admired and cherished.

I must say that they finally came around and saw the truth of what I was saying. They knew I was sincere and serious about it. From then on, we really had the most inspiring and exciting rehearsals. In fact, first they all went to the other extreme: they threw themselves into the scenes and spirituals so wholeheartedly, with such torrential abandon that the whole pattern of direction and the control of action was com-pletely lost. It all became too realistic and formless.

It took quite a while to achieve the combination of the two equally vital elements on the stage: mental and emotional spontaneity with strictly controlled action—especially in view of the fact that I was styl-izing all the action. The Porgy performance was rhythmic and stylized from beginning to end. A lot of movements, positions, and group-ings were utterly unrealistic. It took a little doing for the cast to get used to it. The objective of stylization is that all passions, feelings, and thoughts of the actors are real, even though their postures and move-ments are stylized. When inner emotions are genuine, then the cor-rectly stylized position is the most expressive one, and to the audience it appears to be completely realistic.[24]

Though Leigh Whipper had spent some time in Charleston as a child, the Gullah dialect that flavored the Heywards' script was unfamiliar to Mamoulian's "Gullahs." A South Carolina authority on Gullah culture, Samuel Gaillard Stoney, was engaged to coach the cast. Mamoulian, meanwhile, was observed by the Guild's Helburn working "in detail on almost every single word with an actor who lacked previous . . . training"; he "gave you a sense of knowledge and experience . . . beyond his actual experience." Howard Barnes, in *Theatre Magazine*, compared Mamoulian's method with that of the Guild's preeminent director, Philip Moeller. Moeller worked collaboratively, whereas Mamoulian "enters the rehearsal period with the entire course of his direction carefully planned out in advance and waits patiently for his project to be realized, spending an immense amount of time on stage movement."*

Production photographs of *Porgy* document the painstaking preci-sion and detail of Mamoulian's stagecraft—and also his flair for "styliza-tion." In the hurricane scene, the massed Gullahs assumed the shape of a triangular wedge registering the thrust of the storm; they comprised a wave of humanity whose crest has just peaked against a shoal. Stage left, bodies were flung to the floor, feet forward. Further from the open stage-left door, other bodies rose ever higher, arms tossed upward and tilted toward the stage-right wall, halting the backward human surge. No realistic blocking could so potently or aesthetically have conveyed

---

*According to Leigh Whipper, however, *Porgy* was never set in stone, and retained an improvisa-tional quality throughout the run.

the terror of these huddled victims. Many Mamoulian tableaux bristled with individual detail; he knew and instructed every cast member by name. At Robbins's funeral, the fervent singing of "Oh I'll Meet 'um in de Promis Lan!" gathered force in correlation with the swaying and clapping of the mourners, variously choreographed, and also with increasingly gigantic shadows cast on the back wall by three downstage spotlights—an effect that Moeller (if Mamoulian is to be believed) greeted with such enthusiasm "he just couldn't control himself, [shouting] 'This is great!' 'This is great!' "[25]

The complexity and novelty of the undertaking equally bred anxiety. Every Sunday the six Guild directors attended a run-through. On one such occasion, while Mamoulian drilled an actor on his lines, Lee Simonson exclaimed, "Not again! I can't stand it!" Simonson asked Helburn, "How much have we sunk in this damned thing?" "Too much to go back now," she replied. In letters to his mother, Heyward registered an ebb and flow of conflicted expectations. At one rehearsal, "everything went wrong. The Negroes got rattled and left out important lines. When they remembered them they said them woodenly like school children reciting." Heyward also wrote: "The cast is scarcely more than amateur." They learned "terribly slowly" and forgot overnight "what Mamoulian bangs into them each day." And, as October loomed: "Mamoulian has been superhuman. . . . I do not see how the play can fail to be impressive. It will probably get some criticism, and it will be for things we can't help—inexperienced cast, etc. But there are several scenes that will be unique in the American theater." Mamoulian, years later, recalled feeling "utter distress" at the final dress rehearsal.[26]

The Guild chose to postpone the premiere by a week: from October 3 to October 10. The morning of the 11th, the Heywards read Brooks Atkinson's mixed *New York Times* review—and were asked by the Guild to rewrite the last act. Arriving at the theater, revisions in hand, they discovered a long line of ticket-seekers standing in pouring rain. The act was not revised.

THE REVIEWS

Atkinson took a more positive view of *Porgy* in his Sunday column—joining a chorus led by the famously pungent Alexander Woollcott:

> The skill, the imagination and the generosity with which [*Porgy*] has been brought to glowing life on the stage . . . make of it an evening of new experience, extraordinary interest and high, startling beauty. In a dozen years of first nights I have not seen in the American theatre an example of more resourceful and enkindling direction. In the dusk of the auditorium, one peers at the program to find out the name of the man who could take this wild, untrained, tatterdemalion horde of players and weave a pageant so fluent, so thrilling. . . . In the ballet of the mourners' shadows upon the wall "Porgy" reaches one of the most exciting climaxes I have ever seen in the theatre. . . . The Guild has begun its tenth season magnificently.

Woollcott, in the *World*, was not the only critic for whom Mamoulian's conception of Robbins's funeral was a defining moment. In the *New Republic*, Stark Young wrote: "When the dead man lies on the bed and the neighbors sing the spirituals to fill the saucer with money to bury him, and the excitement rises to dancing and wild music, the dramatists must have their due credit for what must be one of the high points of this or any season." Atkinson wrote in the *Times*: "For the curtain of one of the early scenes [the direction] rises to splendid theatrical generalship. . . . Gradually the singing becomes more and more preternatural. In the violence of the religious orgy . . . the stage is illuminated only from the front, and the pale wall behind quickly swarms with a myriad of dancing, swirling, leaping shadows." Alan Dale wrote in the *New York American*: "To hear the spirituals sung as they were is worth twice the price of a seat at the Guild Theatre. There were the fervor, the hysteria, the emotionalism, and the curious abandon that must accom-

pany such outbursts. All the colored 'folks' raised their voices, gesticu-
lated, gyrated, as they joined in the volcanic choruses. It was something
new to most of us—may I say to all of us."[27]

For Woollcott, excepting *The Emperor Jones*, *Porgy* was "the first good
job the American theatre has done with the Negro and certainly the
finest performance of a play I have ever seen from a Negro troupe."
For other critics, a powerful black spectacle proved alien or discomfiting. In *Billboard*, Gordon Leland predicted that "the teeming canvas of
this sprawling nigger slum will not enjoy the continued success of other
Guild plays, such as *The Second Man*, or *Ned McCobb's Daughter*." Percy
Stone, in the *Herald Tribune*, found the characters of *Porgy* to be "the
nearest approach to the eternal verities of primitive living in our country
since the Red Savage was systematically exterminated." Other writers
presciently detected Mamoulian weaknesses: the tendency of "stylization" to lapse into artifice and excess; a command of spectacle and mass
shortchanging the individual. "The play does not set off individual acting in high perspective," Atkinson wrote. "It runs more to an exposition
of group psychology." Young, in the *New Republic*, was a native of Mis-
sissippi. "None of the acting is in itself very important, and sometimes it
is very poor," he thought.

> The whole quality is thinned down from the Southern real thing. . . .
> Mr. Mamoulian's directing . . . is sure to attract attention. . . . It is
> indeed admirable in many spots, . . . exhibiting a stage sense that goes
> far ahead of most directors.
>
> It ought to be . . . equally clear that this is often the wrong directing
> for this play of "Porgy." And this is true not because that quick, obvi-
> ously disciplined and drilled movement and sound . . . are not true to
> Negro quality, and could never achieve, of course, the rich languor of
> physical rhythm or voice or emotion that is natural among Negroes.
> The director, as an artist, must have a right to be as false or as true as

he chooses to the material that he works in. But such a style is wrong because it disturbs the nature of the play Mr. Mamoulian is creating into stage terms. If "Porgy" seemed, as we watch it there on the stage, less active, whisked up, competently direct and sharp, we should have more room for that relaxed logic, for those childlike and unruled fires and for the vagaries of mood, beauty, whim and story. . . .

Whatever *Porgy* was, it was self-evidently Mamoulian's show. "Mamoulian should be considered almost solely responsible for the success of the new play *Porgy*," wrote the *Brooklyn Daily Eagle*'s George Halasz. It would have been "difficult to sit through without the Guild's lucky discovery of its new director," testified John Mason Brown in *Theatre Arts Monthly*. "To [Mamoulian's] vivid direction may be ascribed much of the play's popularity," opined Percy Hammond in the *Herald Tribune*.[28]

Porgy ran for 217 performances on Broadway, then took to the road. When it returned to New York in April for 137 more performances, Woollcott returned as well and reported that he liked *Porgy*—the play and the performance—more than ever. John Mason Brown returned and wrote: "To this day 'Porgy' as a play is largely a matter of [Mamoulian's] direction. Its strength comes not so much from what the Heywards have actually written as from the manner in which Mr. Mamoulian has treated the scenario they have given him."

Mamoulian was by now a star. His admirers included James Weldon Johnson, a seminal African-American artist and intellectual for whom *Porgy* "loomed high above every Negro drama that had ever been produced." Johnson also wrote: "In *Porgy*, the Negro performer removed all doubts as to his ability to do acting that requires thoughtful interpretation and intelligent skill. Here was more than the achievement of one or two individuals who might be set down as exceptions. Here was a large company giving a first-rate, even performance, with eight or ten reaching a high mark. . . . The play carried conviction through its sincere simplicity. . . . at times it rose to heights of ecstasy and tragedy; and always it was suffused with Negro humour." The *Age*, an important New York City African-American weekly, reprinted Woollcott's review from the *World* with a commendatory note. Max Reinhardt, who saw *Porgy* seven times, told the *World* that it was one of his "great experiences in the theater"; it combined "convincing truth with the utmost stylization" and possessed "a luminousness that originates not with single stars but with the intensity of the entire ensemble." (According to Mamoulian, in later years Reinhardt adapted Mamoulian's "shadow ballet" for a Shakespeare production and credited *Porgy* in a program note.) When the Theatre Guild premiered *Marco Millions* on January 9, 1928, the director—Rouben Mamoulian—was chosen by the playwright: Eugene O'Neill.[29]

SCRIPT REVISIONS

If Mamoulian had done nothing more than galvanize the Heywards' *Porgy* with "enkindling direction," he would have remained crucial to the play's success. But he did much more than that: the final script was greatly reshaped by his interventions. At the time of its Broadway run, Mamoulian took no credit for the script in comments to the press. Rather, Dorothy Heyward, in articles and interviews for years after, emphasized the contributions she and DuBose had made to the casting and mounting of their play. Hollis Alpert, in *The Life and Times of Porgy and Bess* (1990), acknowledged that

> Mamoulian had ideas about the script that meant more work for the Heywards. The part of Porgy, he felt, needed to be strengthened in a way that would bring him closer to his more sensitive, mystical, and philosophical counterpart in the book. Porgy should also show an earlier interest in Bess to sharpen the conflict between him and her lover,

Crown. He wanted more made of Sporting Life and the "happy dust" with which he lures Bess to her unknown fate.[30]

In fact, the Guild's Theresa Helburn participated in the many revisions undertaken by the Heywards. As for Mamoulian, he was an auteur. He invariably introduced changes to the plays and films he directed; it was part of his method. In the case of *Porgy*, he testified in 1958 that the script he was first shown was

> not satisfactory . . . ; it still remained basically a narrative, a novel, though . . . in dialogue form. . . .
>
> I went back to the Guild and told them that I thought the play wasn't dramatized enough. They asked me to put in writing what . . . I thought should be done. This I did, on fifteen pages. They sent these pages to DuBose and Dorothy Heyward, who were at the time in London. A cable came back from them saying that they both fully agreed with every point I made and that they would start re-writing at once. This made me very happy. So I signed a contract to direct *Porgy*.

According to Mamoulian's further recollections, he obtained a more optimistic ending for the play, and clarifications and simplifications of speech. He also had the parts of Sporting Life and Crown enlarged in order to dramatize the forces impinging on Bess. And, to further enlarge Bess's tragic stature, he intensified the community's hostility toward her.[31]

The published version of the *Porgy* script, dated 1927 (and reprinted by the Theatre Guild in 1955 as "the complete text" and again in 1959 in *Famous American Plays of the 1920s*, selected by Kenneth MacGowan), shows a play in four acts. Mamoulian's working script for *Porgy* is a typescript. The typescript differs substantially from the published play. With Mamoulian's *additional* handwritten changes—including dialogue and action entered or effaced, and compression into three acts—the typescript differs *fundamentally* from the published play. Although changes in Mamoulian's hand are not necessarily changes conceived wholly by Mamoulian, it so happens that they embody, in detail, the changes he later remembered requesting (his 15-page memorandum of 1927 seems not to have survived). They also include the addition of the daybreak "Noise Symphony"* that we know was part of *Porgy* at the Guild Theatre. It may be reasonably inferred that, in comparing the thrice-published play to the annotated typescript, the nature of Mamoulian's contributions may be gleaned. In summary, such comparison shows that, as a Broadway exercise in integrated musical theater, *Porgy* as revised by Mamoulian was both unprecedented and *sui generis*; that Mamoulian's interventions created a dramatic template essentially different from that of the novella or the original play; and that thus—and only thus—Mamoulianized, *Porgy* already strikingly resembles the operatic *Porgy and Bess* of 1935.[32]

If Mamoulian is to be believed, Ravel called *Porgy* an "opera." It is indeed a Wagnerian *Gesamtkunstwerk*. The polyphonic texture of the action is instantly established. Before the curtain rises—for that matter, before the rise of every curtain—the bells of St. Michael's Church chime the hour. It is 8 P.M. We see the dilapidated Catfish Row courtyard, with its twenty shuttered windows and florid southern vegetation. The courtyard echoes with Gullah banter. A guitar is heard, an urchin dances. Gradually, language becomes decipherable; the last Gullah line, spoken by Maria, reads: "Enty onah yeddy 'bout huccum Porgy ma done title um?" Then Mingo says, "Yo' is all too talky round hyuh. A nigger can't get time tuh read de bones atter he done t'row um"—and a craps game ensues. The men grunt, chant, whistle, snap their fingers. Mingo sings: "Ole snake-eye, go off an' die. Ole man seben, come down from Heaben." Porgy, "in a sort of sing song chant," coaxes "Oh, little stars, roll me some light."[33] Exclamations punctuate each roll of the dice: "Made um," "Dat's de point." The game escalates. Crown snatches a

---

*See p. 224.

bottle, downs the contents, and shatters it on the flagstone floor. Earlier in this multifarious scene, Clara paces the courtyard with her baby, singing a lullaby: "Hush, li'l baby, don' yo' cry. Fadder an' mudder born to die." Her husband, Jake, snatches the child and sings:

> My mammy tells me, long time ago,
> Son, don' yo' marry no gal yo' know.
> Spen' all yo' money—eat all yo' bread,
> Gone to Savannah, lef' yo' fo' dead.

Several men join in the last line. Jake declares the child asleep. It wails. The men laugh. Clara takes the baby to her room. With Clara and the infant out of the picture, with the drunken Crown joining the men, the craps game increasingly focuses the courtyard's ceaseless activity, which also informatively introduces Serena, Robbins, Sporting Life, Maria, and Peter (among other Catfish Row denizens of lesser importance), setting in motion each relationship and conflict that will ignite the story at hand.

Everything I have just described may be found in the Heywards' published *Porgy* script with one exception: Mamoulian's annotated typescript is the source of Maria's Gullah line cited above, and of Mingo's response. Mamoulian's first significant intervention occurs just after Crown throws down a coin and threatens: "I'm talkin' to yo' mans. Anybody answering me?" In provocative counterpoint to the intensifying contrapuntal male banter, Mamoulian has Bess, Serena, and Mingo reprise "My mammy tells me."* "Shet yo' damn mout!" Crown explodes, clapping his hand over Bess's mouth as all three stop singing.[34] At such protean moments—and there are many—*Porgy* less resembles a play with incidental music than what Ravel dubbed it: opera.

In overview, Mamoulian's additions to the sonic world of *Porgy* are of

---

*In *Porgy and Bess*, Clara memorably reprises "Summertime" over the craps-game shouts.

two types: musical and extramusical. The music of the play begins with its speech: a line such as "What yo' bring dat 'oman here fo'?" (memorably set by Gershwin) invites an eloquence of rhythm and pitch even when spoken. Then there are the spirituals. As published in 1928 by Bibo, Bloedon & Lang, the *Porgy* spirituals are simple voice and piano arrangements by George Shackley. The music for the a cappella choral versions sung by the *Porgy* cast has apparently not survived. Mamoulian's annotated typescript shows that when the play went into production, the proportion of music to speech increased. The "new" numbers include a picnic song—"Satan led me to the window"—that provokes Jake to protest: "Nobody knows whether yo' getting religion round here or doin a juba dance so cut it out will you please?"* Mamoulian also interpolates Leigh Whipper's Crab Man song:

> I'm talking about devil crabs
> I'm talking about steam crabs

Finally—crucially—Mamoulian adds a closing chorus to the show:

> I'm on my way to heavenly land
> Oh lord, I'm on my way!

The ultimate point to be made about Mamoulian's musical reconception of *Porgy* is that for him "music" is a universal category of sonic experience: his notion of sound is virtually Cagean. In *Porgy*, a detailed sonic tapestry is always in play. In act 1 alone, there are specified moans, shuffles, whimpers, shouts, grunts, sobs, hand-claps, foot-pats, finger-snaps. Shutters bang. Rain pummels a roof.

In fact, two of the four biggest "musical" set pieces emphasize noise. One, ending act 2, is the hurricane: choreographing a range of specific sound cues, Mamoulian creates a crescendo of fervor as articulate as

---

*This, then, is the seed of Gershwin's picnic scene song "It Ain't Necessarily So."

the huddled chorus. The second, in act 3, is a "Symphony of Noises" calibrating the awakening of communal life. The play's other two major set pieces are Robbins's funeral in act 1, and the act 2 picnic, with the Jenkins Orphanage Band that Mamoulian imported from Charleston. All four deserve to be described in sequence, and in detail.

ROBBINS'S FUNERAL

During the act 1, scene 1 craps game, Crown accuses Robbins of cheating. They fight. Crown slays Robbins with a cotton hook and flees. Scene 2—Robbins's funeral—is the *Porgy* episode that New York's critics found the most astonishing. It is, in its entirety, a musical composition crafted by Mamoulian.

We hear St. Michael's chime 7 P.M. A dirge commences. The curtain then rises on Serena's room; she is Robbins's widow. Robbins's body, under a white sheet, lies on a bed. A large saucer rests on his chest. Mamoulian instructs that the singers are softly clapping hands and swaying, that shadows are cast by a lantern on the floor. The mourners drop coins in the saucer in rhythm to the music.

> Deat', ain't yuh gots no shame, shame?
> Deat', ain't yuh gots no shame, shame?
> Deat', ain't yuh gots no shame, shame?
> Deat', ain't yuh gots no shame?
>
> Teck dis man an' gone, gone,
> Teck dis man an' gone, gone,
> Teck dis man an' gone, gone,
> Deat', ain't yuh gots no shame?

"How de saucer stan', Sistuh?" asks Jake, over the chorus. Dialogue ensues. Mamoulian specifies that the dirge here diminish to a "soft moan." Peter begins a call-and-response prayer, with the crowd "swaying and moaning."

> PETER: Gawd gots plenty coin' fo' de saucer.
> SERENA: Bless de Lo'd.
> PETER: An' He goin' soften dese people heart' fo' fill de saucer till he spill over.
> SERENA: Amen, my Jedus!
> PETER: De Lord will provide a grabe fo' He chilun.
> CLARA: Bless de Lo'd!
> [etc.]

Porgy and Bess arrive. There are objections to Bess because of her past association with Crown. The singing resumes ("few start, others join," writes Mamoulian):

> Leabe dese chillum starve, starve,
> Leabe dese chillum starve, starve,
> Leabe dese chillum starve, starve,
> Deat', ain't yuh gots no shame?

The sound of rain commences; the spiritual grows ("move from single to double swaying," Mamoulian annotates).

Suddenly, three white men—a detective and two policemen—burst into the room. All music ceases abruptly. The exchange that follows—during which Peter is detained as a witness to the murder—doubles the residual impact of the funeral chant by imposing the antimusic of blunt white speech.

> DETECTIVE: Um! A saucer-buried nigger, I see! (To SERENA.) You're his widow?
> SERENA: Yes, suh.
> DETECTIVE: He didn't leave any burial insurance?

SERENA: No, boss. He didn't leabe nuttin'.
DETECTIVE: Well, see to it that he's buried tomorrow.

"A moment of desolate silence" punctuates the departure of the three outsiders with Peter miserably in tow. To transition back to the funeral, Mamoulian begins by restarting the rain. "Dere go Peter fo' be lock up like t'ief, an' here lie Robbins wid he wife an' fadderless chillum," Porgy observes. Mamoulian instructs that Porgy's next sentence—"An' Crown done gone he was fo' do de same t'ing ober again somewheres else"—be moaned. He next writes: "Crowd takes up moan and raises it like an organ vox humana until it vibrates." A new spiritual—"What' de mattuh chillum?"—comes next. Mamoulian has Maria sing the first verse while "others hum." Then, as the song builds, Mamoulian has the rows of mourners on either side "double sway" in succession until by the final verse all are double-swaying.

The black undertaker bustles into Serena's room. The singing dies away, but the swaying does not. To soft moans, he briskly inquires, "How de saucer stan' now, my sistuh?" Moaning stops at the prospect of Robbins's body being seized by the board of health for medical students. The undertaker relents and agrees to bury Robbins. Mamoulian has the pleading Serena lie flat on the floor with her arms around his ankles; he also choreographs the crowd's relaxation when the undertaker gives in.

Bess, squatting, now commences a final, triumphant song:

> Oh, I gots a little brudder in de new grabeyahd
> What outshine de sun,
> Outshine de sun.

This is the moment for which Mamoulian has been waiting. "Crowd starts moaning with rising tone, until Bess rises to her knees with outstretched arms." The lights dim. A lamp on the mantel "flickers and goes out." An amber spot, downstage center, is cued to Bess's exclamation, "I will meet um in de Primus Lan'!" The full chorus, basses predominating, ignites. "Double swaying," says Mamoulian, "rows on each side of bed rise starting from back and 'shout.' Serena rises and clasps hands tightly above head. Three counts after she spreads them open." All are on their feet, swaying and clapping. Bess leads the "shouting." Cries of "Alleluyah" and "Yes, Lord" swell the song as gigantic shadows are cast upon the back wall by three downstage spotlights; as the singers move closer to the stage lip, the tumult of gyration is gradually magnified till the curtain's fall. This shadow ballet, which would become a Mamoulian signature, visually magnified the "musical" parameters of his style: rhythm, diminuendo and crescendo, ritardando and accelerando.

Some of what I have just described—including the white "anti-music"—may be found in the Heywards' script. Mamoulian's supplementary role is here twofold. He heightens and stylizes the action (the coordinated squatting, kneeling, and standing, the culminating shadows—all vital to his design—are wholly unrealistic). And he composes. The entire scene was doubtless directed with a metronome controlling tempo ("METRONOM [*sic*]," reads an initial Mamoulian annotation). Even the mute typescript, with his annotations, makes his mastery of transition and climax self-evident. It should be recalled that Mamoulian's formative professional experience, in Rochester, was mainly operatic. In fact, *Porgy*'s three other primary set pieces are "musical" numbers of his invention.

PICNIC AND HURRICANE

Mamoulian's compression of *Porgy* from four to three acts resulted in a first act with two scenes, a second act with four, and a third with three. Act 1, scene 1, ends with Robbins's death; scene two is the funeral. In act 2, scene 1, everyone leaves for the picnic on Kittiwah Island. Scene 2, on the island, is the picnic itself, after which Bess is captured by Crown.

In scene 3, fishing boats set out and a hurricane looms. Scene 4 is the hurricane. Porgy kills Crown in act 3, scene 1. In scene 2, detectives take Porgy away and Sporting Life accosts Bess with happy dust. In the final scene, Porgy returns to find Bess gone. (The opera adopts the same blueprint.)*

Like the novella *Porgy*, the Heywards' script is full of music. (Heyward—and not only in *Porgy*—adored the black songs of the south.) But the original *Porgy* script contains not nearly enough consolidated music to balance the sung lamentation and exaltation of Robbins' funeral. As Mamoulian's annotations document, he created a musical structure for the play; superimposed upon the script, it transforms texture and reshapes trajectory. In act 2, scene 1, he focuses and amplifies the role of the picnic band. To the culminating act 2 hurricane, he adds a symphonic conception of devastation. For the final scene of act 3, he invents an extended musical pantomime and interpolates a closing chorus. These numbers are cunningly distributed to articulate a megarhythm for the show. If *Porgy* were a symphony, the funeral would be movement one (a Mahlerian touch). The picnic band would be the scherzo, the hurricane the tortuous central climax, and the pantomime/final chorus a healing finale with coda.

The picnic musicale is the simplest and—in terms of the central narrative—the most tangential of these revisions. Mamoulian (it will be recalled) was introduced to the celebrated Jenkins Orphanage Band in Charleston and there resolved to bring it to New York for *Porgy*. In the novella *Porgy*, what could only be the Orphanage Band—"two score boys attired in several variations of the bandmaster's costume"—launches (as we have observed)† "daring and individual excursions into the realm of

---

*In the original four-act script (as published, but not as performed), act 1 (with two scenes) is the same. Act 2 is two scenes: the picnic departure; the picnic. In act 3, scene 1, the boats depart; scene 2 is the hurricane. Porgy kills Crown in act 4, scene 1; in scene 2, Porgy is detained; in scene 3, Porgy returns but Bess is gone.

† See p. 22.

sound." In the Heywards' script for the play, an unidentified band takes part in act 2, accompanying the song

> Sit down! I can't sit down!
> Sit down! I can't sit down!
> Sit down! I can't sit down!
> My soul's so happy dat I can't sit down!

Mamoulian's annotation here reads: "Band enters, 2×2, march down center. Dancing etc. Band wheels and exits. Crowd follows. Jake and Annie last, doing cakewalk." The Heywards, in their published four-act script, next had Porgy, left behind, shadowed by the buzzard who brings bad luck. Frantically, impotently, he waves his arms. "Get out ob here! Don' yo' light. . . . Oh, Gawd! . . . 'Tain't no use now. . . . He done lit." Porgy looks up "with an expression of hopelessness as the curtain falls." Mamoulian deletes this encounter so that the scene ends with the departing band—which is next heard, curtain down, performing a newly added entr'acte song, "All de Gold in de Mountains" (later sung by the picnickers). At the picnic (act 2, scene 2), the band is initially heard offstage, playing "Ain't It Hard to be a Nigger?" The party proceeds, after which Crown has his confrontation with Bess. Mamoulian deletes the scene's final instruction: "The band is still playing but grows faint in the distance." The Jenkins band, then, becomes a compact, unadulterated diversion, a happy interlude.

Charleston's Jenkins Orphanage Band had by 1928 performed in the inaugural parades of Theodore Roosevelt and William Taft. It had been heard in Paris, Berlin, Rome, London, and Vienna. As many as five Jenkins Orphanage Bands were on tour at any one time. A November 22, 1928, Fox Movietone short* makes singularly obvious Mamoulian's rea-

---

* Accessible via YouTube.

sons for transporting the band to Broadway, and the degree to which its presence necessarily focused the musical energies of the play. The uniformed rapscallions gravely blowing and pounding their huge instruments, the grinning bandmasters shuffling and mugging, would be the center of attention on any stage.

If the picnic scene, revised by Mamoulian, becomes a raucous divertissement, the hurricane becomes the play's sonic climax. Throughout the Heywards' published script, Mamoulian ruthlessly excises dialogue in pursuit of a schematized, stylized reading that supports a superimposed musical structure. Foregrounding the hurricane, his pencil is itself a hurricane of destruction: nearly all the dialogue the Heywards furnished for act 2, scene 4, is scratched out. Cheryl Crawford's compensatory offstage orchestra, listed in Mamoulian's hand, here includes two wind machines, a thunder drum, and a tin sheet. The sound effects listed by Mamoulian include a wood crash, a timber crash ("block of wood on top of ladder that is thrown over"), a glass crash, a "sea effect," two "lightning effects" and seven revolver shots. In combination with three spirituals and a song, this arsenal of noise is deployed with precision to craft an elemental sound design: a single crescendo; sudden silence; curtain.

Mamoulian's crescendo begins at the end of the preceding scene. The courtyard is empty. The wind begins softly. The hurricane bell tolls ("very different," the script tells us, "from the silver tone of St. Michael's"). Clara, whose husband's fishing boat is far out to sea, rushes to the gate shrieking "Jake! Jake!" Mamoulian here replaces pages of dialogue with these instructions: "Wind louder. Crabman in distance and boat whistles start and continue to curtain. Shutters bang. Wind loud. Women yell for children. Roll of thunder. First whistle = cue for electric fan that blows clothes on line. Women and children running. Curtain." The sounds of wind and water continue while the set is changed. A spiritual commences:

> We will all sing togedduh on dat day
> We will all sing togedduh on dat day
> An' I'll fall upon my knees an face de risin' sun,
> Oh, Lord, hab mercy on me!

The curtain rises on Serena's room, dimly lit. The door is stage left. A downstage spotlight supplies shadow effects. The spiritual continues. The roaring swells. A second spiritual begins:

> Dere's somebody knockin' at de do'
> Dere's somebody knockin' at de do.'
> Oh, Mary, oh, Mart'a,
> Somebody knockin's at de do'.

The song swells and accelerates. There is shouting. Peter exclaims: "I hear dea' knockin' at the door." One by one, the singers cease. The knocking grows louder. To shrieks of terror, the door opens against the wind. It is Crown, come for Bess. "Yo' stick 'round here, yo' sure to get killed sooner or later," Serena warns. Crown laughs: "Ef Gawd want to kill me, he got plenty ob chance 'tween here an' Kittiwah Islan'. Me an' Him been habin' it out all de way from Kittiwah; first Him on top, den me. Dere ain't nuttin' He likes better'n a scrap wid a man. Gawd an' me frien'!" The wind roars in reply. A third spiritual begins:

> All I know
> Got to meet de Jedgement

Above the singing, addressing the wind, Crown shouts "at the ceiling": "Dat's right, drown um out! Don' yo' listen to um sing! Dey don' gib yo' credit fo' no taste in music. How 'bout dis one, Big Frien'?" He now sings a lewd ragtime song, "Hesitation Blues":

> Ashes to ashes, dust to dust
> Show me a 'oman dat a man can trust
> Oh, Honey, how long do I have to wait
> Oh, can I get yo' now or must I hesitate

Mamoulian annotates: "This song and spiritual in counterpoint with each other, the spiritual becoming faster to keep the half time." The wind peaks. Surmounting the din, Crown roars: "Don't yo' hear Gawd A'mighty—laughing up dere? . . . Gawd laugh, an' Crown laugh back!" Mamoulian instructs: "Crash/all effects." Clara rushes out, wildly seeking Jake. Crown follows, intent on rescuing Clara. A sudden silence engulfs the room. The stage grows lighter. Everyone crowds toward the single window, peering through the slats of the closed shutters. Fast curtain.

Excising a dance number and various vicissitudes of the storm, distributing and redistributing the singers in discrete massed configurations, retaining only the least dispensable snatches of speech (such as the passages I have cited above), adding Crown's lewd ragtime, imposing his single sonic crescendo, Mamoulian transforms the Catfish Row storm into a stark metaphoric epic: Judgment Day, with Crown's Satan taunting the wrathful Gawd all others fear. As we shall see, the epic implications of this dramatic redesign were part of a Mamoulian master plan.

FINALE

Like the Jenkins band, the "Symphony of Noises" that Mamoulian interpolates in *Porgy* as the third act's central "musical" event resulted from the initial Charleston reconnaissance with his designer Clarence Throckmorton. Mamoulian fastidiously listed eighty-four characteristic outdoor sounds he encountered. His catalogue records rug-snappers and pillow-beaters, knife-sharpeners and hammering shoemakers. An elaborate choreography of these daybreak noises replaced the nondescript 2 P.M. beginning of the play's final scene as first scripted by the Heywards, with "Negroes . . . coming and going about their tasks," Maria serving food, and Serena singing a lullaby—after which Porgy arrives and calls furtively to the boy Scipio to open the gate.

The previous scene has ended with Bess slamming her door on Sporting Life. The curtain is now down. We hear snoring and the pounding of a hammer. The curtain rises. A woman enters, sweeping with a broom. It becomes apparent that these sounds have from the start been rhythmically cued, with the hammer on beat one, the snore on beat three, and the swish of the broom on beats two and four, the rise of the curtain having occurred on the first beat three. It is morning; all shutters are closed. Mamoulian's noises accumulate one by one in the course of the next four minutes. The governing meter shifts from 4/4 to 2/4 to 6/8—in effect, an accelerando. The courtyard fills.[35] Shutters open on cue. Noise, dialogue, and stage action amass a density of detail both formidable and precise.* As the "Symphony" peaks, two men beat a Charleston rhythm on boxes and a vegetable vendor enters calling out his produce. A police bell sounds offstage. Cries of "Porgy!" are heard. Porgy appears at the gate accompanied by a policeman, who exits. Mamoulian's interpolation here meshes with the Heywards' script. In "a joyous but guarded voice," Porgy says: "Shhh, don't nobody let on yet dat I is home again. I gots a surprise fo' Bess, an' I ain't want she to know till I gots eberyt'ing ready." He does not notice that the others are silent and embarrassed.

Mamoulian later recalled that he conceived the "Symphony of Noises" because what struck him most about the black lifestyle in Charleston was "its almost musical fluency and rhythm." He claimed that he would invariably rehearse his noises with a baton.

---

*For the complete script of the "Symphony of Noises," see Appendix A.

One hot summer morning, as I was conducting . . . in the large room at the top of the Theatre Guild building, two of the Guild management dropped in to watch the rehearsal. The picture they saw must have appeared odd. Here was the whole cast in an attitude of utter and alert concentration making incredible noises, and here was I facing them with a baton, making out I was Toscanini. I will never forget the look on their faces. They stayed a few minutes, then silently left the room. A little later a note was delivered to me asking me to come and see them in their office. . . .

They demanded that I cut this scene out of the production. It didn't make any sense, they said . . . I liked the idea too much and thought that my instinct was right and they were wrong. Finally, I said, "If you cut this scene out, then I'm out. . . ." After a long pause, with expressions that looked painfully stoical, they said: "All right keep it, and let the audience teach you a lesson." So the audience did. . . . The Noise Symphony became one of the highlights of the show.[36]

Mamoulian adored his daybreak symphony. He recapitulated it in Paris in *Love Me Tonight* (the best evidence of what it looked and sounded like in *Porgy*). And he inserted it in *Porgy and Bess*. But *Porgy* is the show that most requires it. In terms of musical structure, it balances the weighty numbers of acts 1 and 2; in terms of dramatic structure, its crescendo prepares Porgy's final entrance and the cruel irony of his disappointment. What is more, like the hurricane, the "Symphony of Noises" is metaphoric. Robbins and Crown have been murdered. Lives have been lost at sea. But life goes on. Daybreak here asserts the daily resilience of the human spirit. What *Porgy* needs next—and last—is a redemptive moment consummating Crown's extinction. The novella *Porgy* ends in quiet despair. The Heywards' published script ends with Porgy learning that Bess has gone to New York (an inspiration generally credited to Dorothy):

PORGY: Which way dat?

LILY: (Pointing.) Up Nort'—past de Custom House.

(PORGY turns his goat and drives slowly with bowed head toward the gate.)

MARIA: Porgy, I tells yo' it ain't no use!

LILY: Dat great big city. Yo' can't find um dere!

SERENA: Ain't we tells yo'—

(But PORGY is going on toward gate as if he did not hear, and they cease to protest and stand motionless watching him. As PORGY reaches the gate, SCIPIO silently opens it. PORGY drives through and turns to left, as LILY pointed. St. Michael's chimes the quarter-hour. The gate clangs shut. Curtain.)

Mamoulian required an ending less realistic, more effulgent. And he needed music. In fact, throughout his career his predilection was to brighten "unhappy" endings. His rhapsodic style craved the redemptive flush. Of all the additions to the Heywards' script in Mamoulian's hand, none is more crucial than what comes last:

PORGY: Bring m' goat.

MARIA: What you wants wid' you' goat. Yo bes' not go any place.

PORGY: Bring m' goat!

SERENA: You bes' stay wid yo' frien', Porgy—a little rest it make you feel better.

PORGY: Wont nobody bring my goat. (It is brought.)

MARIA: Aint we tell you, you can't find um.

SERENA: For Lawd's sake, Porgy, where yo' goin'.

PORGY: Aint you say Bess gone to Noo Yawk. Dats where I goin'. I gots to be wid Bess. I gonna find her. I'm on my way.

(MARIA starts to sing softly.)

LILY: Porgy, Porgy.

MINGO: Don't go Porgy.

LILY: You best stay wid us.

(PORGY raises his hands—prays silently and repeats: "I'm on my way"—then the others realize there is a spiritual to fit the occasion and all start singing as he crosses to goat cart, exits off Right.

SERENA: May the good Lord be wid you.

(Singing continues.)

> I'm on my way to heavenly land
> Oh lord, I'm on my way
> I'm on my way
> To heavenly land
> I'm on my way
> To heavenly land
> I'm on my way
> To heavenly land
> Oh, Lord, I'm on my way!*

MORALITY PLAY

This, then, is the second aspect of Mamoulian's reconception of the Heywards' script. In addition to extrapolating and organizing its "music," he transcends its naturalistic and anthropological tendencies with an epic thrust. The polar world of the spiritual—of travail and redemption—supplies a refreshed dramatic template. *Porgy* is no longer about Gullahs. Rather, the Gullahs stylize a universal condition of humankind.

Mamoulian's ecstatic ending would have been preposterous in Heyward's novella. Heyward's Porgy would no more have attempted to drive his goat cart to Manhattan than would his Gullahs have synchronized their morning sounds, or assumed an expressive wedge in the face of a hurricane. With his stentorian command, "Bring m' goat!" the Porgy of

---

*To compare the endings of the novella, the play, the revised play, and the opera, see Appendix C.

the revised play attains iconic stature—and so, in the play, do Sporting Life and Crown.

Heyward's novella, it will be recalled, paradoxically intermingles naturalism with a state-of-nature fable. Mamoulian is no naturalist. And, as his revisions to *Porgy and Bess* would confirm, he had no use for Heyward's "Golden Age" framework. Even so: though Catfish Row may not be Eden, happy dust remains Sporting Life's apple of temptation. A snake in the grass, he insinuates a subcurrent of sin. If he obtains nothing comparable to the two songs Gershwin would memorably compose for him, he becomes a more prominent presence in rewrites of the script that give him much more to say. He is no longer, as in the novella, a mere cameo player. As for Crown, Mamoulian's streamlining of the hurricane scene, expunging most of the dialogue, elevates Crown's "Gawd" invocation to a mythic moment. In his 15-page memorandum to the Heywards, Mamoulian had proposed that the forces impinging on Bess be intensified. As Sin, as Satan, Sporting Life and Crown are more central to the action of the play than to the world of the novella.

And there are further new challenges for Bess: Mamoulian's annotations underline the hostility excited by "Crown's Bess." In act 2, scene 1, Bess is first observed living with Porgy. Serena, Jake, and Maria debate this development. Bess enters and crosses "with an air of cool scorn." Mamoulian, in his annotations, here interrupts before she can reach Porgy's door: he has Serena, Maria, and Lily begin gossiping about Porgy's "luck" at craps.

BESS (rushes at LILY): You say Porgy t'ief?

LILY: I going to run dat little hussy out ob dis court.

MARIA: No you aint. An I hope she teach you to keep yo' mout' off Porgy. . . . (MARIA pats BESS on back. Whole court gathering or leaning out of windows. When MARIA pats BESS on back, she turns on her like a wildcat and MARIA backs, first scared, then laughing. BESS goes in PORGY'S house with head up, defiant.

In Heyward's novella, Bess is less prepossessing than this. She does not accompany Crown to the craps game, as in the play. Rather, she materializes subsequently as a sordid apparition:

> Through the early night a woman had lain in the dust against the outer wall of Maria's cook-shop. She was extremely drunk and unpleasant to look upon. Exactly when she had dropped, or been dropped there, no one knew. . . .
>
> The visitor measured the distance to the next bench with wandering and vacant eyes, plunged for it, and collapsed, with head and arms thrown across a table. . . . An ugly scar marked her left cheek, and the acid of utter degradation had etched hard lines about her mouth. . . .
>
> "Who lib in dat room 'cross de way?"
>
> "Porgy," she was informed, "but such as yuh ain't gots no use fuh he. He a cripple, an a beggar."
>
> "He de man wid goat?"
>
> "Yes, he gots goat."
>
> The woman's eyes narrowed to dark, unfathomable slits.
>
> "I hyuh say he gits good money fum de w'ite folks," she said slowly. . . . She crossed the narrow drive with a decisive tread, opened the door of Porgy's room, entered, and closed the door behind her.[37]

Living with Porgy changes Bess. "Her gaunt figure had rounded out, bringing back a look of youthful comeliness, and her face was losing its hunted expression. The air of pride that had always shown in her bearing, which had amounted almost to disdain, that had so infuriated the virtuous during her evil days, was heightened, and, in her bettered condition forced a resentful respect from her feminine traducers." Bess tells Maria: "I gots tuh be decent 'bout somet'ing, 'less I couldn't go back an' look in Porgy face." But she also confesses, to Porgy: "W'en I tek dat dope, I know den dat I ain't yo' kin'. An' w'en Crown put he han' on me dat day, I run tuh he like water. Some day dope comin' agin. An' some day Crown goin' put he han' on my t'roat. It goin' be like dyin' den. But I gots tuh talk de trut' tuh yuh. W'en dem time come, I goin' tuh go." Bess's fatal moral weakness is of course retained in the play, but there is more to offset it.

Porgy, too, is less infirm in body and spirit, transposed to the stage. If Bess, onstage, is less debased, Porgy is less passive. Here is Heyward on Porgy, in the book:

> There was something Eastern and mystic about the intense introspec-
> tion of his look. He never smiled, and he acknowledged gifts only by a
> slow lifting of the eyes that had odd shadows in them. . . . Unless one
> were unusually preoccupied at the moment of dropping a coin in his
> cup, he carried away in return a very definite, yet somewhat disquiet-
> ing impression: a sense of infinite patience, and beneath it the vibra-
> tion of unrealized, but terrific, energy.
>
> There was a touch of grey in the wool above the ears, and strong
> character lines flared downward from the nose to corners of a mouth
> that was, at once, full-lipped and sensuous, yet set in a resolute line
> most unusual in a negro. With the first indications of age upon it, the
> face seemed still alive with a youth that had been neither spent nor
> wasted.

As for the "change in Porgy" wrought by Bess: "The defensive barrier of reserve that he had built about his life was down. The long hours when he used to sit fixed and tense, with the look of introspection upon his face, were gone. Even the most skeptical of the women were begin-ning to admit that Bess was making him a good mate. Not that they mingled freely with the other residents of the court. On the contrary, they seemed strangely sufficient unto themselves."[38] Mamoulian's Porgy is more prepossessing.

Taken literally, Mamoulian's revised ending is ludicrous—or, more precisely, absurdist: Porgy will never make it to New York with his goat.

His resolve is of course symbolic. Bess has made him a happier man: he sings; he is kind to children. Killing Crown has made Porgy the cripple into a whole man. A purgative act, it embodies the strength of goodness and simplicity. Catfish Row, to be sure, is no Paradise: Bess, the agent of Porgy's self-realization, is gone. And yet *Porgy*, stylized by Mamoulian, is—unforetold by the novella—a morality play.

AN OUTSIDE PERSPECTIVE

A final topic: the choice of Mamoulian to direct *Porgy* excited surprise because he was young and foreign. But the incongruity of this assignment ran deeper. DuBose Heyward was a regional Charleston writer testing his conservative pedigree. Mamoulian was a cosmopolitan experimental auteur.

In the novella *Porgy*, exotics inhabit a fringe culture dwarfed by a white world they neither know nor understand, persevering at the mercy of fate and the weather. Heyward's refined, even hyperrefined style risks vitiating his subject matter. He marvels at the novelty and quaintness of what he observes. His detachment is both social and aesthetic.

The robust physicality of the play *Porgy*, and of its music, is inherent to theater: we see and hear a people and their songs. Incidental characters in Heyward's novella—Jake, Mingo—become visual fixtures, plying their destiny. And, supervising a cast of sixty-six, Mamoulian is a director equally obsessed with the mass and the individual: he painstakingly superintends every cast member; his annotations expand many a "minor" role.

If Heyward is a genteel southern regionalist, Mamoulian is a student of Russian theater and an immigrant from Europe. In *Porgy*, both these identities ultimately matter. Some New York critics discovered verisimilitude in Mamoulian's Gullahs. The Theatre Guild itself, in advertisements, called *Porgy* "an authentic picture of Southern life." "It just killed me," Mamoulian once recalled, groaning at the memory of misguided accolades. "Because [*Porgy*] was utterly stylized." Equally, Heyward's African-American play was not in Mamoulian's view an agent of reform. Heyward struggled with the "Negro question"; all his work bears on issues of social justice in a segregated society. For Mamoulian, social justice was not a reason for art. "I will certainly never do a play only because it's a Negro play," he told an interviewer years later.

> My profession is to do something worth doing on the stage. But if it happens to be potentially a worthwhile production, if it happens to be "humanistic" from that point of view . . . then you have a united impulse. But as far as the humanistic impulse is concerned, if you want to be "humanistic," then you'll send them some money or help them in some other ways, but you're not going to play havoc with your profession and do something that is not good theater simply because it is humanistic.

Was Mamoulian's *Porgy* method "Russian"? Oliver Saylor, an authority on Constantin Stanislavski's Moscow Art Theatre (first seen on Broadway in 1924), inferred a Stanislavski influence:

> In its crescendo, retardando, diminuendo and crescendo again, *Porgy* has been orchestrated as nothing seen on our stage since Stanislavsky first showed us Tolstoy's *Tsar Fyodor Ivanovitch*.
>
> Stanislavsky's direction of [Rimski-Korsakov's opera] *The Snow Maiden* . . . suggests strong parallels with the hurricane and wake-up scenes of *Porgy*.
>
> Imagine the number of people necessary to create the storm effect: actors, stage hands, supernumeraries, and even office help were given whistles, castanets, and other peculiar machines for the purpose of making noise. Some in our backstage [*Snow Maiden*] "orchestra" even used their feet. . . . When the sound reached its highest note, a snow-

storm composed of white confetti blown by large ventilators was let loose upon the stage.[39]

Mamoulian did not endorse Stanislavski's penchant for naturalism (or the "method" of his American disciples). But Stanislavski's masterful handling of the crowd—"every actor in the scene [from *Tsar Fyodor*] is no less an individual than the Tsar himself," wrote one American reviewer[40]—resonates with Mamoulian's Gullah community.*

Porgy made Mamoulian. Never again would he receive such singular personal acclaim for a stage production. Never again would he be assigned a play so appropriate to his integrated aesthetic of stylized rhythm and pictorial composition. By imposing rhythms and meters for speech and action, by conceiving elaborate *tableaux vivants*, Mamoulian felt empowered to convey emotional truth. "In 1927, I was King of Harlem," he told an interviewer in the 1970s.[41] "They had parties for me, it was wonderful."

Other outsiders to the American experience had with clear minds and open ears seized on the black vernacular as a New World bellwether. Around the turn of the twentieth century, this was Dvořák's discovery, and also that of Frederick Delius on a Florida orange plantation; both predicted that black Americans would create a great American music. On Broadway in Mamoulian's time, George Balanchine (native to St. Petersburg) directed Ethel Waters, Katherine Dunham, and Todd Duncan (Gershwin's Porgy) in *Cabin in the Sky* (1940), with songs by Vernon Duke (born Vladimir Dukelsky in Belarus) and sets by Boris Aronson (a

---

*Virtually unremembered today is that Stanislavski was as much a director of opera as of theater. He initially aspired to become an opera singer. He formed his Opera Studio in 1918 (in which year Mamoulian left Moscow) to improve the acting at the Bolshoi Opera. His Opera Studio itself produced operas beginning in 1918 with Rimski-Korsakov's *May Night*. In Stanislavski's staging of Puccini's *La bohème*, individual chorus members "had to know who they were, their names, and whether they came to the Café Momus on their own or were invited." In Stanislavski's staging of Tchaikovsky's *Eugene Onegin*, each chorus member was assigned a character drawn from Pushkin. See David B. Rosen, "Stanislavski's *La bohème* (1927)," in Roberta M. Marvin and Hilary Poriss, eds., *Fashions and Legacies of Nineteenth-Century Italian Opera* (2010).

rabbi's son from Kiev). Nine years later, Kurt Weill (a cantor's son from Dessau) composed a black musical powered by a narrative chorus: *Lost in the Stars*.

It is true that Mamoulian took scant interest in the politics of culture, or culture as national expression. But, feted in Harlem, he knew the Harlem Renaissance firsthand. It was Mamoulian who would direct Todd Duncan in *Lost in the Stars*—and also Pearl Bailey in her Broadway debut in *St. Louis Woman* (1946). With Weill, he began an adaptation of *Huckleberry Finn*; as a moral compass, Mark Twain's Jim parallels Mamoulian's redemptive Porgy.

The son of Russian Jewish immigrants, George Gershwin was an outsider to the world of the Carolina Gullahs. In his quest for "American" opera, he would purposefully spurn the Eurocentric Met. He had already plunged into Harlem. His *Porgy and Bess* collaborators would include the conductor Alexander Smallens (a.k.a. Alexander Smolensk, born in St. Petersburg), the designer Serge Sudeikin (born in Smolensk)—and the director Rouben Mamoulian.

Gershwin saw *Porgy* with Kay Swift. "He cheered it enthusiastically," she remembered in her ninetieth year, "and still wanted to convert it into an opera." He also would call *Porgy* "the most outstanding play that I know about the colored people." That was in 1935—by which time Mamoulian's *Porgy* was imprinted upon Gershwin's *Porgy and Bess*.[42]

CHAPTER 2

EXPERIMENTS IN MUSICAL THEATER

To realize why opera has never really taken root here, why its audience is one-twentieth of what it should be, and why so few American composers have written grand operas, try to imagine the state of the American theater today if it had faced the conditions under which its sister art has had to struggle. Suppose that, fifty years ago, a group of public-spirited New Yorkers had built a magnificent theater and installed therein a company of first-rank actors, prepared to give the finest plays written. For fifty years, then, this company has been presenting the works of Moliere, Racine, Rostand, Hauptmann, Sudermann, Schiller, Goldoni, Ibsen, Shakespeare, and other playwrights. None of these plays, however, has been done in English. The French plays have been played in French, the German ones in German, Ibsen in Norwegian, Dostoyevsky and Tchekoff in French or Italian—never English—translations. The company, which at first was entirely European, is now about one-third American. Most of these American actors have received their training in Europe, and know their roles only in foreign tongues; for even Shakespeare, in this imaginary theatre, is played in Italian.[1]

THIS 1937 THOUGHT EXPERIMENT by the composer-critic Deems Taylor encapsulates why George Gershwin said no when Otto Kahn proposed that the Metropolitan Opera premiere *Porgy and Bess*. Gershwin felt Broadway was a better place for an American opera.

Kahn's offer, and Gershwin's refusal, embellished a tangled and sporadic American history—today, mainly buried—of opera in English. In the second half of the nineteenth century, operas were commonly given in Italian, French, and German throughout the United States. Opera in English by touring troupes was also commonplace. In 1873, the soprano Clara Louise Kellogg became the first American to create a prominent English-language troupe, preaching "opera for the people" and singing as many as 125 performances annually. Emma Abbott, the "populist prima donna," founded a comparable company six years later; it toured extensively in the far West, playing six and seven times a week. The Metropolitan Opera, founded in 1883, initially performed in Italian, French, and German. When its artistic leader, Leopold Damrosch, died suddenly in 1885, one of the company's tenors—Anton Schott—proposed reconceiving the Met as an English-language house specializing in German repertoire.

Though Schott's proposal went nowhere, opera in English remained a fervent cause. The same year, Jeannette Thurber established her National Conservatory of Music, which under the directorship of Antonín Dvořák (1892–1895) would influentially spearhead Thurber's crusade for an "American school" of composition. Less well known is that—also in 1885—Thurber established an American Opera Company that for two seasons widely toured opulently produced opera in English. The singers, mainly American, were obscure. The conductor and orchestra—Theodore Thomas and the Thomas Orchestra—were world-class and famous. The project failed: it started too big, it lacked glamour, it ran out of money. (Thurber was a keen advocate of federal arts funding—which might have buttressed her lost cause.)[2]

By 1900, opera in America, once a variegated mix of art and entertainment, was fast becoming "grand opera" headquartered at the Met:

big voices, a cavernous space, foreign tongues. Oscar Sonneck, the pioneer historian of American music, summarized in 1905:

> To-day we are as far from American opera of artistic importance as we ever have been. Not that our composers lack the power to write dramatic music, but our operatic life has been trimmed into a hot-house product. The one Metropolitan Opera House in New York supplies the whole country with opera.* . . . Under these circumstances there is neither place nor time for the production of American operas, and our composers have almost stopped trying their hands at this sadly neglected branch of our art. The struggle against the apathy of the public, . . . against the commercial cowardice and avarice of the managers, seems hopeless.[3]

Three years later, New York's pre-eminent music critic, Henry Krehbiel, groaned that opera in America would remain "experimental" until "the vernacular becomes the language of the performances and native talent provides both works and interpreters. The day is far distant, but it will come."[4] Krehbiel—and not only Krehbiel—reasoned that in Italy, Germany, France, and Russia, distinct operatic cultures had evolved alongside distinct native repertoires; that particular vocal and compositional styles had materialized grounded in Italian, German, French, and Russian speech; that—preliminarily, necessarily—audiences had consolidated around opera in translation: they were accustomed to understanding the words. But opera in translation never took hold in the United States. Instead, American operagoers clung to snob appeal—which required glamorous foreign-born vocal stars. Opera was not, as so often abroad, an essentially theatrical genre.

After World War II, a late abortive effort to popularize opera in

---

*The Met toured vigorously beginning in the nineteenth century; its last national tour took place in 1986. Its Saturday afternoon national radio broadcasts began in 1931.

English was impressively mounted by the NBC Opera Theatre (1949–64). But the New York City Opera, which might have become an opera-in-English bastion comparable to London's English National Opera, was at best ambivalent about opera in translation. The advent of operatic supertitles in the 1980s orphaned opera in English for good—and at the same time belatedly restored theatrical possibilities long preempted by foreign languages; suddenly, such bold musical dramatists as Berg and Janáček made sense at the Met, and Wotan's monologue became more than endurable.

This little-known narrative omits a chapter even less known: the Rochester American Opera Company of the 1920s. Perhaps no American opera in English enterprise, before or since, has been infused with such idealistic theatrical panache. As its prime movers included Rouben Mamoulian, the *Porgy and Bess* story cannot be told without it.

ROCHESTER RENAISSANCE

> The American time was very happy for a renaissance. It was in the early half of the twenties. We were getting over the War and were still sensitive enough to use our imaginations. The arts seemed to be a happy outlet for that future civilization we were going to have, in which there would be no more killing and exhausting of a whole race. The first step towards the new Golden Age was culture. . . .[5]

The "renaissance" here described took place in Rochester, New York, and began in 1923. The describer is Paul Horgan, later the recipient of two Pulitzer Prizes for books of American history. Horgan was barely out of high school in the 1920s, yet in Rochester contributed his services as a scenic designer and translator for Mamoulian's productions. Others there would also make big names. The local conductors were Eugene Goossens and Albert Coates—subsequently, high-profile music directors in Cincinnati, Sydney, and London. Martha Graham danced and taught dance. Vladimir Rosing—an inimitable Russian tenor already celebrated abroad—taught opera. Otto Luening—later, a pioneering figure in tape and electronic music—composed. Nicolas Slonimsky— later, a widely esteemed musical lexicographer—was Mamoulian's chief répétiteur.*

The 1925–26 musical season in Rochester is worth describing in overview. Goossens directed the Rochester Philharmonic in matinee and evening concerts. The guest conductors included Willem Mengelberg and—early in his tenure as director of the Eastman School of Music—Howard Hanson, who led a program of unpublished American works. The Eastman School had an orchestra of its own. There was also an amateur Rochester Symphony, giving three concerts annually. The Rochester American Opera Company offered half a dozen productions. The visiting recitalists included the singers Maria Jeritza, Tito Schipa, John McCormack, Sigrid Onégin, and Ernestine Schumann-Heink; the pianists Josef Hofmann, Ossip Gabrilowitsch, Myra Hess, and Josef Lhévinne; the violinist Mischa Elman; and the Flonzaley Quartet. A 90-piece orchestra (overlapping in membership the Rochester Philharmonic) performed six days weekly when the Eastman Theatre served as a temple for cinema. And the Metropolitan Opera performed *Rigoletto* and *Tosca* on tour.

The first cause of the Rochester renaissance was Rochester's omnipresent first citizen, George Eastman (1854–1932). Self-educated in the American manner, he invented roll film (a direct precursor of motion-picture film) and perfected the Kodak camera. He founded the Eastman Kodak Company. He gave away something like $100 million. His chief beneficiaries included the University of Rochester, Mechanics Institute (later the Rochester Institute of Technology), and (as the anonymous

---

*Horgan remembered Slonimsky as "almost insolently efficient. . . . While accompanying the rehearsals with his hands on the keys, he would read Dickens, never missing either a note, a cue, a cut in the opera; or a word, a chuckle, or a trial pronunciation of a new word in the novel." (Slonimsky, who was learning English at the time, attested in his memoirs that he merely "pretended" to read fiction while accompanying opera.)

"Mr. Smith") the Massachusetts Institute of Technology. Paul Horgan knew him—everybody did—and later wrote:

> He gave his character, that rational, dry, cool, shrewd and modest view of life which, combined with his industrial originality, and his immense fortune, made him an extraordinarily effective man— though like all men occasionally he had unaccountable opinions which in his case were magnified by his powerful position from the merely personal to the official and compelling. . . . He set by his mere presence in the town a standard of decorum, self-respect and prestige which reached down through every level of Rochester society.[6]

A lifelong bachelor, Eastman was famously austere in his personal affairs. His speech was terse and precise. He did not flaunt his feelings. His known pleasures included big game hunting and—surprisingly— classical music. The activities enlivening the sober magnificence of his mansion were known to include large parties with music performed by Eastman's personal organist on a concealed console. At breakfast, which lasted exactly 35 minutes, the organ again entertained (Bach, antipathetic to Eastman, was proscribed). Eastman would also engage chamber musicians to perform unseen for $35 (then a lordly sum) apiece. He financed Rochester's principal public concert venue: the 3,300-seat Eastman Theatre, built in 1922 by a great architectural firm: McKim, Mead & White. The same building houses the Kilbourn Recital Hall (named after Eastman's mother), and offices, studios, and classrooms, the whole of which comprises the Eastman School of Music, endowed by George Eastman as a privileged precinct of the University of Rochester. The Rochester Philharmonic, supported by George Eastman, also performed—as it does today—at the Eastman Theatre. Over a colonnade of pilasters at the front of the building are engraved the words FOR THE ENRICHMENT OF COMMUNITY LIFE.

Eastman claimed no special knowledge of music. Its value, to him, was pedigreed by its appeal—measured in earning power. If the citizenry wanted a first-rate orchestra, and if he did not have to support it alone, he pledged large sums. When Vladimir Rosing convinced him that Rochester should be the seat of America's first modern opera company, Eastman agreed to back it for three years—after which it would be on its own. Rosing was doubtless an irresistible advocate. Born in St. Petersburg in 1890, exiled by the revolution, he had by 1921 given more than a hundred recitals in London. George Bernard Shaw ranked him with Fyodor Chaliapin as one of the two "most extraordinary singers. of the twentieth century." Rosing's tenor art is preserved on dozens of recordings. In common with Chaliapin, he prioritized words and meanings; he sustained an actor's command of verbal nuance; he seized interpretive extremes of color and dynamics—including rarified "head voice" effects—other singers shunned. When he sang Mussorgsky's *Songs and Dances of Death*, he made his face a cadaver; singing Mussorgsky's "Song of the Flea," he scratched himself all over. Rosing's sometime accompanist Ivor Newton later wrote:

> Rosing had one of the vividest and most magnetic personalities I had ever come across; rarely have I known anyone who could hold an audience in such a sheer ecstasy of enchantment through a whole recital. A Rosing audience was unlike any other. There was electricity in the air and people crouched forward in their seats as though they were watching some fierce and terrifying melodrama. . . . He acted every song; often he overacted it, sometimes he all but clowned it. The purists were scandalized. . . . But it came off, because, despite all his eccentricities, Rosing was never cheap; in everything he did there was such an overpowering impression of stern, unflinching sincerity.[7]

But Rosing's eventual ambition was to run an opera company dedicated to theatrical ideals he had absorbed in Moscow: the synthesis of music, gesture, dance, and design; a sustained ensemble art transcend-

ing individual contributions. In March 1923, sailing from America, he
met a Rochester music critic, Jack Warner, who was en route to London
to finalize contracting Eugene Goossens and Albert Coates for Rochester. Warner told Rosing that Rochester aspired "to become another
Bayreuth." The two men spoke until daybreak. Warner cabled to George
Eastman. Rosing met Eastman the following June at the penthouse of
the Kodak Building. He persuaded Eastman that opera could become
more than "a bastard art built of compromise" and that Rochester could
lead the way. Eastman gave him two days to prepare a four-year budget;
the result was a two-year contract. Rosing scoured the United States
for young American singing actors who could credibly deliver opera in
English. Some nine hundred auditions resulted in twenty-four chosen
vocalists, each of whom received a full Eastman School scholarship.
Eastman would also supply a chorus, an orchestra, coaches, costume and
set designers, and theaters. It was Rosing who enticed Slonimsky, who
had served as his accompanist in 1921 and 1922. And it was Rosing who,
with Eastman's blessing, brought Mamoulian from London.[8]

Mamoulian was all of twenty-five years old. He was tall, slender,
pale-faced, black-haired. His old-fashioned pince-nez was soon replaced
by spectacles. He also wore London suits, black fedora hats, fur-lined
overcoats, and spats. He carried a gold-headed black walking stick. Two
or three dried violets were typically pinned to his lapel. A slave bracelet
adorned his wrist (a local critic successfully disabused him of the intention to add an ankle bracelet to his leg). Horgan called him "prince."

Mamoulian's exquisite formality and restraint were ameliorated by
the brilliance of his dark eyes and the warmth of his occasional smile. At
work, he was all energy, compacted by intellect and disciplined feeling.
His powers of concentration amazed. As an exercise in "rapid concentration on detail," Mamoulian undertook the following demonstration:

> Seating himself at a table, he recited distinctly, with full dramatic sig-
> nificance, a poem in the Russian language, at the same time writing

a number of stanzas from Fitzgerald's "Omar Khayam," of course in English. The recitation and writing were done rapidly.

Mr. Mamoulian then seated the twenty members of the class in a semicircle giving to each member a pencil and a pad of paper. He started at one end of the semicircle and dictated to one class member a line of a poem in English, to another a line of a poem in French, to another a part statement of fact, to another part of an algebraic formula, to the next a column of figures. He constantly interrupted his round by telling parts of a story, which he completed after he had given each of the twenty students something to write. Then he went rapidly around the circle again and again four times in all completing without error the matter which he had begun dictating in parts of his first round.[9]

Horgan once observed Mamoulian illustrating the importance of "concentration of mind and feeling" on what an actor attempts to represent:

[Mamoulian] said, "I will show you a scene, a commonplace from everyday life. You will not believe what I show you—you won't know what it is—if for a single second I drop my concentration of mind and feeling upon what I am trying to represent. But if at every second and with every gesture I concentrate wholly upon my own dramatic problem, you will see everything and you will believe everything, though I will use no props, no speech, no co-actors, and no program notes. One false move, or false idea, or incomplete memory, and my whole act will fall to pieces. Now watch."

He then took the center of the room and became . . . a barber, receiving, seating, sheeting, and shaving a customer. The whole thing was in pantomime, yet we could see the instruments in his empty hands. We could glance with him out the window at the passing world on the sidewalk. We could hear the soundless conversation of the obsequious barber and the grunts of the reclining victim. We could hear the steam in the sterilizer and the clock on the wall. We could smell the eau de cologne and the bay rum. We had a sense of the shape, size and color of the barber-shop. When the razor was getting dull, we knew it, and winced at its pull, and were relieved when the barber, smiling tolerantly at life's little trials, wiped the blade and stropped it to the singing sharpness. Our spirits rose as the sharpened blade went flashing and expert again at its task on the sodden jowl of the man in the chair. . . . We knew the self-satisfaction, the self-respect and the social character of the barber himself. . . .

The astonishing performance took about fifteen or twenty minutes. It never faltered. There was not a single false note. . . . The real barber, had he been before us, would have made his little fumbles, his inaccuracies of movement; but we would not have remembered him, or known much of anything about him. . . . The difference, of course, was art.[10]

Mamoulian's range of culture and experience clinched his authority. He could tell his American students about their own national literature. Having studied the violin as a boy, he knew music. Horgan testified:

He knew more about the various contributing elements of a stage production than any of the artists separately charged with creating each. . . . He was an amusing draughtsman, and liked to draw . . . on restaurant tables, menus, paper napkins; but beyond this, his love of the art of painting was nourished by a penetrating knowledge of the great graphic art of the European past. . . . We felt that he was closer than anyone we had ever heard of to embodying Gordon Craig's ideal for the regisseur—that he should know more of music than the composer, more of painting than the painter, more of acting than the actor.[11]

Mamoulian instantly registered as a Rochester personage—a dandified genius or certified "nut." With Horgan and Slonimsky, he formed a Society of Unrecognized Geniuses (from which Rosing was excluded for lacking a sufficient propensity for boisterous mischief). According to Slonimsky, Mamoulian and Horgan would "put on monocles, click their heels, and spout torrents of ersatz German in public places." But Mamoulian also acquired identity as an American. He picked up on American slang, vitality, and—notwithstanding his suits and spats—informality. And, like many another adaptable exile, he appreciated things American in ways Americans did not—in Horgan's opinion, one root of his subsequent success appropriating the folk traditions of southern blacks.[12]

The Russians Rosing and Mamoulian were complementary. Both came from aristocratic households suffused with culture. For both, the ambience of Stanislavski's Moscow Art Theatre inspired ideals of concentrated detail and integrated ensemble. Mamoulian—a planner—was considered fastidious. Rosing—a performer—was volatile, improvisational, eccentric. He wore eyeglasses mended with adhesive tape, hairpins, and glue. His theories of stage gesture were predicated on classic statuary; he taught rules for sculpturing body movement. Mamoulian was already obsessed with "rhythm." Like Rosing, he was a choreographer, intent on canceling waving arms and wandering hands. He wrote, in Rochester: "The legitimate theatre of the present day is invaded over measure by literature. Too much emphasis is given to the spoken word . . . and not enough to the dramatic movement, which is the true art of the theatre."[13]

The prescient Rochester American Opera style would minimize scenery and emphasize light, shadow, the psychological use of color. It would abjure the curtain. Money, talent, vision were at hand in abundance. The moment was pregnant with possibility.

AMERICAN OPERA

Rochester's exercise in reforming opera acquired two public faces: interludes during film screenings, and fully staged operatic productions.

Both were novel. Both oscillated between the world of student and professional, Eastman School and Eastman Theatre. The Rochester American Opera Company was formally launched in November 1924 with Mamoulian and Rosing as codirectors. Subsequently, Mamoulian additionally conceived and directed an Eastman School of Drama and Dramatic Action—that is, a theater school, avoiding the terms "acting" and "theater" because for whatever reason they were anathema to Eastman, who put up $13 million. Mamoulian's school merged with the Eastman Theatre Ballet. Dancing, acting, singing shared a unified curriculum.

According to Horgan, "the Eastman Theatre set a standard in those days which has never been equaled for the taste, ingenuity and charm of stage productions on movie bills."[14] This claim is made plausible by a trove of surviving evidence. When the Eastman Theatre screened a film (films, of course, being silent), the program comprised an overture performed by a large orchestra, a newsreel, a solo act, the featured film, and a production number. This extravagant entertainment genre was by no means unique to Rochester. But in Rochester the production number, elsewhere a popular diversion, might be— Mamoulian and Rosing's premiere Eastman Theatre creation, on November 25, 1923—the entire last act of Verdi's *Rigoletto*.

Subsequently, Mamoulian contrived to unify such Eastman Theatre presentations. When in October 1924 the film was *The Phantom of the Opera* with Lon Chaney, Mamoulian created a staged prologue, "The Spectre in Red." A masked ball was enacted, at which a soprano sang the "Jewel Song" from Gounod's *Faust*, the opera in the film. A waltz for the entire company ensued. A sinister figure, clad in red, attempted to abduct the soprano. When the Eastman Theatre screened Erich von Stroheim's silent version of *The Merry Widow* for the week beginning December 17, 1926, Frank Waller of the Rochester American Opera Company composed and conducted an orchestral score for the entire 137-minute film. Mamoulian created an "overture-prologue" for thirty singers and dancers, featuring "Vilja" and other exerpts from Lehár's score. Another Eastman Theatre Mamoulian production was "The Volga Boatman's Song." The singing boatmen, heard from afar, appeared pulling the rope of a barge. Their singing—in Russian—dissipated into the purple glow of a sunset, embellished by a new moon. In a program note, Mamoulian compared the song to the breadth of the Russian steppes; he said that it embodied "Russian land and Russian soul." He also noted: "All the men of the department are engaged in the production. Although it is a 'chorus,' every one of the performers has a role to play and impersonates a definite character."[15]

The formal debut of the Rochester American Opera Company, distinct from its productions on film bills, occurred on November 10, 1924. The program comprised scenes from *Boris Godunov*, conducted by Goossens, and *Pagliacci* complete, conducted by Waller. Rosing and Mamoulian shared both productions. The principal singers include George Fleming Houston as Boris and Charles Hedley as Canio—artists who would become widely known. But the emphasis on ensemble was such that singers with major roles in the one opera became choristers in the other. Howard Hanson, in a prefatory speech, promised "important musical growth" and national influence. Local critics concurred; elsewhere, the debut was widely noticed.

The company's first complete full-length opera was Gounod's *Faust* on January 17, 1925. Preparations included lectures on the Faust legend. Observing Houston's red-clad Mephistopheles, Horgan wrote that he "was properly regarded as the Chaliapin of the company . . . Mamoulian invented marvelous things for [his] cloak to do." The production's spare sets and strong colors abjured realism. A front-page review in *Musical America* reported:

> What made the afternoon unique . . . was a departure from hidebound traditions. In the place of clay figures, singing and acting with strict observance of vocal and histrionic mannerisms that have been handed down for at least two generations, there were seen a delightful

originality and spontaneity. At times, indeed, this zest became almost extreme.[16]

Subsequent productions included *Carmen*, in March 1925, locally reviewed as the company's best effort to date: "The handling of the crowds was masterly in its spirited nonchalance. . . . The performance moved with a precision and smoothness that only could have been accomplished by infinite effort and care."[17] Horgan—by now Mamoulian's indispensable factotum—especially savored *The Pirates of Penzance* and *H.M.S. Pinafore*, each given one act at a time on Eastman Theatre film bills.

Any traditional Savoyard must have died of chagrin and indignation if he ever saw Mamoulian's productions. . . . He brushed off that curious blend of solemnity and low comedy which is the familiar Gilbert and Sullivan idiom. . . . How often has it been remembered that some of Sullivan's most incomparably expressive moments are also outrageous burlesques of Donizetti and the florid school of 19th century Italian opera? Mamoulian of course relished the point. . . . The choruses were massed in delightful pictures. There was a ballet-like precision and flow in the action of the principals as they gave tongue.

Horgan himself was cast as the Major General in *Pirates* and the Admiral in *Pinafore*—the former invested with "the self-pity of the eternal sentimentalist, the darting glance of the uncertain man of authority," the latter "tired, vain, complacent, yet dutiful with social response, and victim of a hollow elegance."

Opera, as mounted by Mamoulian in Rochester, reveled in the detailed correlation of music and gesture, and in exquisite choreography of the crowd. The young people of the company, observed by Horgan, knew that "he was making a new theatrical synthesis."[18]

SISTER BEATRICE

Horgan fictionalized the Rochester Renaissance in his 1933 novel *The Fault of Angels*—an elegantly turned *roman à clef* (it won the Harper Prize) whose characters are based on Eastman, Rosing, Slonimsky, Coates, Goossens, and Horgan himself (Mamoulian is missing). Dorchester, a midsize American city, is made singular by the influence of a terse, officious, withdrawn and yet magnanimous millionaire. Intent on civic betterment, fired with confidence and aspiration, the millionaire directly or indirectly entices a colorful assortment of youthful artist types, mostly foreign-born. They comprise a subcommunity coexisting with provincial or supportive locals. The resulting creative conditions, if evanescent, are effervescent. When in later years Mamoulian campaigned for an "experimental laboratory" in Hollywood jointly funded by the major studios, he doubtless recalled Rochester as a place where experimentation mattered. And he remembered his Rochester production of Maeterlinck's *Sister Beatrice* as his peak achievement.

Mamoulian's assorted private writings and public pronouncements in the press, all of which he assiduously amassed,[19] eventually acquired a pathetic redundancy; intellectually, he long endured a terminal condition of stalemate. His Rochester writings and pronouncements are fresher than any that came after, percolating with discovery and cocksure self-discovery. Sprinkled with allusions to Greeks and Romans, to Indian puppetry and Japanese marionettes, to commedia dell'arte and Shakespeare's Globe, to Stanislavski and Bernhardt, they amass a polemic addressing the world history of theater and its proper fruition. Theater, he argues, is a synthesis of the arts indifferently defined. Its essence eludes contemporary practitioners. What is that essence? A thought experiment reveals that theater may exist without words, without scenery, without music, even without living actors. Its essence, therefore, is action, gesture. The art of acting "is mainly the art of silence and movement." "One can better discern a fine actor when he is acting in a foreign tongue." Present-day theater too much attends to words, not enough to music and dance. "To me, theatrical action means both dramatic and dance movement. It must be expressive, plastic and rhythmic. And, if this be so, music comes closer to drama than even the spoken word."

The actor must " 'burn' with the desire to act," must "inflame himself." Artists like Chaliapin, Duse, and Salvini "are endowed by nature itself with a boundless creative energy"; rather than "perform," they "live" onstage. Others, less endowed, must and can consciously learn how to acquire such inspiration. The crucial ingredients include concentration and freedom of movement. Children are an "ideal example of acting"—"but the minute they become conscious that some grown-ups are watching them, they begin to 'perform.' "

The entire enterprise, riddled with dilettantes, requires integration, organization, and instruction. The play is only a "canvas" awaiting a "creative design."

> The director and the actors receive from the playwright only the spoken word. On the stage, and through visible movement, they bring those to the soul of the audience, using the words only as a finishing touch in order to make it easier for other people to understand their artistic creation. The interpretation of their parts, their movement, must be bound into a perfect harmony and unified into an artistic design.

Hence the crowning role of the "stage director."[20]

When Mamoulian conceived his Eastman School production of *Sister Beatrice* as a "new form of theatrical art," he put into practice all the theorizing and experimentation that, however tendentiously or immodestly, ignited his precocious Rochester career. Maurice Maeterlinck's notion of "static drama" was a fit for Mamoulian's aspirations. Maeterlinck dwelt on external forces, not inner lives. The mystic aura of his poetic prose, its dreamlike tales and characters, suited the Mamoulian predilection for gesture and tableau. As we have seen, one of Yevgeny Vakhtangov's signature productions, in rehearsal at his studio from 1916 to 1918, was of Maeterlinck's play *The Miracle of St. Anthony*. Mamoulian—never generous in acknowledging what others taught or inspired—doubtless scrutinized Vakhtangov's treatment of Maeterlinck's St. Anthony of Padua materializing at a modern funeral to raise the dead. When in Rochester Mamoulian preached that "dance and drama were united in the early days of the theater," the context was the forthcoming Maeterlinck spectacle, with its minimal text and miraculous plot. He entrusted Horgan with a fresh translation of the unrhymed alexandrines of the French original. Otto Luening's organ score, composed during the rehearsal process, would accompany the play throughout its three acts, precisely cued to the action. The cast of thirty-five actor-dancers was supplemented by a chorus drawn from Eastman's Opera Department, plus a solo soprano for the "Song of the Virgin." The venue was not the Eastman Theatre, but the intimate Kilbourn Recital Hall. Given January 15 and 16, 1926, the production marked the debut of Mamoulian's School of Drama and Dramatic Action. That is: Mamoulian's authority, sans Rosing, was virtually limitless, as were his resources and preparation time. The drumbeat in the local press was prolonged and loud. The program was headed:

"RHYTHMIC DRAMA TO MUSIC"
A new form of theatrical art
conceived and developed by Rouben Mamoulian

Presented through the medium of
"SISTER BEATRICE"
A Play in 3 Acts by Maurice Maeterlinck

Production directed by Rouben Mamoulian
Musical score composed by Otto Luening
Play especially translated by Paul Horgan

A program note explained that "Rhythmic Drama to Music" was "based on the belief that the art of the theatre has for its medium the expressive, rhythmic, plastic movement of the actors, coordinated into one creative design by the stage director, with the spoken word, the art of the painter and the music constituting supplementary elements rather than actual necessities."[21]

Set in a fourteenth-century French convent, *Sister Beatrice* is a 1901 miracle play—which is to say, it adapts a medieval genre combining religious tableau and song. It adapts the same legend as Max Reinhardt's famous production of *The Miracle*, first seen in 1911. Sister Beatrice, a young novice, has secretly fallen in love with Prince Bellidor. They elope. A statue of the Virgin Mary comes to life to take her place. The nuns discover the statue missing, not the sister. Twenty-five years later, Sister Beatrice returns, deserted by Bellidor; the sisters discover the missing statute returned to its rightful place. Sister Beatrice, to whom they attribute the miracle, is beatified. Luening's organ score, performed by Guy Fraser Harrison (later conductor of the Oklahoma City Symphony from 1951 to 1972), suggested Gregorian chant. Horgan's prose translation was undertaken in close collaboration with Mamoulian; the result, less formal (and archaic) than the extant blank verse English version by Bernard Miall, was nonetheless superbly rhythmic—as in Bellidor's wooing speech:

O Beatrice! How beautiful you are when you approach thus to meet the stars which await you all a-tremble, in the doorway. . . . They know at last that a great happiness is born; and, like golden grains of sand that are spread in silence before the step of a queen, they scatter themselves all along the misty roads which we are going to travel![22]

Mamoulian conceived stylized gestures inspired by French medieval prints and paintings. Production photographs, in which the young director's coiffed hair, bow tie, and pipe clash with the plain décor and costumery of the individually posturing nuns, evoke a presentation oscillating between theater, dance, and opera. A local critic reported that Mamoulian appeared beforehand "and assured the audience something new in theatrical art was about to be disclosed, so evidently it was." Luening, decades later, remembered *Sister Beatrice* as revolutionary; he said Mamoulian "sculpted the whole production with a psychic force" and likened the result to 1960s multimedia theater. Horgan—in later life a writer of no mean critical gift—wrote in 1946 that Luening's score "supported and defined the mood as arches lift and give shape to a stone vault," that the presentation as a whole "was an artistic success of the truest quality," that Mamoulian "still carried the hope that he may some day produce our Rochester *Sister Beatrice* before a wider public."[23]

Though *Sister Beatrice* was far from Mamoulian's final Rochester effort, it may have marked the limits of what he felt he could achieve there. In any event, he was itching to move on to Manhattan. Lawrence Langner of the Theatre Guild visited Rochester periodically on business. There Mamoulian "walked my legs off, racing the streets . . . , telling me all he planned to do in the theater if I would only bring him to New York."[24] Meanwhile, Mamoulian had a falling-out with the director of the Eastman Theatre. As their sporadic correspondence shows, his relationship with Rosing also soured. In June 1926, he resigned his Rochester appointments and moved to New York to direct at the Theatre Guild School in the New York City suburb of Scarborough.

The Eastman School of Drama and Dramatic Action died with Mamoulian's departure; the Rochester American Opera Company lived on another four years under Rosing. It toured to western Canada. It presented Mary Garden in *Carmen* in February 1927. After George Eastman's support lapsed the same year, Rosing's troupe debuted in New York performing for a week under Goossens as the independent, professional American Opera Company. It returned to New York in 1928, then toured nationally until the Depression killed its 1930–31 season. During the Mamoulian years alone, the repertoire included operas or excerpts

by Beethoven, Charles Wakefield Cadman (*Shanewis*), Debussy, Gilbert
and Sullivan, Gounod, Lehár, Massenet, Mascagni, Mussorgsky, Ros-
sini, Saint-Saëns, Tchaikovsky, Verdi, and Wagner. The robust Rochester audiences, as reported locally, were "not the older operatic audiences
of the city; they are made up of musical people who plainly . . . like to
hear opera sung in English." In 1963, the *Los Angeles Times* music critic
Albert Goldberg remembered the American Opera Company as his
"first exposure experience with opera in English, and the conversion
stuck." He added: "There has been nothing comparable since."[25]

FILM AND SOUND

What no postmortem of the Rochester American Opera Company could
possibly have predicted is that, via Rouben Mamoulian, it would within
a decade connect to George Gershwin's great American opera. But first
came Mamoulian and *Porgy* the play. Though many on Broadway mar-
veled that a "Russian" had triumphantly undertaken this unusual assignment, with Rochester in mind it may be appreciated that the Heywards'
play was far better suited to Mamoulian than any *Cherry Orchard* or *Uncle
Vanya*. Its pertinence to Mamoulian's Rochester career generally, and to
Sister Beatrice specifically, is in fact self-evident. With its Gullah idiom
and exotic dramatis personae, *Porgy* was already stylized and rhythmic
in the Mamoulian manner. Its large ensemble and dramatic scenario
invited tableau. In Mamoulian's choreography, its gyrating mourners
and hurricane storm-wedge potently illustrated how unrealistic deportment could convey real feeling. When he called his cast members "children," Mamoulian was appreciating the concentration and instinct they
brought to their roles, transcending mere "performance." Stressing the
epic, downplaying the personal, recasting the novella's dour ending as
a redemptive mass finale, Mamoulian nudged *Porgy* toward a "miracle
play" paradigm. He equally extrapolated its "operatic" possibilities. No

more than *Sister Beatrice* could *Porgy* be readily placed within any established theatrical form.

Beyond launching his Broadway career, *Porgy* catapulted Mamoulian toward film. Rochester was again pertinent. Both the Eastman Theatre and Eastman Kodak afforded limitless opportunities to watch and discuss movies; Mamoulian's Rochester associates observed his keen interest in the high art of silent cinema. With the coming of sound in 1927, Hollywood sought help from Broadway directors. New technologies disclosed new aesthetic possibilities: a singular, short-lived window for innovation preceding the reestablishment of norms. *Applause* (1929)—Mamoulian's first film, shot not in Hollywood but at Paramount's Astoria Studios in New York—is an acknowledged landmark in the early history of "talking" pictures. Helen Morgan plays an ageing burlesque queen who sacrifices herself for her daughter. When Mamoulian, contradicting his cameraman, insisted on using two sound channels in order to simultaneously record the mother's song and the daughter's prayer, a new technique was born. Intent on retaining the mobile camera and montage effects of the master silent directors, he equally insisted that the cumbersome early sound cameras, enclosed in bungalows, be made to move. He used split screens and wipes. He filmed outdoors. He relished the cacophony of traffic.*

The film's initial sequence—a Mamoulian tour de force—brandishes its virtuosity. The credits roll to the accompaniment of "Alexander's Ragtime Band," pounded out by a small marching band. The music fades to silence—the band recedes—as the screen goes blank. Then we see a sign—ZEPHYR FEED AND GRAIN SUPPLY COMPANY—on a

---

*Among the jottings of Mamoulian's retirement years is a double-sided page, dated October 15, 1969, listing "new devices" and other points of interest in *Applause*. The list includes "Split screen," "Recording sound on two channels," "Restoring mobility to camera," "Deglamorizing the star [Helen Morgan]," "Shooting in the subway, Pennsylvania Station, Brooklyn Bridge," and "The traffic noises simulated in the studio." I am grateful to Mark Spergel for sharing with me various Mamoulian papers not to be found in the Library of Congress Mamoulian Archive.

shuttered storefront; a distant drumbeat commences. Mamoulian's camera pans back to an empty street. Trash and newspapers blow in the wind, then along the ground. The steady drumbeat builds. Posters fly past. Close-up of a poster: KITTY DARLING—QUEEN OF HEARTS. The drumbeat is now a band, increasing in volume. A dog chews the poster. A girl grabs the dog and runs. Other children are running. Adults are running. The running gets faster; the music gets louder. Everyone crowds forward to watch . . . the band, marching across the screen, with Kitty's carriage in tow. A close-up of the bass drum fades to a close-up of the same drum in a theater pit. The individual faces and instruments of the musicians crowd the screen, defeating any possibility of glamour. Panning upward, the camera discloses fat legs and lackadaisical kicks, then the workaday faces of the bumping and grinding girls. Lascivious trombone slides smear the dance refrain. Kitty enters and sings. Mamoulian pans back to scan the seedy theater, then closes on Kitty and her partner, delivering sotto voce the film's first short burst of dialogue. The number ends. The crowd applauds.

This sequence of three and a half minutes is as informative as it is entertaining. Our filmmaker is a man of action, not of words. And he adores sound. The moving camera precisely registers the relative proximity of music or speech. Filling the frame, the bass drum is suddenly louder than when framed from afar. The girls' banal song is intimate or remote as the dour camera eye moves in or out.* The scene's calibrated crescendo, visible and audible, is an exercise in rhythm. The chewed poster of Kitty is a metaphor for the weary reality of the film's tale to come.

Mamoulian next made *City Streets* (1931)—a gangster picture packed with visual metaphor and city sounds. Mamoulian here invents the voice-over: for the first time, a talking voice is heard without lips being

---

*In a 1937 interview, Mamoulian emphasized that he was particular about the volume level of music on a soundtrack. See Neil Lerner, "The Strange Career of Rouben Mamoulian's Sound Stew" in Neil Lerner, ed., *Music in the Horror Film* (2010), p. 58.

moved. *Dr. Jekyll and Mr. Hyde* (1931), Mamoulian's opus three for Paramount, is widely regarded as the most remarkable screen adaptation of Robert Louis Stevenson's novella. The beginning is famous: the camera's eyes and ears and Jekyll's are one and the same. The shadow of a head, cast on a musical score, is the first thing we see, then hands on a keyboard (unlike Stevenson's, Mamoulian's Jekyll plays Bach on the organ). A knock, a voice, and our gaze moves to the right to glimpse Jekyll's butler. In the ensuing sequence, we don our coat and look in the mirror—at which point Jekyll's face first appears. (A typical Mamoulian touch: the butler's voice grows louder as Jekyll approaches.) Because the visual field of the human eye does not scan a firm rectangle, Mamoulian shades the corners of the frame for the three and a half minutes that the first-person camera is maintained.

Even more celebrated is the film's first transformation sequence. Through the use of filters, Fredric March's face changes into a hideous Neanderthal visage in a single take—at which point the first-person camera is resumed and we experience Jekyll/Hyde's disorientation: the room blurs and turns; snatches of memory materialize and dissolve. In place of music, Mamoulian here applies a sound collage combining a recorded heartbeat with uncanny metallic sounds. Accounts of this sonic concoction mention candlelight photographed directly onto the soundtrack, and a gong's reverberations played in reverse.

In short, Mamoulian's first three films thrive on innovation. They bristle with originality. They imply that artistry demands novelty. At the same time: as in Rochester, where he had to satisfy George Eastman's criterion of popular appeal, Mamoulian's is a popular art. It aims to please—and also to uplift. Notwithstanding an abundance of grit and adversity, *Applause, City Streets*, and *Jekyll and Hyde* are all morality plays with positive endings. And all three transcend emerging film genres. The tragic lives and sordid musical numbers in *Applause* violate nascent norms for "musicals." In *City Streets*, the killings are offscreen and a love story ultimately takes precedence over the gangster plot. With its earnest philosophizing about man and nature—about the consequences of instinct repressed and distorted—*Dr. Jekyll and Mr. Hyde* is and is not a "horror film"; it aims not to frighten, but to entertain and disturb.

If these aspects of creative cinema are sources of pleasure and fascination characteristic of Mamoulian's best work, the three films also illustrate Mamoulian weaknesses. With the exception of Helen Morgan's tattered burlesque diva, there is not a single memorable performance here. Much of the acting is formulaic. The delivery of dialogue is stiff. Even the leading characters are for the most part one-dimensional and emotionally remote. To be sure, Fredric March is intensely cruel as Hyde. As Jekyll, however, his love scenes with his fiancé are cast in cardboard. In fact, the more realistic the words and action, the more Mamoulian's stylization risks seeming mannered or otherwise obtrusive. The ocean waves embellishing a moonlit tryst in *City Streets* are a cliché. The madly accelerated velocity of the same movie's culminating chase is merely silly.

But Mamoulian's fourth film is fundamentally synthetic, comprehensively musical, purely an exercise in style. In the absence of filmed documentation of Mamoulian's *Sister Beatrice* and *Porgy*, or of his Broadway *Porgy and Bess*, *Oklahoma!* and *Carousel*, *Love Me Tonight* (1932) makes visible and audible the techniques of rhythmic direction that made Mamoulian a singular practitioner of Broadway musical theater. To glean what gifts Mamoulian brought to Gershwin's operatic masterpiece, a close analysis of Mamoulian's screen masterpiece is a gripping exercise.

LOVE ME TONIGHT

Was Mamoulian's cinema style, brandishing conspicuous artistry, good box office for Paramount? *Applause* was a critical success merely, but *City Streets* pleased a mass audience. Thus empowered, Mamoulian both directed and produced *Dr. Jekyll and Mr. Hyde*—and also *Love Me Tonight*.

Even within the studio system, he was for a short time able to exercise something like complete artistic control. According to a Mamoulian story, when Paramount—in the person of Adolph Zukor—"begged" him to do a musical with Maurice Chevalier and Jeanette MacDonald (both with big salaried contracts), Mamoulian protested that Ernst Lubitsch "had done well with these players in the past" and that Zukor should approach him.[26] But Lubitsch was busy with other projects. Mamoulian liked to feel implored and cajoled. In fact, he had every reason to attempt a Hollywood musical. From his Rochester days, he was already an old operetta hand—which is to say, he had already experimented with new ways to stage light opera.

At a party, he acquired a story idea he liked: a fairy tale about a tailor who marries a princess. Chevalier would be the tailor, MacDonald the princess. Paramount offered Oscar Straus for the music and Samson Raphaelson for the script—stylish purveyors of a Lubitsch milieu steeped in Viennese nostalgia. Mamoulian replaced Straus with the fledgling song-writing team of Richard Rodgers and Lorenz Hart. Hart was a scathing ironist whose future output would include a Shakespeare parody. Mamoulian wanted from Rodgers something he had never thought to attempt: a score comprehensively including song, dance, and incidental music. For a principal writer, he picked Samuel Hoffenstein, with whom he had worked on *Dr. Jekyll and Mr. Hyde*. Hoffenstein produced a script combining a parodistic edge as acute as Hart's, a "miracle" ending in the Mamoulian manner, and a whimsical reprise of the *Dr. Jekyll and Mr. Hyde* theme of instinct repressed by convention. Maurice Courtelin is a tailor owed 40,000 francs by the ne'er-do-well Viconte Gilbert de Varèze (Charles Ruggles). Maurice embarks for the country estate of Gilbert's uncle the Duke (C. Aubrey Smith), who holds the family purse strings. At the Duke's castle, Maurice encounters Princess Jeanette, who languishes from snobbish boredom and disuse because she cannot marry beneath her station. With the connivance of Gilbert, Maurice passes as a baron and successfully woos Jeanette. Then he designs her riding habit and is unmasked. Though true love ultimately redeems Jeanette from self-imprisonment, the film is more concerned with sex and with certain amusing effects of sexual deprivation.

The singular musical-comedic texture of *Love Me Tonight* can only be conveyed in detail. It begins with a one-minute overture: a medley of tunes to come. What follows is the daybreak "Symphony of Noises" from *Porgy*, transferred to Paris. A clock strikes six. A workman pounds a hammer. The rhythmically coordinated sound ingredients, added one at a time, include snoring, sweeping, knife-sharpening, and shoemaking. A radio is turned on—and this music becomes a synchronized symphonic soundtrack to the growing din. A seamless edit—the camera dollies into a small apartment—introduces Maurice, who pronounces: "Love song of Paree, you're much too loud for me." He closes his windows, the music diminishes, and he sings his "Song of Paree." It is punctuated by residual poundings, and traffic horns. Meanwhile, the orchestra adds split-second sound cues supporting Maurice's sung list of such non-Parisian sounds as a nanny goat, a Viennese waltz, and a Spanish fandango.

When Maurice undertakes a brisk stroll, his ongoing "Paree" song becomes a series of exchanges with passersby and vendors.

> Bonjour Mr. Cohen
> How are things goin'?

He reaches his shop: a musical codetta. Emil, a client, arrives to pick up his suit. "It's like poetry in a book. Oh, how beautiful I look!" The rhyming continues. The orchestra reenters. Maurice sings:

> My face is glowing
> I'm energetic,
> The art of sewing
> I find poetic.

We are irresistibly in the throes of one of the film's great numbers: "Isn't It Romantic?" It propels Maurice onto the street, where a man is hailing a cab:

> Emil: Isn't it romantic?
> Oh, no, I need some air.
> Isn't it romantic?
> Driver: At last I've got a fare!

The man turns out to be a composer—he is both singing and *composing* "Isn't It Romantic?" in the cab's back seat. Next our composer shares a chugging train compartment with a battalion of singing soldiers. Bayonets appear. The soldiers break the horizon in formation. Now the tune barks to trumpets and drums:

> Isn't it the right foot?
> Isn't it the left?
> That town is full of dames.
> So we lift a light foot!
> Marching full of heft
> And give your right names.

A passing Gypsy rhapsodically absorbs the refrain on his violin and sprints to an encampment complete with cimbalom: a picture framed and shaded as artfully as any canvas. The itinerant melody, cheerfully begun by Maurice, is finally wafted to Jeanette's balcony, where she earnestly warbles:

> Isn't it romantic?
> Music in the night,
> A dream that can be heard.
> Isn't it romantic?

That a hero might
Appear and say the word.

The song cadences to the slap of a ladder. The elderly Count de Savignac (Charles Butterworth), gripping a flower stem in his teeth, has ascended to serenade Jeanette.

"Princess? Jeanette? I just came to join you in a little chat before dinner."

"Count, why the ladder?"

"Oh, it's more romantic. . . . I brought my flute, hoping to entertain."

"No, count, not tonight."

He loses his balance and falls to the ground.

"Oh, I'll never be able to use it again."

"Oh, count, did you break your leg?"

"No, I fell flat on my flute."

This concludes scene 1 of *Love Me Tonight*.*

Scene 2 transpires at the Duke's palace: a portrait of ennui; a new musical palette. Three elderly aunts—a tittering parody of the witches in *Macbeth*—are brewing a potion to ward off Jeanette's fainting illness. They chant to a *misterioso* refrain embroidered by harp arpeggios. The Duke is introduced by a lumbering march. A second such march introduces his decrepit footmen. His guests, semicomatose, are playing bridge in slow motion to the accompaniment of "A Hot Time in the Old Town Tonight," also in slow motion. Suddenly, Gilbert arrives

---

*This and other sequences here described are easily accessed via YouTube.

from Paris in pursuit of a loan: a skittering Presto. The Duke says no. To close the scene: a reprise of the aunts' *misterioso* theme, with the aunts casting a spell to entice a "Prince Charming as of old" (and thus invoke the Sleeping Beauty fable Mamoulian has here lightly reinterpreted as a discourse on libidinal repression). To close the entire act: a distended reprise of "Isn't It Romantic?" with Jeanette in bed. Mamoulian pans away from the bedroom to the castle exterior as introduced at the beginning of scene 2. Full cadence. To commence act 2: the Paris skyline exactly as at the beginning of act 1; the orchestra recapitulates Maurice's "Song of Paree."

As in *Porgy*, narrative structure and musical structure here prove one and the same. "Isn't It Romantic?" has supplied a varied musical journey linking Maurice with Jeanette, so far away in style, mood, and caste. In scene 1, with Jeanette on the balcony, it forecasts the story to come; in scene 2, with Jeanette in the bedroom, it furnishes closure and an explicit prediction of intimacy.

What I have just described approximates an engaged initial viewing of the film's first twenty-four minutes. Subsequent viewings of this "act 1" disclose a great deal more. To begin with, Mamoulian's prioritization of music is ingeniously sustained. No more than Luening's score for *Sister Beatrice* was Rodgers's score for *Love Me Tonight* composed after the fact. Rather, Mamoulian recorded the orchestral soundtrack before he filmed his singing actors: what we see and hear is therefore the actual singing. That is, music creates the conditions for words, not the other way around. Even more important: Chevalier and MacDonald can sing and act more expressively than if they were mouthing songs they had already dubbed. *Love Me Tonight* may be a fabrication of life, but its musical content is a study in veracity. A typical Mamoulian touch: the first hammer blow of the "Symphony of Noises" is less resonant than the second, because with the second blow we are in close-up. Equally typical: our Gypsy violinist is doubtless no Gypsy (of the "Frenchmen" in the film, only Maurice is French), but self-evidently he actually plays the violin.

Where the music stops, Mamoulian's metronome and baton take over: the dialogue in *Love Me Tonight* is itself unfailingly musical. Maurice's rhymed exchange with Emil sets the *Allegretto* for "Isn't It Romantic?" The entire song is a musical exercise in transition. The soldiers slow the tune to a dotted-rhythm march. The Gypsy's *tempo rubato* slows it some more. Jeanette's culminating version, embellished by the Gypsy's obbligato solo violin, is a languorous *Andante*. Never mind that the ensuing minisequence on the balcony contains no music as such (other than the Count's fluting): it functions as the song's ironic coda. In maximum contrast to Jeanette's swooning vocal climax (with the unseen fiddler riding on top), Mamoulian secures a brisk, clipped delivery of the ensuing repartee, synchronizing the Count's foolish eagerness with Jeanette's officious rebuffs. In *Love Me Tonight* generally, words do not impart information; rather, their function is to entertain and—just as crucial—to further calibrate pace and transition.

At Eastman, Mamoulian would administer exercises in walking. Precise concentration, he demonstrated, dictated exactitude of gait, including the number of steps required to properly traverse a given distance. In *Love Me Tonight*, walking is never a random activity. When Maurice struts along the boulevard, the tempo of his feet matches that of "The Song of Paree." The Duke's footmen march lethargically in time to "Hot Time in the Old Town." When Gilbert, propelled by Rodgers, races through the castle antechamber, his twelve steps, five hops (to change direction), and thirteen more steps convey him to a staircase where the lounging Countess Valentine (Myrna Loy) stops him in his tracks: his right foot lands on step one the split-second the music cadences.

Later, in act 2 of *Love Me Tonight*, Mamoulian has a horse canter in tempo to a song. Jeanette has burst into view driving a carriage and singing a terrific waltz. Rodgers would also compose terrific waltzes with Oscar Hammerstein, but never one incorporating such horseplay as:

> Lover
> When you find me,
> Will you bind me
> With your glow?
> Make me cast behind me
> All my WHOA!
>
> Kiss me
> He'll be saying
> Gently swaying
> I'll obey
> Like two children playing
> in the HEY!*

The song ends with the recalcitrant horse cantering into a ditch and disgorging its driver. As surely as Mamoulian's tramping French soldiers, this cheeky yet bewitching number is an operetta send-up; waltzes are for dancing. Upon reaching the Duke's castle, Jeanette faints. "Can you go for a doctor?" Gilbert asks the luscious Valentine. "Certainly, bring him right in," she replies. Otherwise summoned, a doctor materializes. As Jeanette disrobes, they share a song composed (as Rodgers's score confirms) mainly to be spoken in rhythm: "A Woman Needs Something Like That." "You're not wasting away," the doctor diagnoses. "You're just wasted." A lyric expunged by censors† amplifies:

---

*"Lover" was published with different lyrics, unrelated to Jeanette's horse
†The guidelines of the Motion Picture Production Code were established in 1930; a period of stricter enforcement began in 1934.

A doorbell needs tinkling
A flower needs sprinkling
And a woman needs something like that.

A car needs ignition
To keep in condition
And a woman needs something like that.

All inventions of Edison
And medicine would leave you flat.
A peach must be eaten
A drum must be beaten
And a woman needs something like that.

Love Me Tonight is the rare film musical without dance. Instead, Mamoulian supplies a ballet pantomime with animals. The musical-dramatic set piece of act 3, scene 1, is a hunt whose racing dogs and horses align with a brisk march with horn calls, plus pizzicatos for a bounding deer. To test his alleged pedigree, Maurice is supplied with a horse named Solitude because "he always comes back alone." Horse and rider rocket out of sight: a fast-motion blur (drumroll and cymbals). Maurice somehow survives and befriends the deer. "Shhh! The stag, he is asleep," he tells the Duke. "We must go back, he is very tired. Quickly and quietly, on tiptoe." The hunters obediently gallop away in exquisite slow motion: a poetic denouement sealed by a somnolent Rodgers waltz laced with glissandos. The delicacy of this departure pervades the shimmer of light, sound, and décor throughout; Mamoulian's art director Hans Dreier, who for *Jekyll and Hyde* contrived a teeming and claustrophobic London of angles and shadows, supplies the ersatz French aristocrats with a milieu itself gracefully musical.

In an essay, "The Psychology of Sound,"[27] Mamoulian extolled "anti-realism." His principal example was (of course) the transformation scene in *Dr. Jekyll and Mr. Hyde.* When in act four of *Love Me Tonight* the aunts learn that Maurice is no baron, they bustle about the castle emitting high-pitched exclamations reinforced by the yaps of the family lap dog. Entering the drawing room in which the Duke has assembled assorted aged family members and guests, they upset a small vase, which shatters on the floor with the thunder power of a bomb. This figurative explosion—of the Old Order—ignites an incensed ensemble number. Scanning the archaic castle hierarchy, "The Son of a Gun Is Nothing but a Tailor" is sung in turn by the Duke, the aunts, Gilbert, a butler, a maid, a cook, and a laundress. Next—our climax—Jeanette sees Maurice leaving. A montage sequence juxtaposes or superimposes remembered song and dialogue ("I love you!") in voice-over; Jeanette cogitating and weeping; and Maurice at the train station: the arriving locomotive, the locomotive departing. Jeanette runs to the stable and gallops after Maurice's train. Train and horse hurtle toward the camera. A bellowing smokestack alternates with a heaving equine head, churning wheels with churning hooves. The music accelerates apace. Jeanette dismounts. Head back, arms akimbo, she faces the charging locomotive, a moment more phallic than romantic. To whistle blasts and trombones, the train halts, Maurice leaps to Jeanette, and all is enveloped in steam. Mamoulian's early films reflect close study of the German and Russian silent cinema. This over-the-top finale is nothing if not an Eisenstein parody.

In addition to speech, rhymed speech, rhymed speech to music, and sung speech, *Love Me Tonight* specializes in rhythmic speech. The film closes with the three aunts. "Please put into verse the end of the picture," Mamoulian had instructed Hoffenstein.[28] Hoffenstein supplies lines to be conducted, beginning:

> Once upon a time—
>   And not long ago
> There was a prince—
>   Who yet was not a prince

A compressed reprise of the aunt's *misterioso* motif, a compressed reprise of "Love Me Tonight," a fanfare, and we are done.

How considered is the film's musical structure? The principal set piece of act 1 (24 minutes) is "Isn't It Romantic?" which returns as a coda. Act 2 (22 minutes) begins with the same skyline and music as act 1; it ends with a reprise of "Mimi," sung by Maurice 10 minutes earlier. Act 3 (24 minutes) begins with the Duke snoring—a distinct sonic whiff of the initial "Symphony of Noises." An elaborate ensemble reprise of "Mimi" ensues. At the close of the act, Jeanette and Maurice mutually declare their love. "Love me tonight," Maurice implores—and the orchestra whispers a tune to come. Act four (20 minutes) begins with the same perky refrain that began act 1, scene 2. Maurice and Jeanette then sing "Love Me Tonight"—the title song first intimated moments earlier, and reserved for this romantic consummation: a virtually Wagnerian move.[*]

BEYOND CATEGORY

The cultural fluidity of *Love Me Tonight*—the promiscuous ease with which Mamoulian intermingles art and entertainment; his playful invocation and repudiation of genre—was variously noted or ignored. American and British reviews—as copiously collected by Paramount—offer a foretaste of the reception history of *Porgy and Bess*. The question "What is it?" is differently asked and answered. Frequent comparisons are made to Lubitsch, whose film musicals to date included *The Love Parade* (1929) and *One Hour with You* (1932) with Chevalier and MacDonald, and also to René Clair.[†]

---

[*]The division of *Love Me Tonight* into four acts is my own, based on unmistakable structural, musical, and visual cues.

[†]In Clair's *Under the Roofs of Paris* (1930), a song migrates from household to household—like Mamoulian's itinerant "Isn't It Romantic?" in *Love Me Tonight*. Clair also uses music to articulate the film's structure. He shares Mamoulian's delight in the creative deployment of camera and sound. Like Mamoulian, he strives to wed artistic novelty with popular appeal. The relative anonymity of Clair's 1940s films for Hollywood studios, compared to the dazzling freshness and

American film critics adored *Love Me Tonight*. For many, it seemed Chevalier's best vehicle. For a lesser number, it was something else: a Mamoulian tour de force. Categorized as Hollywood fare, it provoked scarcely a single attempt at sophisticated appreciation or analysis. A partial exception was the *New York Telegraph*'s Al Sherman, who recognized that Mamoulian aimed "to make cinema history." A singular vacillating assessment was that of Mordaunt Hall in the *New York Times*, who found "frequent signs of . . . straining for effect."

A newspaper review by a theater critic—the *Cleveland Plain Dealer*'s William F. McDermott—brought to bear a different context and a higher critical intelligence. McDermott knew *Porgy* and the Theatre Guild. He had seen Chevalier in Parisian revues. He had encountered MacDonald, Butterworth, Ruggles, and C. Aubrey Smith on Broadway. He knew Hoffenstein from his days as a Broadway press agent. He wrote:

> This picture is genuinely distinguished by the standards of the highest-class stage drama. . . . Mamoulian uses precisely the same methods with "Love Me Tonight" that he used in transfiguring "Porgy," but he bends his technique to suit the requirements of an entirely different type of story and he makes extraordinarily complete use of the special advantages the films have over the physically limited and inflexible stage.
>
> Roughly speaking, the Mamoulian method is to substitute stylization and synchronization of sound and movement for literal realism. To put it more concretely, he begins "Love Me Tonight" as he began an act of "Porgy." . . . The scene mounts to a crescendo, like a musical composition. . . .
>
> Music and timing are used more adeptly than I have ever seen

---

originality of his work during the inherently experimental early years of sound, is not irrelevant to Mamoulian's eventual American fate. Though Mamoulian never (to my knowledge) mentions Clair as an influence or inspiration, I am informed by my colleague Kurt Jensen that he saw fit to visit Clair in Paris in 1932.

them used in the films. The piece has a distinctive tempo and flavor and, within its little ribaldries, a kind of delicacy.

The British clippings collected by Paramount occupy a different critical milieu. Keying on Mamoulian, they do not classify *Love Me Tonight* as a generic Hollywood product. Here, for instance, is Ernest Betts in London's *Evening Standard*:

Mamoulian, who is a Russian, and offers caviar to the general, made "City Streets" and "Dr. Jekyll and Mr. Hyde." He is a great stylist in direction, a connoisseur in the disposal of corpses and the dispensing of epigrams. . . .

The satin-like sheen in which he envelops his material, even when it drips with blood, shows him to be a likely candidate for sophisticated fame.

Mamoulian, I honestly believe, could direct anything. He has directed Hollywood towards his own line of advance, which constitutes a record in movie history. . . .

Paramount, in permitting him to direct Maurice Chevalier, have chosen brilliantly. They may not be aware of it, but they have done something for the screen. . . .

The *Times* of London:

The difference between this production of Mr. Rouben Mamoulian . . . and even the most ingenious works of the same kind can only be explained by the fact that Mr. Mamoulian is an artist. . . . The film musical comedy, when it is not unbearable, is usually rescued by precision and speed. This film is at least as ingenious as any of the same sort that have preceded it, but this is the point where Mr. Mamoulian begins, not where he ends. . . . He has the artist's gift of discovering formal relations in any material, and by so doing, by some mysterious and recondite process, he lifts the squalid yearnings and base humour which the musical comedy is intended to express into another and far more delicate world. . . .

It is characteristic of his skill that he is able to introduce an exquisite pastoral ballet, a most romantic deer-hunt, which moves in time to music—even the deer somehow leaps in time—without any break or discontinuity in the performance. Even the star actors and actresses are, if not suppressed, at any rate kept strictly in their place, and yet M. Chevalier is allowed to do everything which his public would wish him to do. For the stars are inevitably compelled to take their part in the elaborate and subtle system of relations, visual, auditory, and intellectual, which Mr. Mamoulian contrives to extract from what one might well have thought the most refractory material.

The *Daily Telegraph*:

Mr. Mamoulian has composed a rhythmic satire. . . . [His] sense of style is unfailing. The opulent chateau might have been simply vulgar—an affair of gold plate and gigantic bathrooms in the Cecil de Mille manner. Instead, Mr. Mamoulian has achieved, by the use of chiaroscuro, an atmosphere of lightness and grace which I have never seen equaled on the screen, and never approached on the stage.

For the *New Statesman*, Francis Birrell produced an essay, "The Art of Mamoulian."

The film industry has produced many men of talent, but few artists. . . . With Chevalier [Mamoulian] has worked marvels. Lubitsch, a man of immense talent, seemed to fit Chevalier like a glove. There is in all Lubitsch's screen-work a coarseness of line, a commonness of treatment that suited Chevalier perfectly. In Mamoulian's hands Chevalier develops a refinement we should have thought impossible without sacrificing his innate high spirits. . . .

This film is the opposite of a talkie. For the noise dictates the speech, not the speech the noise. The noise also dictates the movement, of which the speed is never for long the same. He uses the sound as the basis of everything. . . .

It would be pleasant to see Mamoulian less tied to Hollywood, not always making bricks out of other people's bad straws. . . . With complete freedom he might do anything; for he is a man of genuine invention. . . . We have seen him at his finest, perhaps, not in film work at all, but in his production of "Porgy."

Love Me Tonight was also released in France, with French subtitles. Most French critics of course received it as a Chevalier film. But not *La Cinématographie Française*:

Mamoulian has fashioned . . . a masterpiece of grace, charm, spirit, and also novel technique. By structuring his film in a continuous balletic mode, by his use of sound as a means of expression, by the ongoing research into [modes of] staging, Mamoulian has truly created a new style of musical cinema. . . . The movement and finesse of the images, as well as the catchy music, complete the miracle.[29]

To this day, *Love Me Tonight* resists categorization—or submits to the category that most confines it: the Hollywood musical as contemporaneously defined by Lubitsch, a New World homage to the sly conspiratorial charm and teasing subject matter of Viennese operetta. That Lubitsch supplied Mamoulian with a template is no more obvious than Mamoulian's tactic of using that template as a toy. The densely agglomerated aural and visual layers of the Mamoulian style cancel the possibility of operetta sentiment, let alone Viennese nostalgia. And Mamoulian himself, unlike Lubitsch, had no anchored past—as time would tell, he was a deracinated twentieth-century exile mutually susceptible to assimilation and estrangement. The greater difference between Lubitsch and Mamoulian, however, is between creating a film with music and composing a film musically.* For a variety of reasons, re-creating *Porgy* for the stage, directing *Porgy and Bess*, were assignments as unthinkable for Lubitsch as they proved susceptible to the Mamoulian touch.

---

*To pick another deracinated immigrant, fired by the artistic cauldron of early-twentieth-century Moscow and St. Petersburg: *Love Me Tonight* actually bears comparison with George Balanchine's choreographic genius for newly exploring the synergies binding sound and gesture.

CHAPTER 3

PORGY AND BESS

ROUBEN MAMOULIAN was experimental by conviction. Though he invariably downplayed the influence of the Russian avant-garde on his thinking—though he characteristically took full credit for himself—his formative years in prerevolutionary and revolutionary Russia, and his exposure to Stanislavski and Vakhtangov, must have predisposed him toward a concentrated and original brand of creativity. For him, art dictated newness and novelty.

George Gershwin was experimental by habit. Though he thirstily obtained formal or informal instruction from a variety of teachers—though his genius was eagerly and overtly acquisitive—his formative apprenticeship was essentially self-made, self-invented in the American manner. For him, art was restless and unpredictable.

These disparate yet aligned creative personalities further converged in their relative disdain for lineage and past practice. The story Mamoulian told about himself extolled personal vision overcoming obstacles, subverting or transcending received wisdom: he told cameramen what a camera could do; he conducted actors with metronome and baton. Gershwin comparably said: "There is no such thing as tradition for me. Whatever I know about music, I've wrenched out for myself. I had no parents to stand over me and encourage me in the little tunes that I used to make up. No one ever urged me on by telling me that Mozart was a great composer when he was eleven."[1]

A further aspect of experimentation, as practiced by Mamoulian and Gershwin, was cultural fluidity. Disdaining the hierarchies of "high" and "low," Mamoulian directed Maeterlinck and Mickey Rooney; he prepared a "new version" of *Hamlet*. "It's just as difficult to write popular music as it is to write serious music," Gershwin said.[2]

Mamoulian's training was mostly self-training, on the job in Tbilisi, London, and Rochester; on Broadway and in Hollywood. Gershwin's early self-training was on Tin Pan Alley. That he was neither systematically nor formally schooled in composition did not, however, make him an unschooled composer. All his life, his musical passions recorded a wide range of knowledgeable affinity: Berg's *Lyric* Suite, a Hindemith string quartet, an Art Tatum set.

Gershwin was something like ten years old when he heard a schoolmate, Maxie Rosenzweig, play Dvořák's G-flat major *Humoresque* on the violin. "A flashing revelation of beauty," he later called it. That the Dvořák *Humoresque* was a first cause is pregnant: its blue notes and dotted rhythms point equally to the jazz club and the concert hall. In 1912—a few years after Maxie's Dvořák—Gershwin acquired his first significant teacher, the composer-pianist Charles Hambitzer, who is said to have been one of the first Americans to play Schoenberg's Opus 19 piano pieces. The pieces Hambitzer assigned Gershwin included preludes by Bach and Chopin. (Gershwin in later life hoped to compose his own set of twenty-four preludes.) At fifteen, Gershwin quit school and became a Tin Pan Alley song-plugger—that is, he sold other peoples' songs by playing and singing them for customers. He was a Broadway rehearsal pianist by the age of eighteen. Edward Kilenyi seems to have entered the picture a couple of years later. Kilenyi was scholarly and progressive; he knew (and partly translated) Schoenberg's theory text *Harmonielehre*. Gershwin's harmony and counterpoint lessons with Kilenyi were not casual. Rubin Goldmark, the Dvořák pupil whose works included symphonic appropriations of "Negro melodies," taught Gershwin next. A fourth formidable mentor, Joseph Schillinger, instructed Gershwin in his novel mathematical composing methodology beginning in 1932.[3] While this narrative remains somewhat patchy, it adds up to a substantial pedagogical sequence.

From an early age, Gershwin was an avid concertgoer. Stravinsky's *Petrushka* was one of his favorites (and he heard the composer conduct it). He also liked Shostakovich's First Symphony. Concurrently, he was a member in good standing of a collegial songwriters' community; his admiration for Irving Berlin and Jerome Kern was boundless.

And so the two streams of music that Gershwin absorbed from his teenage years bonded Europe and America. Like any son of immigrants, he was predisposed to ponder New World identity. A mission to find American identity in music, fusing New World and Old, came naturally to him. He thought and wrote about it. In 1929, assaying "Fifty Years of American Music," he said of American music that it "must express the feverish tempo of American life." It had to give voice to "our masses," to glimpse "our skyscrapers, "to convey "that overwhelming burst of energy which is bottled in our life."[4] In the same essay, Gershwin treated Irving Berlin's "Alexander's Ragtime Band" (1911) as a lodestar: "the first real American [musical] work." In Gershwin's opinion, Berlin was fortunate not to have studied abroad after the fashion of most "serious" American composers of his time. In 1934, Gershwin's search for America directed him to Charles Ives, whose songs and *Concord* Sonata he found inspirational (but who did not respond to Gershwin's overtures). Gershwin's writings on jazz seal its American identity without sidestepping misgivings—mistaken misgivings issuing from the Old World half of his fused creative personality—about its permanence. In 1933, he wrote:

> Jazz is the result of the energy stored up in America. It is a very ener-
> getic kind of music, noisy, boisterous and even vulgar. One thing is
> certain. Jazz has contributed an enduring value to America in the sense

that it has expressed ourselves. It is an original American achievement which will endure, not as jazz perhaps, but which will leave its mark on future music in one form or another. The only kinds of music which endure are those which possess form in the universal sense and folk music. All else dies. But unquestionably folk songs are being written and have been written which contain enduring elements of jazz. To be sure, that is only an element; it is not the whole. An entire composition written in jazz could not live.[5]

Everything Gershwin knew, believed, and experienced conditioned him to seek "American" variants of the "high" musical genres. As early as 1913, he composed a piano piece, "Ragging the Träumerei," pairing ragtime with Schumann. If "ragging the classics" was no novelty, *Blue Monday* was. This twenty-minute one-act "Opera Ala [*sic*] Afro-American" was created for George White's revue *Scandals of 1922*. Unlike Rouben Mamoulian's 1920s Rochester experiments rethinking European grand opera, Gershwin's experiment was more carefree than considered. *Blue Monday* was composed in five days. It begins with a vocal Prologue parodying the Prologue to Leoncavallo's *Pagliacci*; it ends in an avalanche of minstrel sentimentality; its seams—inconsistencies of style and tone—are mended with Scotch Tape. Gershwin's next approach to the "higher forms," two years later, was already *Rhapsody in Blue* for Paul Whiteman's "Experiment in Modern Music" at New York's Aeolian Hall. The Scotch Tape still showed—in fact, with its myriad incarnations, this episodic score yields no final form. But the materials are irresistible—and so is the driving trajectory binding rambunctious American energies with its signature tune, a swooning Russian love song.

A year later, a "real" conductor, Walter Damrosch, commissioned from Gershwin a real piano concerto. Gershwin complied with a thirty-minute work in the standard three movements, orchestrated—for the first time—by himself. Gershwin was no newcomer to piano concertos. And yet the first movement of his Concerto in F does not attempt the customary sonata form. Its very beginning is "experimental": a "modern" tattoo for percussion, a jaunty Charleston snatch, a drumroll, and—curtain up!—a cadenza for the soloist. Liszt and Brahms, among others, had launched piano concertos with stentorian cadenzas. But the Broadway milieu of Gershwin's preamble is something new, and so is the sauntering gait of the solo pianist. As in *Rhapsody in Blue*, Gershwin's fingers-on-the-keys composing style spontaneously fosters a multitude of thematic relationships. In the second movement, a blues, the result is a sublime theme song organically prepared and cannily delayed (like the Russian "love song" in *Rhapsody in Blue*, it enters two-thirds of the way through).

When in 1927 Gershwin made his Lewisohn Stadium debut, performing *Rhapsody in Blue* and the Concerto in F at Manhattan's major summer concert venue, an audience of 15,000 broke the previous Stadium attendance record (set by Beethoven's Ninth).[6] Both works have intoxicated multitudes ever since. Their eclectic appeal mutually registers cultural fluidity and stylistic fluidity. The *Rhapsody* is equally a brisk American diversion with band, a Slavic miniconcerto with orchestra, or a protean nightclub topic. The piano concerto is in various renderings akin to James P. Johnson, Ravel, or Rachmaninoff. Many local premieres surrounded it with short "pops" numbers by Rimsky-Korsakov, Smetana, Chabrier, and the like. Others, however, took Gershwin "seriously." Damrosch, at Carnegie Hall, premiered the concerto alongside a symphony by Glazunov and a suite by Henri Rabaud. In St. Louis, Vladimir Golschmann (who in Paris had already conducted the concerto to resounding popular and critical acclaim) positioned it after Tchaikovsky's *Pathétique* Symphony. Fritz Reiner, in Cincinnati, coupled it with Beethoven's Seventh, Strauss's *Till Eulenspiegel*, and *Rhapsody in Blue*. Meanwhile, Leo Reisman and Paul Whiteman widely toured the Concerto in F with their respective jazz orchestras. Even jazzier were much later versions with the Sauter-Finegan Orchestra and with the Marcus Roberts Trio. The embedded songs of Gershwin's style, the improvisatory élan of his composer's fingers, have ever promoted a singular range of interpretive possibilities.

The same fluidity factor, however, jinxed critical reception. If *Rhapsody in Blue* generally excited admiration amid questions about craftsmanship, the Concerto in F more fundamentally challenged the status quo. The reviews defied consensus—Gershwin was courageous and original; Gershwin was crude or immature. New York's two most prominent music critics were disappointed for different reasons. Lawrence Gilman in the *Herald Tribune* called the concerto trite and conventional—"we heard a facile and anxiously conformist youth talking the stale platitudes of the symphonic concert hall." Olin Downes in the *Times* felt Gershwin lacked the technique to write a work of symphonic dimensions. Over in the intellectual camp, Paul Rosenfeld, writing in 1927, favorably compared Aaron Copland's jazz-infused Piano Concerto to the "hash derivative" compositions of Gershwin. Virgil Thomson, writing in 1935, thought the concerto's charms did not disguise its lack of professionalism and depth. A further perspective: the violinist Winthrop Sargeant (later a *New Yorker* music critic) reported from within the ranks of Damrosch's New York Symphony that the musicians "hated Gershwin . . . with an instinctive loathing. . . . [They] pretended to regard Gershwin's music humorously, made funny noises, and played it, in general, with a complete lack of understanding of the American idiom."[7]

And so in the face of avid and self-evident popular acclaim, Gershwin's critics found his concert idiom too vulgar or too tame—too jazzy or not modern enough. In retrospect what most impresses about these early judgments is their patronizing tone. It did not sufficiently occur to the writers, or to Damrosch's musicians, that Gershwin might be a consciously innovative concert composer, and that his strategies of innovation might choose to ignore modernist dogma—that Gershwin might be at one and the same time an artist of genius and a popular artist. Certainly, he sought originality. Certainly, he sought to appeal—as he once put it—"to the great majority of our people."[8]

The history of *Porgy and Bess*—and of its critical reception—would follow suit.

. . .

It speaks volumes that a composer as naturally and fearlessly creative as Gershwin should have declared himself unready to set *Porgy*. When in 1926 he wrote to DuBose Heyward with instructions to proceed without him in bringing *Porgy* to the stage—that the opera could wait—he was doubtless aware of the usual fate of first operas, even those of great opera composers. He also reasoned (as we have seen) that a play could be a useful forerunner for the larger project he had in mind; it would provide a text, maybe even a template. Heyward and Gershwin first met in November 1927, when *Porgy* was in production. "My first impression of my collaborator remains with me and is singularly vivid," Heyward wrote eight years later. "A young man of enormous physical and emotional vitality, who possessed the faculty of seeing himself quite impersonally and realistically, and who knew exactly what he wanted and where he was going. This characteristic put him beyond both modesty and conceit. About himself he would merely mention certain facts, aspirations, failings. They were usually right."[9]

Gershwin's first crack at a full-length opera, as it turns out, was to be an adaptation of Szymon Ansky's *The Dybbuk*, commissioned by the Metropolitan Opera. But Gershwin was unable to secure the rights. He and Heyward began work on *Porgy and Bess* in fall 1933—by which time Gershwin's concert catalogue included *An American in Paris* (1928), the Second Rhapsody for piano and orchestra (1931), and the *Cuban* Overture (1932). Concurrently, his Broadway shows had been moving toward a tighter integration of story and music.[10]

Gershwin had for some time envisioned creating a "jazz opera." "I think it should be a Negro opera," he wrote in 1925.

"Bring m' goat" and "I'm on my way"—two crucial revisions to the published *Porgy* script, in Mamoulian's hand.

Cleon Throckmorton's set for *Porgy* (1927).

Rouben Mamoulian instructing his *Porgy and Bess* cast (1935).

Porgy and Bess (1935): The mourners' shadows at Robbins's funeral.

Porgy and Bess (1935): Bess restrains Crown moments after he has murdered Robbins.

Porgy and Bess (1935): The orphans' band.

Porgy and Bess (1935): The residents of Catfish Row try to drown out the hurricane with their singing.

Rouben Mamoulian, ca. 1935.

Rouben Mamoulian, 1984.

The mood could change from ecstasy to lyricism plausibly because the Negro has so much of both in his nature. The book, I think, should be an imaginative, whimsical thing, like a Carl Van Vechten story; and I would like to see him write the libretto.

That type of opera could not, I am afraid, be done at the Metropolitan. It is a typical opera comique venture. I would like to see it open as an opera comique on Broadway. I would like to see it put on with a Negro cast. Artists trained in the old tradition could not sing such music, but Negro singers could. It would be a sensation as well as an innovation.[11]

Heyward's novella inspired Gershwin to undertake a black opera far less whimsical in tone. So did *Porgy* on Broadway.

The novella and Mamoulian's production were already saturated with music; both Heyward and Mamoulian were themselves "composers" of a sort. Collaborating with Gershwin, Heyward wrote verse that would endure as his peak literary achievement. "Summertime," "My Man's Gone Now," and "A Woman Is a Sometime Thing" are among the opera's lyrics that are considered wholly his. With the exception of "Bess, Oh Where's My Bess?" Ira is thought responsible for songs of lighter tone or lesser depth, including "It Ain't Necessarily So." "Bess, You Is My Woman" and "I Got Plenty O' Nuttin'" were cowritten by the two lyricists. The libretto's recitatives—often closely based on the play's script—were Heyward's. The opera's nine scenes correspond precisely to the nine scenes of the Heywards' play, abridged for singing.

Ira later recalled that George was flattered when Otto Kahn, the Metropolitan Opera's enterprising board chairman, offered to mount the forthcoming *Porgy* opera at the Met. But the Gershwins decided to sign with the producers of *Porgy* the play: the Theatre Guild. In late 1934, Gershwin offered the Guild a list of prospective directors, including Heyward's first choice: the young John Houseman, who earlier that year had directed a black cast in Virgil Thomson's *Four Saints in Three*

Acts. Heyward had found Mamoulian mercurial and harsh with cast and crew in 1927. But the Guild had never produced anything like Gershwin's fledgling opera, and neither had Houseman (*Four Saints* having been a modest production endeavor). Warren Munsell of the Guild wrote to Heyward favoring Mamoulian over Houseman. The Guild's Theresa Helburn, with whom Mamoulian had worked closely on *Porgy*, successfully pushed for Mamoulian with Gershwin. Heyward acquiesced.[12]

Correspondence with the Guild confirms Mamoulian's claim that while in Hollywood he committed to *Porgy and Bess* without having heard a single note. He subsequently visited the Gershwins in New York and heard the brothers play and sing the entire score. But he spent months haggling with the Guild over financial terms before signing his contract. He had last directed on a New York stage in 1930. He had directed four Hollywood films subsequent to *Love Me Tonight*: *The Song of Songs* (with Marlene Dietrich, 1933), *Queen Christina* (with Greta Garbo, 1933), *We Live Again* (a forgettable vehicle for the forgettable Anna Sten, 1934), and *Becky Sharp* (a pioneering venture in Technicolor, 1935).

Mamoulian's 1938 account of his private audition at the Gershwins' is the most memorable and affectionate of his many published writings. Both the opera and the brothers impressed him inordinately. Close observers of Gershwin the man, generally, recorded the disarming frankness and sincerity of his self-appreciation, and the unusual intimacy of his bond with Ira. His supreme ego seemed immune to pettiness or envy. The critic Alexander Woollcott is one of many who testified that Gershwin "had no habit of pretense," that he was "above" and "beyond" posturing. At the same time, Gershwin appeared gregarious yet shy, outgoing yet unknowable, boyish yet studied, carefree yet melancholy. His brother and collaborator was an anchor, even an alter ego; decades after George's death, Ira would argue with him in his sleep, with Ira wanting to depart the world and George insisting that he stay.[13]

Mamoulian's essay "I Remember," for a Gershwin memorial volume edited by Merle Armitage, adds some characteristic anecdotes to reams of Gershwin portraiture. Late to meet Gershwin for dinner, Mamoulian was unshaven. "George said, 'Rouben, don't apologize. Personally, I love you when you're unshaven [because] when you're unshaven you look like me.'" Like a child, George would laugh loudly and delightedly at the same repeated jokes. He could also resemble a patriarch, these being his extremities of character. In between "there was much in him that was neither as simple nor as clear, nor perhaps, as happy. George did not live easily. He was a complicated, nervous product of our age. . . . He searched for a solution of himself." Distinctive to Mamoulian's reminiscence is his account of the audition itself. Initially, he had been shocked to learn that *Porgy* would be set to music; he found the play already complete. But he also felt that if anyone could make *Porgy* operatic, it could only be Gershwin. Thus disposed, he was handed a highball by the brothers and directed to a leather armchair. All three men trembled with excitement. George sat down at the piano. Ira "stood over him like a guardian angel." George made excuses that playing an opera on the piano was difficult. Mamoulian said he understood.

The next second I was listening to the opening "piano music" of the opera. I found it so exciting, so full of color and so provocative in its rhythm that after this first piano section was over, I jumped out of my armchair and interrupted George to tell him how much I liked it. Both brothers were as happy as children to hear words of praise, though heaven knows, they should have been used to them by then. When my explosion was over and they went back to the piano, they both blissfully closed their eyes before they continued with the lovely *Summertime* song. George played with the most beatific smile on his face. . . . Ira sang—he threw his head back with abandon, his eyes closed, and sang like a nightingale! In the middle of the song George couldn't bear it any longer and took over the singing from him. To describe George's face while he sang *Summertime* is something that is beyond my capacity as a writer. "Nirvana" might be the word! So it went on. George was the orchestra and sang half of the parts, Ira sang the other half. Ira was also frequently the "audience." It was touching to see how he, while singing, would become so overwhelmed with admiration for his brother, that he would look from him to me with half-open eyes and pantomime with a soft gesture of his hand, as if saying, "*He* did it. Isn't it wonderful? Isn't *he* wonderful?" George would frequently take his eyes away from the score and watch me covertly and my reaction to the music while pretending that he wasn't really doing it at all. . . . We all felt exultantly happy. The next morning both George and Ira had completely lost their voices.[14]

In contract negotiations with the Guild lasting some six months, Mamoulian was promised 2 percent of box-office receipts per week over $7,000, plus a salary of $500 per week.[15] These terms further financially encumbered a production that would require a 43-piece orchestra—more than twice the size of the usual Broadway pit ensemble—in addition to a huge cast and an elaborate set. Mamoulian also emphasized to the Guild that he would leave the show if there were fundamental disagreements about staging, and that he was to be bothered with pre-production work as little as possible.

In engaging Rouben Mamoulian, the Gershwins and the Guild acquired an expensive director with a deserved reputation for taking over whatever he touched. He routinely revised scripts and inflicted novelties. He had already formidably experimented with opera in English. He regarded the Theatre Guild *Porgy* as his personal offspring. On Broadway, in Hollywood, he had imposed notions of "rhythmic" speech, gesture, and construction as a veritable *idée fixe*. We have already observed that the play *Porgy* substantially refashioned the novella *Porgy*, and that Mamoulian was a crucial agent of this transformation; that Heyward's regional Gullah cameo, which was also a state-of-nature fable, acquired universal resonance as an epic tale of sorrow and redemption. As *Porgy and Bess* would be fundamentally based on the play, and not the book,

Mamoulian's inherent impact far exceeds what previous accounts of the opera's gestation have acknowledged. This, and his further impact on the Gershwin opera in rehearsal and performance, are the central topics of the present chapter.

MAMOULIAN'S SET PIECES

Gershwin finished both a vocal score (i.e., voices with piano) and a full score (voices with orchestra) before *Porgy and Bess* went into production. To this day, the published score for *Porgy and Bess* is Gershwin's original vocal score, issued in 1935.[16]

Mamoulian arrived on the scene as a celebrity. During the rehearsal period, he added to Gershwin's vocal score and subtracted from it. According to his usual practice, he actually choreographed it, changing or ignoring Heyward's published staging notes at will. There is no evidence that Heyward was part of this process. Gershwin, however, was present for an hour or two nearly every day. He conferred frequently with Mamoulian and with his conductor, Alexander Smallens. Nothing was done without Gershwin's consent. Four decades later, when memories of the premiere production had long faded, *Porgy and Bess* revivals by the Cleveland Orchestra (1975), Houston Grand Opera (1976), and Metropolitan Opera (1985) were proclaimed "complete" by virtue of presenting the published score in full or nearly in full. But this claim is no more legitimate—in fact, arguably less so—than calling the Theatre Guild production the "real" *Porgy and Bess.*

How to analyze Mamoulian's impact as director of *Porgy and Bess*? A starting point: as musically structured by Mamoulian, *Porgy* was anchored by the four set pieces earlier explored:* Robbins's funeral, the picnic celebration with its orphans' band, the hurricane, and— opening the final scene—the daybreak "Symphony of Noises." Balanc-

---

*See pp. 45–57.

ing the upbeat tone of the Noise Symphony, the play concluded with Porgy's ecstatic resolve to find Bess en route to "heavenly land." The orphans' band, the "Symphony of Noises," and the ecstatic close were all Mamoulian inspirations. The funeral scene was indelibly choreographed by Mamoulian. The hurricane was amplified by Mamoulian as another noise symphony. All of these components were reprised in *Porgy and Bess*—but with varying degrees of emphasis. The orphans' band, the "Symphony of Noises," the Mamoulianized ending—"Bring m' goat!"—were operatically adapted. The funeral again excited a singular choreographic intervention. The hurricane scene was eventfully expanded. Each of these episodes deserves a close look.

Of Mamoulian's additions, the orphans' band and "Symphony of Noises"—neither to be found in the published vocal score—were for decades essentially forgotten. Only beginning in 1987 did the Gershwin scholars Charles Hamm and Wayne Shirley exhume the pertinent Theatre Guild materials. A 2006 reconstruction of the Theatre Guild *Porgy and Bess* by the Nashville Symphony, conducted by John Mauceri, followed (and was recorded by Decca).

It will be recalled that Mamoulian thought of adding the Jenkins Orphanage Band to *Porgy* as a result of a reconnaissance trip to Charleston, and that in the play it furnished some necessary musical heft in between the choral effusions of Robbins's wake and of the hurricane. The 1935 vocal score for act 2, scene 1, of *Porgy and Bess* mentions a "stage band" first offstage, then leading the picnickers in a rousing ensemble: "Oh, I Can't Sit Down!" The chorus finishes, then "band turns and leaves, followed by picnickers." And Gershwin in fact scored music for an 11-piece stage band—a further manuscript bound into the manuscript full score. However, the published conductor's score omits this music, and no instrumental parts were published for it. For decades, it was wrongly assumed that the orphans merely pantomimed playing their instruments.[17] So this is an instance where a Mamoulian inspiration—the onstage band—was embraced by Heyward and Gersh-win, then abandoned.

Does it much matter? The ragamuffin impact of the orphans—aurally and visually—was memorable in 1927. The opera, by compari-son, already has its own pit orchestra; the onstage band—following a venerable tradition that includes *Don Giovanni*, *Rigoletto*, and (to mention an opera of special significance to Gershwin) Berg's *Wozzeck*—is in a sense an extravagance. It did not even comprise Carolina orphans, as in 1927. Rather, young New York musicians played its clarinet, two alto saxophones, tenor saxophone, three trumpets, trombone, snare drum, bass drum, and string bass. There were also a drum major, a dancer, and a third, nonplaying band member whose function is unclear. Shirley observes that, with the addition of the band, "the moment of greatest bustle" directly precedes "the moment of greatest tranquility"—Porgy contentedly awaiting Bess's return from the picnic.[18]

Mamoulian's "Symphony of Noises"—which in *Porgy and Bess* is titled "Occupational Humoresque"—is altogether more ambitious. Hey-ward, in his opera libretto, remembers Mamoulian's 1927 "Symphony of Noises" when he prescribes:

> The stage is empty except for one negro asleep at foot of steps. Grad-ually noises of stage start and grow in volume until in about two minutes the stage is alive with color, movement, and sound. This awakening assumes, unconsciously, the character of a racial and occu-pational symphony. The first sounds being slow and widely spaced, the tempo quickens, built up of the strokes of a broom, the snore of the sleeping Negro, the pounding of a hammer. Two carpenters come on and work on steps, their hammer and saw entering into the rhythm and shooting it up into a rapid jazz. Voices call good mornings from windows, and a woman comes out on Serena's balcony and beats a rug. Scipio and four small boys enter and engage in a game of tag[,]

their shrill cries adding to the volume. When tempo and volume have reached their peak, the steady, approaching clang of the bell of the patrol wagon cuts across it, plunging the court into a listening silence [underlining by Gershwin].[19]

But Gershwin instead composed a daybreak pantomime (including "sleeping Negro," "man with broom," "man with hammer," and "man with saw") that in no way resembles the 1927 "Symphony of Noises" Heyward intended to invoke. Perhaps Gershwin had no means of remembering Mamoulian's rhythmic "Noise Symphony" (although *Love Me Tonight* could have instructed him). In any event, his daybreak pantomime and chorus is formulaic and episodic.*

The "Occupational Humoresque" composed by Mamoulian in rehearsal was discovered by Shirley—but, like the onstage band, was unperformed between 1938, when Mamoulian's production last toured, and 2006, when the Nashville forces performed and recorded it. A $\frac{4}{4}$ count is established by thuds and snores on beats one and three. A broom is added, then a knife-sharpener, a saw, a washboard, and so on. A crescendo of sound and stage activity drives the rhythm to $\frac{2}{4}$, then to a Charleston rhythm. At this moment, a portion of what Gershwin had composed is activated; Mamoulian has created a pattern of noises that synchronize with Gershwin's chorus and orchestra.[20] The result is not just a Mamoulian obsession (though it is also that); Mamoulian has replaced Gershwin's preamble with a calibrated crescendo and accelerando culminating with Mingo running to the gate and exclaiming "It's Porgy coming home!" Mamoulian's intervening hand is invisible: the revised sequence has not more but fewer seams. It is tighter than what it replaces, shorter (by two minutes), better.

---

*Hamm calls it "somewhat disjointed"; "not top drawer Gershwin," Shirley says. (Charles Hamm, "The Theatre Guild production of *Porgy and Bess*," *Journal of the American Musicological Society* 4, no. 3 (Autumn 1987), p. 515. Shirley, "The 'Theatre Guild Version' of *Porgy and Bess*," unpublished paper, 2009.

The opera's brief final scene, as in the play, contains only three events: Porgy returns, Porgy learns that Bess is gone, Porgy departs. Buttressing the play (as we have seen), Mamoulian here added his "Symphony of Noises" and—to balance this "musical" preface—a redemptive final chorus ("I'm on my way to heavenly land"). In place of the novella's dour conclusion and the relatively subdued leave-taking in the Heywards' original script, *Porgy and Bess* retains this Mamoulianized finale. Here, Heyward's libretto closely follows Mamoulian's script revisions to the play.* As for Gershwin: appropriating the play's spirituals, he composes spirituals of his own invention, with occasional allusions to the traditional tunes. "Ah'm on my way,"† as employed in *Porgy* the play, is an upbeat tune whose rhythmic motto is three eighth notes plus a longer note:

Gershwin's "Oh Lawd, I'm On My Way" turns the rhythmic motto upside down—so that it rises:

Gershwin's great tune and its deployment mate marchlike resolve with uplift, grandeur with concision (another repetition would be self-indulgent). For the final choral cadence, he has his sopranos leap an octave on "Lawd" to sustain a high B—a note previously unattained in the entire act—for five measures, while everyone else is singing "It's a

---

*See Appendix C.
†I here use the spelling preserved in the sheet music for the play, different from Mamoulian's handwritten insert.

long, long way." The Grandioso symphonic tag drives Porgy's bluesy leitmotif to a soaring culmination.

Mamoulian's choreography characteristically underlines this tightly construed ascent. At the close of Porgy's ultimate lament, "Oh, Bess, Oh Where's My Bess?," "People turn gradually and slowly come down and spread to final positions, never taking their eyes off Porgy." Heyward and Gershwin, in the published vocal score, next have Serena tell Porgy that Bess is "worse than dead . . . but she still livin', an' she gone far away," after which Porgy, to trembling, trilling chords, mightily exclaims "Alive, Bess is alive!" Mamoulian eliminates this passage: it interferes with his trajectory; it preempts his climax. Where Porgy first barks "Bring my goat," Mamoulian writes, "simple request." When Porgy repeats "Bring my goat," Mamoulian writes, "commandingly," and adds to Porgy's lines: "No! I'm going!" Porgy is resolute: strong. Just before Porgy launches "Oh Lawd, I'm On My Way," Mamoulian instructs: "All hands raised to Porgy as in blessing." Porgy sings with "hands to heaven." The choristers, meanwhile, pray with hands raised or on their chests, then with all hands raised. Then they kneel. Amid ecstatic song, Porgy is lifted onto his cart (a stage direction ineffectually *preceding* "Oh Lawd" in the Heyward script). Porgy exits and the curtain falls with the choral cadence. The curtain rises again for the seven-measure symphonic postlude, then descends again on the final chord. With its ever-mounting tide of rapture, this religious ending—to which Mamoulian contributed at least as much as Heyward—is a cosmic summons unglimpsed in Heyward's novella or the Heywards' original *Porgy* script. Porgy has endured solitude, found love, and uncovered betrayal. His resilient growth in character is sealed by a community's pride and exaltation. The "Heav'nly Lan'" toward which he ascends embodies new moral stature, shedding the indolence and happy dust of his ghetto origins.*

---

*For more on the musical content here, see pp. 6–7.

Unlike the orphans' band or "Noise Symphony," the hurricane is a momentous set piece in *Porgy and Bess*. It impacts impressively but haphazardly. Revising the Heywards' act 2, scene 4, script for *Porgy*, Mamoulian ruthlessly expunged most of the talking; what was mainly left were three spirituals and a song, Crown's ragtime "Hesitation Blues." Thus streamlined, the scene built swiftly to an elemental apex, then a sudden silence—the hurricane's eye—and a fast curtain.* Gershwin's complex operatic scene proved less readily susceptible to surgery. As originally composed and published, it begins and ends with an effect Gershwin discovered in a Hendersonville, South Carolina, church: six superimposed solo prayers ("Oh, Doctor Jesus"). Clara reprises "Summertime." Crown's titanic forced entrance into Serena's room, with its huddled mass of humanity, leads to shouted expostulations and to a relatively intimate encounter between Crown and the hostile Bess. Then, ragging the storm, Crown sings "A Red-Headed Woman." Throughout, outbursts of thunder and lightning alternate with pleading choral interventions. This mixture of ritual, lullaby, and private altercation, of plantation song and ragtime, of quiescence and turbulence, challenged Mamoulian's fixation on rhythm and transition. By eliminating the massive opening prayer, with its tense layers of song, he made the scene begin not *forte* but *piano*: a hushed starting point ("Oh, De Lawd Shake De Heavens"). And Mamoulian markedly accelerated the cumulative momentum by eliminating Crown's return to "A Red-Headed Woman." The closing "Doctor Jesus" expostulations were greatly compressed. Though Wayne Shirley, for one, considers the Ivesian onslaught of the "Doctor Jesus" choruses "one of the great twentieth-century representations of humanity crying de profundis," Mamoulian is striving, successfully or not, for a "long line." He is also trimming an overlong act—a topic to which we will return.[21]

---

*See pp. 51–53.

ROBBINS'S FUNERAL

In 1927, Robbins's funeral, its choreographed swaying and clapping amplified as a shadow ballet, was the *Porgy* episode that excited the most astonishment.* In *Porgy and Bess*, the corresponding sequence—the ceremony of lament and keening widow's song—comprises the opera's most sustained set piece. Nothing else in American musical theater so formidably unites human and epic tragedy. Nothing else in *Porgy and Bess* so silences criticism of Gershwin's operatic craftsmanship.

In *Porgy* the play, this second scene of act 1 incorporates three choral spirituals. "Deat', ain't yuh gots no shame?" is the monotonous dirge the mourners have been singing for hours; some are lulled into a coma. After the police take Peter away as a witness to Robbins's murder, the singing grows more emphatic: "What' de matuh chillum? . . . Pain gots de body, an' I can't sit still." The undertaker agrees to bury Robbins: a victory yielding the ecstatic "Oh, I'll meet um in de Primus Lan'!" In *Porgy and Bess*, Heyward's libretto links four numbers. "Gone, Gone, Gone" is now the weary funeral chant. "Overflow" is an exhortation to fill the saucer with coins enough to inter Robbins. "My Man's Gone Now," Serena's aria, is a solo moment not to be found in the novella or play. And "Oh, the train is at the station" seizes the undertaker's consent to "see you through."

Gershwin knits these four musical episodes into a quasi-symphonic structure. "Gone" ("marcia funebre") is a study in mortal ennui: the refrain sinks slowly, ineluctably, perpetually. "Overflow" is a contrasting scherzo. "My Man's Gone Now," the funeral's pounding centerpiece, is a different type of dirge, mining more personal sorrows; it culminates in a full close, inviting applause. "Oh, the train is at the station" (accelerating to animato) is compensatory, a jubilant catharsis. All the junctures are well considered. The fatigued chromatics of "Gone" make

---

*See p. 45.

it harmonically unstable—Gershwin's basses must reiterate their low G thirteen times to bring it to a G minor halt before "Overflow" is suddenly and "fanatically" activated in another key (E-flat major) by a series of self-commands: "Come on, sister, come on, brudder, fill up de saucer til it overflow." Its chromatic instability renders the slithering "Gone" refrain transitional and modulatory—and Gershwin regathers this woeful undercurrent three times more as binding; both Serena's lament and the ecstatic communal "train" are so prepared, with the final reprise a cumulative brass threnody with pounding marcato dotted rhythms.[22]

Supporting Gershwin, Mamoulian interposes a completely different form of binding: stylized ritual informs his staging of the entire scene, securing a gestural patina of formality and timelessness not otherwise suggested. This singular contribution is instantly obvious: the curtain rises on a room without a ceiling. A bed with a corpse is flanked on either side by a row of three mourners on chairs, then a row of three more on stools; the chairs are graduated in height, rising toward the back; other mourners are situated on the floor. No actual funeral was ever so punctiliously configured. As in a ballet, this opening tableau is the premise for every subsequent variation. The mourners precisely regroup. They clap or pat their feet; they sway on the beat or in syncopation (scrupulously notated by arrows penciled above the pertinent vocal line); they squat or rise to their knees; their hands and arms are up or down, stationary or atremble.

Thus, as Gershwin begins to build his climax in "Overflow," Mamoulian has everyone stop swaying and gradually sit straight. "Bless de Lawd!" is shouted by two rows of mourners, "Oh, my Jesus!" by four rows, and so on. He then creates a stage picture of kneeling figures with the tallest in the center and gradually diminished height to either side. Gershwin's transition to "My Man's Gone Now" comprises a surging reprise of "Gone," then a torrential marcato scale in the orchestra plunging to the new E minor tonic. Mamoulian's mourners lean backward, heads to heaven, swaying slowly with eyes closed. As Serena commences her lament, Porgy and Bess sit back to back, heads together "like masks";* all others "sway ovally." At "Ole Man Sorrow, sittin' by de fireplace," Gershwin adds sopranos and altos singing "Ah!"; italicizing a Gershwin marking, Mamoulian wants them to accent their sixteenth-note upbeats: a stabbing inflection.

For Serena's wailing glissando ascent to a high B, all lean forward, heads to knees. For the ensuing wailing choral glissando, Serena sweeps the floor with her right hand as she circles and rises to a standing position (readers familiar with the music should pause to envision this inspiration). All heads slowly rise. When Serena commences her final keening descent: "All hands up"; "Ross, Yeates, Hines, McLean [four chorus members] fall flat on floor." Serena finishes her song and collapses sobbing.

As in 1927, Mamoulian reserves his signature shadow play for the scene's final chorus, variously illuminated by an amber mantel light, a lantern, and white, amber, and blue footlights. Characteristically, he streamlines this charging "train" number, compressing the hurtling trajectory and eliminating a spot where the heavenly land locomotive stops and starts again. The buildup: "Right side double sway; left side single

---

*The music critic Irving Kolodin, observing this moment in rehearsal, recorded that Mamoulian found Bess's swaying movements too vigorous. "You are the accompaniment, not the melody," he told her. "What we want here is an obbligato."

sway and profile of hands up." "All shout jump clap hands noisily ad lib, etc." A group of three women "screams at intervals til curtain;" two men shout. Clara and Maria move toward the footlights to project ever more looming, more gyrating shadows. Eight men clap a Charleston, another eight a simpler rhythm, stamping and swaying. Finally, with the ecstasy of "Until we meet our brudder in the Promise' Lan,' in the Promise' Lan'!," Serena rises slowly and moves to her downstage "lamp mark," creating the most colossal of the shadows overwhelming the ceiling-less room on three sides. The mourners are now spread across the stage. Those on either end fall to their knees. All arms are raised. In a production photograph of this final tableau, the stark, featureless wall images suggest pagan or primitive statuary. Gauguin's Tahiti is a plausible frame of reference. So is Gershwin's favorite painter, George Roualt, who could be barbaric and Christian at the same time. A November 1935 *Stage* magazine description by Ruth W. Sedgwick is vividly evocative:

> At first the lights pick up fingers, transform them into tongues of black flame darting through the air. Then faces, raised, and beautiful with quiet resignation, take on the flat quality of Italian primitives. Finally the lamp goes out, the white spots in the footlights come on, and voodoo shadows begin their dance of death along the wall. At the end Lord Jesus has entirely gone, and the sultry soul of Africa broods over the room.

The curtain falls. To end on a peak dynamic, Mamoulian kills the orchestra's postlude; its chugging locomotive decrescendo could only undercut what has transpired onstage.

At such moments, the collaboration of Heyward, Gershwin, and Mamoulian becomes remarkably evenhanded. In Charleston, Heyward recorded the rites of a local Carolina subculture. Gershwin, in New York, stirred Heyward's findings into a black melting pot. Mamoulian has no secure geographic base; rather, his grounding (potentially precarious) is personal and professional: a theater-history narrative into which he ambitiously situates himself as an agent of change. For him, the Gullahs' communal mourning ritual resonates not with Folly Island or Harlem, but with thespian roots in Africa or classical Greece; with Negroid masks and tribal dances; with the omnipresent chanting choruses of Aeschylus, which observe and gesticulate, punctuate and opine.

FURTHER MAMOULIAN TOUCHES

The singers cast for *Porgy and Bess* ran the gamut from show business to opera. John W. Bubbles (Sporting Life) was a vaudeville star; in rehearsal, his inability to read or remember music caused consternation, but the antioperatic Bubbles style was what Gershwin wanted; Mamoulian had him dance the entire role and even added (to "It Ain't Necessarily So") a dance number accompanied by humming and guitars. Todd Duncan (Porgy), Anne Brown (Bess), Abbie Mitchell (Clara), Ruby Elzy (Serena), and Edward Matthews (Jake) were all classically trained singers. Both Duncan and Mitchell had recently starred in Mascagni's *Cavalleria Rusticana* with New York's black Aeolian Opera. Brown had studied at the Peabody Institute in Baltimore and at the Juilliard School, Elzy at Juilliard. Matthews, a graduate of Fisk University, had sung in *Four Saints in Three Acts*. In rehearsal, these artists proved strangers to the black southern dialect Heyward had adapted. Duncan later confessed that they also did not know that Sporting Life's "happy dust" was cocaine. At an early rehearsal and recording conducted by Gershwin (July 19, 1935), Mitchell—whose teachers had included Jean De Rezske in Paris—renders "Summertime" with rolled R's. Duncan's *Porgy and Bess* studio recordings (1940, 1942) are plangent and sympathetic; he lightens his timbre and even indulges in some embellishments of "Oh Lawd, I'm On My Way" (Gershwin cheerfully permitted such digressions from the score). Brown is a vulnerable, notably decorous Bess whose colloquial diction sounds learned for the show. Duncan and

Brown are heard to better advantage at the Hollywood Bowl Gershwin Memorial Concert (September 8, 1937). At this charged public occasion, "Bess You Is My Woman" is plastically shaped by sentiment. Elzy pours out "My Man's Gone Now," her inflections, vocal and verbal, aching with pathos, her high silvery soprano long sustaining the stratospheric B's of the opera's grandest climax.

But the most memorable (and least known) sound documentation of these original cast members is a Sunday afternoon radio broadcast—*The Magic Key of RCA*, December 1, 1935—from the stage of the Alvin Theatre shortly after the show opened. Mitchell is heard in "Summertime" (still rolling her R's), Duncan and Brown in "I Got Plenty O' Nuttin'" and "Bess, You Is My Woman Now." The orchestra (presumably led by Smallens) is tight and pliant. In the duet, the lovers share their affection intimately, at tempos molded to carry the words. The revelation is Porgy's song: its smiling inflections; its mounting ecstatic surge. Lines like "Oh dere's no use COMplainin'" and "What the hell, I'm alive! Oh, I got plenty o' nuttin'!" are not sung or spoken; they are shouted, imitating the quasi-Caribbean Gullah shouts Gershwin retained in his ear from his Carolina visit of 1934. This special radio performance, before a live audience when the show was fresh, today survives as the single most revealing *Porgy* recording ever made.[23]

Duncan, Brown, and many other cast members reported their happiness with *Porgy and Bess*, with Gershwin, and with Mamoulian. In a 1938 Gershwin tribute, Duncan recalled an early rehearsal of Serena's prayer (act 2, scene 3):

Mamoulian was working like mad with the actors setting the entrances, positions, the music and action. This is a very quiet scene, one of profound religious fervor. We singers were very tired, tired enough fortunately to set up the exact atmosphere required for the prayer. . . . Miss Elzy (Serena) went down on her knees as if her own mother had been ill for weeks; she felt the need of prayer. Two seconds of silence inter-

vened that seemed like hours, and presently there rose the most glorious tones and wails with accompanying amens and hallelujahs for our
sick Bess that I ever hope to experience. This particular scene should
have normally moved into the scene of the Street Cries, but it did not.
It stopped there. The piano accompaniment ceased, every actor (and
there were sixty-five of them) had come out of his rest position, sitting
at the edge of his seat and R.M. was standing before us quietly moving his inevitable cigar from one side of his mouth to the other, his
face lighted to sheer delight in realization, and then, George Gershwin like a ghost from the dark rows of the Guild theatre appeared
before the footlights. He simply could not stand it. He knew then, that
he had put down on paper accurately and truthfully something from
the depth of soul of a South Carolina Negro woman who feels the
need of help and carries her troubles to her God.

In later years, Duncan and others recalled the high morale of the rehears-
als, and Mamoulian's "brilliance." The great Russian stage actress Alla
Nazimova, whom Mamoulian had directed in Turgenev on Broad-
way, sent a telegram wishing ALL SUCCESS TO YOU AND YOUR
CHILDREN AND THANKS AGAIN FOR ALLOWING ME TO WIT-
NESS THE MOST THRILLING AND INSPIRING REHEARSAL IN
MY MEMORY—and Nazimova would have remembered the Moscow
rehearsals of Stanislavski and his associate Nemirovich-Danchenko.[24]

As with *Porgy*, Mamoulian was intent on treating the choristers as
individuals; his annotations identify many of them by name. Irving
Kolodin, tracking *Porgy and Bess* in rehearsal for *Theatre Arts Monthly*,
reported "Mamoulian's objective to establish . . . the feeling that only
an accident of fate kept [the chorus members] from being prime factors, rather than mere bystanders, in the drama. Any one of the men
could have been Robbins, slain by a blow from the drunken Crown; any
one of the women, the widowed Sarina [*sic*]." The artist Peggy Bacon,
sketching Mamoulian in rehearsal for *Stage* magazine, observed:

Dark eyes, intent, clever, vigilant

Adventurous mouth; lips flexible, curling slightly in private appraisal,
> as though inwardly estimating the merits of a peppermint

Tall, trim figure, bent forward eagerly like a sporting spectator

Speech . . . an executive rasp buttered with persuasive tact. Personality
> as effective as an ancient Assyrian out lion-hunting: alert, preda-
> tory, smooth as a knife[25]

Even in a book about Mamoulian and *Porgy and Bess*, it would be
fruitless to attempt to comprehensively catalogue his contributions to
the Gershwin opera. We have just glimpsed Mamoulian in rehearsal,
and examined his role in fashioning or refashioning musical set pieces
he had earlier fashioned or refashioned directing *Porgy*. In chapter 1,
we explored other Mamoulianized aspects of the 1927 play that would
influence *Porgy and Bess*—including augmented roles for Bess, Crown,
and Sporting Life; a first scene lullaby later reprised (as would be "Summertime"), and a picnic song (that would become "It Ain't Necessarily
So"). Mamoulian's working script for *Porgy and Bess* is densely marked
with changes, additions, and cuts. There is also a plethora of production
photographs recording the elaborate tableaux in which he delighted. As
the 1935 Catfish Row set was bigger than in 1927, and the cast commensurately larger, Mamoulian had more space to embellish, more bodies,
more windows. When Crown attacks Robbins, the crowd—as recorded
by Mamoulian's annotations—"weaves in and out like a serpent, following them, coming in close and backing to walls again." The fatal blow—
struck by a knife rather than the fish hook designated by Heyward—is
suddenly illuminated by a red spotlight. "All rush around body hands
up in horror. Serena screams, crosses to body and throws herself on it.
All look at Serena." Bess crosses to Crown. The spot fades just before
Crown speaks to Bess ("Where you goin' hide?"). Every witness to this
event—on the courtyard floor, in doorways, pressing forward on win-
dowsills—participated. In the hurricane scene, Mamoulian similarly

enlarged his *Porgy* choreography: the terrified community is a human wedge, thrust forward in supplication or propelled backward by Crown's forced entrance (to a pistol shot—a crack of thunder—punctuating the storm symphony).

The most densely annotated pages of the vocal score belong to "I Got Plenty O' Nuttin'." Mamoulian's instructions show a complex audio-visual accompaniment, virtually a sotto voce symphony of noises. The musical instruments include a dishrag, a shoe rag, a hammer, and two rugs. The props include soap bubbles floating from a high window, and empty rocking chairs on strings. All this activity selectively starts and stops. When Porgy sings "I got no lock on the door," Mamoulian freezes the shoe rag, the hammer, and the rocking chairs. For Porgy's first forte reprise of "I got plenty o' nuttin'," the chairs resume rocking with women now sewing in time. For the women's choir ("Porgy change since dat woman come to live with he"), all rhythmic activity ceases. When Porgy returns to his tune, joined by humming tenors and basses, Mamoulian restarts his rhythmic implements—only louder, with sleeping men wiggling their feet in time to the music and the rocking chairs at "two counts to the bar." The rockers next further accelerate ("double time four to the bar"). The sleepers awake with a jerk for Porgy's culminating "got my song!" While he holds his final note, the men rise in slow motion, stretching and yawning. During the applause: "general movement and chatter."[26] Gershwin had already made this banjo song, with its choral interjections, a community moment. What is more, he had jotted on a typescript of the lyrics an instruction he likely shared with Mamoulian: "Entire stage affected by rhythm of Porgy's song."[27] Mamoulian transforms "I Got Plenty O' Nuttin'" into a sustained ensemble, with Porgy—who understands the value of "nuttin'," versus locks and cars—an agent of moral instruction and communal euphoria. The redemptive catharsis he ultimately inspires is here whimsically forecast.

Of countless tiny Mamoulian alterations, some are merely sensible.

Where in the craps game Heyward has Sporting Life produce his own dice in an attempt to cheat, Mamoulian has him say "I got some dice—look at these" lest we fail to notice. Mamoulian's sly redeployment of "happy dust" in act 3, scene 2, is transformative. Heyward has Bess accept the cocaine just before Sporting Life croons and struts "There's A Boat That's Leaving Soon for New York." Mamoulian has Bess reject the powder. Instead, Sporting Life takes it himself, so that Bubbles's preening song of enticement—doubtless a tour de force—is freshly coked (an interpretation serendipitously supported by Gershwin's slithering bass line). He then deposits some happy dust for Bess on a step leading to Porgy's room. She runs into the room and slams the door. Sporting Life exits. Heyward keeps the stage empty while the orchestra grandly reprises Sporting Life's song (Maestoso, fortissimo). But Mamoulian has Bess return: "[She] comes out, looks around, and hesitates; suddenly, she grabs powder and goes in house, slamming door." The resulting counterpoint of music and gesture—the grandiose peroration juxtaposed with Bess's pathetic capitulation—is pure Mamoulian, a savage ironic flourish foreign to Heyward and Gershwin both. The orchestra's wicked laughter unexpectedly produces one of the opera's saddest moments.*

THE "MAMOULIAN CUTS"

Porgy and Bess was given a weeklong trial run at Boston's Colonial Theatre, opening September 30, 1935. The reviews would prove a foretaste of New York: they praised Mamoulian and patronized Gershwin. They also broach our next topic: the "Mamoulian cuts."

Elinor Hughes, in the *Herald*, and Helen Eager, in the *Traveler*, were thrilled by Mamoulian's direction. The *Christian Science Monitor*'s L. A. Roper conceded that Gershwin's success was "not insignificant,"

---

*The very opposite is achieved by present-day directors who have Sporting Life and Bess cheerfully exit together, arm in arm—a simplistic inspiration.

given his irregular training. He credited to Mamoulian the production's artistic unity, pointing toward "a correlation of the arts, dreamt of by Wagner but never realized by him or by any of his successors." The *Post* sent both a theater critic, Elliot Norton, and a music critic, Warren Storey Smith. Norton found Mamoulian's achievement "almost staggering." Smith wrote: "Even if his score almost never rises above the level of incidental music . . . it displays a craftsmanship which we would not have expected of the Gershwin of a few years ago. . . . That this music scales tragic heights may hardly be said. It is not yet within Mr. Gershwin's power to write significantly."[28]

Hughes, Roper, Holland, *Billboard*, and *Variety* all found *Porgy and Bess* too long.[29] And Gershwin was prone to "write long." Both *Rhapsody in Blue* and the Concerto in F were abridged by the composer. In the case of *An American in Paris*, Gershwin cut three minutes—one seventh—of what had been a 21-minute score. Heyward's *Porgy and Bess* libretto was itself an exercise in abridgment, vis-à-vis the play; Gershwin snipped some more of it in producing the vocal score. What further cuts preceded the Boston premiere cannot be reliably determined, but there were some.[30] The cuts immediately following the Boston run are usually estimated to have comprised 30 to 35 minutes of music. In any event, *Porgy and Bess* in Boston was said to last about 4 hours, including two intermissions—about the length of an unabridged performance. "Mamoulian's" *Porgy and Bess*, as re-created on Decca in 2006 by the conductor John Mauceri, lasts 2 hours and 25 minutes—to which two intermissions must be added. The Broadway norm was an 8:30 curtain and dismissal by 11:20 in consideration of commuters; *Porgy and Bess* remained long for a "show." Whether the New York cuts helped or hurt, and who exactly inflicted them, remain questions of interest.

Duncan recalled many conferences between Mamoulian, Gershwin, and "the musical heads" (presumably the conductor Alexander Smallens and the vocal coach and assistant conductor Alexander Steinert) dealing with wholesale cuts required before the opera could move on to

Broadway. Not only was *Porgy and Bess* too long; there were issues of vocal stamina. Gershwin wrote to Ira about one deleted passage: "You won't have a Porgy by the time we reach New York. No one can sing that much, eight performances a week." Duncan recalled: "All that last part that I sang [presumably, Porgy's arioso "Tell me quick, where's Bess," "Oh Bess, Oh Where's My Bess?" and "On My Way"] Gershwin wrote for my voice. . . . But it was just too much for one man to sing at the end of an opera." Porgy's role in the final scene rises repeatedly above the staff to E and F—and Duncan, even on studio recordings, did not have an easy top voice. Finally, there were artistic considerations— places where the score seemed prolix, redundant, or otherwise improvable with scissors.[31]

Mamoulian (of course) was ever of the opinion that Gershwin was sensibly amenable to snipping. "Very often people who seem so modest about their work would all but tear you to pieces if you suggested cutting anything out of what they had written, considering every word of it as well-nigh sacred," he wrote in 1938.

> Yet George, who loved his own stuff as much as he did, never hesitated to make any cuts that were necessary. . . . He did this because he had no false vanity about his work and also because George was one of the best showmen I have ever known. He knew the theatre, he knew the audience. His showmanship was so keen that no matter how well he loved a musical passage or an aria (like the Buzzard song in *Porgy and Bess*, for instance), he would cut it out without hesitation if that improved the performance as a whole.[32]

In his 2006 biography *George Gershwin*, Howard Pollack—no friend of the cuts (as we shall see)—lays stress on Duncan's testimony that Gershwin was "upset in Boston," and "didn't want one beautiful blessed note cut." Kay Swift, a close friend of the composer, reportedly considered the cuts "anathema to Gershwin" and felt "he may have been too conciliatory, and a little to easily manipulated." But pain, in this case, is not necessarily incompatible with genuine acquiescence; and the notion of a manipulable Gershwin deserves to be treated with skepticism. Certainly, Gershwin agreed to the cuts. Two days before the October 10 New York premiere, he transcribed a bar of the act 1 piano music Jasbo Brown never got to play and gave it to Mamoulian as a birthday present. On another occasion he presented Mamoulian with some rolled-up pages of the score, tied with a ribbon, as a "thank you for making me take out all that stuff in Boston." Gershwin telegrammed Mamoulian on opening night: I CONSIDER IT A PLEASURE AND A PRIVILEGE TO HAVE YOU DIRECT MY FIRST OPERATIC EFFORT LET'S DO IT AGAIN SOMETIME. Ten days later, Gershwin wrote in the *New York Times*: "It was Mr. Mamoulian who staged the original production of 'Porgy' as a play. He knew all of its values. What was even more valuable, he knew opera as well as he knew the theatre and he was able to bring his knowledge of both to this new form. In my opinion, he has left nothing to be desired in the direction." A note from Gershwin in Mamoulian's scrapbook reads: "Rouben I've been thinkin' that Porgy and Bess is your masterpiece and that we must get together again—and soon." Ira Gershwin wrote to Mamoulian, "Thanks to your direction never have I had so many thrills during rehearsals and even more important—after the show opened."[33]

We have already encountered one of the three most prominent excisions: the curtailment of the six-part hurricane chorus. The other two—eliminating Jasbo Brown and the "Buzzard Song"—have Mamoulian's fingerprints all over them. Heyward's script begins with a pianist performing onstage in one of the Catfish Row flats. "Half a dozen couples can be seen dancing in a slow, almost hypnotic rhythm." They also sing: "Wadeda," "Dooda." The pianist is Jasbo Brown, according to tradition a cabaret musician who gave jazz its name.[34] Though situated within Catfish Row, the scene—combining Tin Pan Alley syncopations with lazy vocal interpolations—conjures a world apart, remote in place and time. Heyward's novella, it will be recalled, starts with a "Golden Age" tableau, fostering a parable of violated innocence[35]—a motif Mamoulian dropped from the 1927 play. That he would again discard it was merely predictable. He also complained (many times) that Jasbo Brown's piano evoked "Harlem," whereas "Summertime" (coming next) was more suitably "southern." These are cogent considerations.

In the published vocal score, the "Buzzard Song" is the closest thing Porgy has to an aria. As in the novella, a buzzard flies overhead; according to local superstition, if it lands it brings bad luck. Porgy's protests—"Keep a flyin' over, take along yo' shadow"—signify new conviction: "Porgy's young again!" Mamoulian felt the song "stuck out like a sore thumb," and he was right: inserted in the first scene of act 2 (otherwise including the love duet and orphans' band), its lachrymose A minor exhortations are musically and dramatically unprepared. Mamoulian also complained to Gershwin that the tune sounded "Russian," and he was right: Gershwin told Anne Brown that Mussorgsky's "Song of the Flea" was here his point of inspiration. That eight years earlier Mamoulian had deleted most buzzard references from the Heywards' script is also relevant. Duncan liked the "Buzzard Song;" at the Hollywood Gershwin memorial concert, he makes it searingly impressive. And some have argued that the "Buzzard Song" is a linchpin in Porgy's maturation. But in fact Porgy matures without it. Mamoulian's cut secures a more integrated musical flow.[36]

Charles Hamm, the first scholar to catalogue Mamoulian's script alterations, extrapolated three Mamoulian objectives: "To match [his] own sense of the rhythm of the dialogue, to eliminate dramatically dead points, or to clarify a certain dramatic situation." Writing specifically of the cuts, Hamm found that they tightened the action, eliminated repetition, and shortened the show. They neither damaged Gershwin's musical design, nor turned his opera into something more like a Broadway

musical comedy. "From Monteverdi through Handel, Verdi, and Wagner and up to the present," Hamm argued, "operatic composers have
tinkered with their pieces"; Gershwin was no exception. Hamm concluded: "Perhaps if Gershwin had been involved in later productions of
his opera with different directors and different casts, and with the entire
first run as a basis for further reevaluation, he would have made other
changes. But his death left the Theatre Guild production as it took the
stage in New York on 10 October 1935 as the only *Porgy and Bess* as he
'intended it to be played.' "[37]

Wayne Shirley, the editor of the forthcoming critical edition of *Porgy
and Bess*, served as an advisor to the 2006 Nashville concert performances
and recording that recreated the 1935 Theatre Guild *Porgy and Bess*. Like
Hamm, Shirley parts company with those who regard the vocal score
as definitive. Rather, he argues that had the uncut version never been
engraved and published for rehearsal purposes, a vocal score published
after the 1935 premiere might have incorporated some of or most of the
Theatre Guild cuts. In general, Shirley views the "Mamoulian cuts" as
Gershwin-endorsed, a product of artistic judgment and exigent circumstance. Like Hamm, he admires the "Occupational Humoresque" and
many other Mamoulian touches. At the same time, he feels that "*Porgy*
the established classic in the opera house can be somewhat more expan-
sive than *Porgy* the Broadway show."*

Howard Pollack in his Gershwin biography, prefers *Porgy and Bess*
uncut. He writes:

> Gershwin cut the work largely in deference to its famous director and
> in response to the exigencies imposed by a Broadway run. The pub-

---

*Shirley, in his unpublished "The 'Theatre Guild' version of *Porgy and Bess*" (2009) has his own list
of the "most painful cuts":
  1. "I hates yo' struttin' style"—"Someone other than Bess must tell Sporting Life off; otherwise
     he seems to be accepted unquestioningly by Catfish Row society."
  2. "I Ain't Got No Shame"—"otherwise the picnic is just a number for Sporting Life."
  3. The six superimposed prayers during the hurricane—"a sound unique in opera."
  4. The second verse of the mourning chorus ("Jake, Jake, don't you be downhearted")—"A
     small cut . . . that robs this music, one of the glories of *Porgy and Bess*, of its proper dimensions."

lished vocal-piano score accordingly can be considered a basic, author-itative frame of reference. . . .

That Gershwin, in his few remaining years, never showed any intention to revise this published vocal score perhaps argues for its authority as well. More to the point, how he could have considered the Broadway version to be anything more than a quick fix remains hard to imagine; for . . . the cuts deprived the opera not only of some won-derful music but of a good deal of dramatic and musical integrity. For instance, the decision to omit most of "Jasbo Brown Blues" . . . not only sacrificed some telling background atmosphere and the introduc-tion of a few germinal motives . . . but compromised the scene's tonal coherence. . . . Overall, the cuts made an already briskly paced work marked by abrupt tonal jolts that much more breathless and jagged.[38]

Opinions will continue to differ. I find only vague circumstantial evidence that Gershwin "deferred" to "a famous director." I do not discover any "telling background atmosphere" in the Jasbo Brown sequence. I agree with Pollack that the truncated transition to "Sum-mertime" sounds "rather lumpish." I agree that "Oh Bess, Oh Where's My Bess?" should not be dismembered. That Mamoulian's treatment of *Porgy and Bess* is an invaluable sourcebook seems to me self-evident. That it implicitly carries Gershwin's imprimatur is useful, too: Gersh-win does "write long."*

Mamoulian brought a singular authority to *Porgy and Bess*. Inevita-bly, inescapably, his production documented his own idiosyncratic tech-niques and ideals—techniques and ideals that, having already permeated the 1927 Theatre Guild *Porgy*, seeped into the themes and aesthetics of

*John DeMain, who has led *Porgy and Bess* more than any other living conductor, has in recent years opted for "about 90 per cent" of the Mamoulian cuts. "When the Houston Grand Opera and I did our historic 1976 production," he says, "the intent was to play as much of Gershwin's music as time would allow; we felt that whether or not this was good theater, it was time for the world to rediscover that it was great music. Now that *Porgy and Bess* has been accepted and performed in the world's major opera houses, I feel less concerned about proving a point and more concerned about keeping the work dramatically tight. The Mamoulian cuts do just that." (Interview with author, Dec. 27, 2011.)

Gershwin's opera. It cannot be regarded as surprising that Mamoulian's input, at every stage, had the general effect of making the opera more resemble the play he had radically and triumphantly reconceived eight years previous.

THE REVIEWS

Porgy and Bess logged 124 performances at New York's Alvin Theatre. With an initial cast of 82 (including 27 children)[39] and an initial orchestra calling for 45 players, the show was costly. The initial weekly box office take of $24,000 covered expenses; subsequently, expenses exceeded box-office revenue; *Porgy and Bess* closed in the red. In the course of the run both cast and orchestra were reduced. A tour ensued to Philadelphia, Pittsburgh, Chicago, Detroit, and Washington, D.C. (where at the cast's insistence the National Theater accommodated an integrated audience).[40]

The Depression was an undoubted factor in the opera's merely modest New York success. So were the reviews. They retain high interest as documentation of the production, of Gershwin's slippery reputation, and of the confusions of cultural fluidity. Also, the Gershwins plainly cared about reviews: they assiduously collected them in scrapbooks.

Certainly, *Porgy and Bess* was received as a significant cultural event. Praise for Mamoulian was widespread. Gershwin's music was adored by many, admired by most, regretted by some. The 1927 *Porgy* was frequently invoked as a standard of comparison: Did the opera enhance or dilute it? The answers varied.[41]

Mamoulian's methods were well known and, in many cases, shrewdly understood (more shrewdly than Gershwin's). In the playbill, "Rouben Mamoulian" appeared in the same font size as "George Gershwin"; Ira Gershwin and DeBose Heyward were smaller names. For at least two critics, *Porgy and Bess* was first of all a Mamoulian show. That this was the view of the *Hollywood Reporter*—Mamoulian in 1935 was primarily a

Hollywood director—perhaps should not surprise: "It was the superior skill of Master Mamoulian . . . which made its presence felt in a sort of golden silence above the musical symphony and the shouts of the dusky operatic thespians; the director embellished the score with notes that were tops." For Walter Winchell, in the *Daily Mirror*, it was Mamoulian's "talented staging and direction that excites the auditor at the Alvin. Several times . . . his groupings . . . take the breath away, and lift the fuzz from the face. . . . the lustiest cheers belong to him."

The most detailed accounts of Mamoulian's contribution appeared in the *New York Post* and *Stage* magazine. Writing for the *Post* under a headline reading " 'Porgy and Bess' Staged Beautifully by Mamoulian," John Mason Brown opined that Mamoulian's take on Heyward's novella

remains one of the most notable feats of virtuoso direction our modern theater has seen. It is Rouben Mamoulian's "Rhapsody in Black"; a production which is filled with a visual music of its own, which is unfailingly rhythmic, which is unforgettable in the ever changing beauty of its groupings, extraordinary in its invention, and amazing in the atmospheric details it employs to recreate the whole pattern of life in Charleston's Catfish Row. . . . [Mamoulian] becomes as much a conductor of Mr. Gershwin's music for the eyes as Alexander Smallens is for the ears. . . . he gives final proof of how rare and masterly is his touch.

For *Stage*, Ruth W. Sedgwick wrote:

Each of the 70 people almost continuously on stage during the three acts of *Porgy and Bess* not only has a plausible and reasonable appearance and behavior but is an individual, with a life of his own and a purpose in living it. . . . You might see the opera a dozen times and still not grasp all the nuances of expression and movement. . . .

Like the brushwork of Gauguin it all looks casual but is painstakingly accurate to the last fraction of detail. There is not even a turn of the head which has not been calculated. The arch of the groupings, constantly changing, always beautiful, is as true as though the medium were marble . . . gesture is constantly used in counterpoint. . . . The hands of the mourners lift and fall in rotation, not unison, at the wake. A widow, with arms extended to form a cross, rises slowly like an organ peal, through the frantic beat of the hurricane motif. . . .

The light plot is a libretto in itself. Mamoulian has used small spots like a paint brush, daubing colors in patterns which are now enchanting, now terrifying.[42]

If insofar as Mamoulian's role was concerned, the tenor of the majority was a paean of unqualified praise,* vigorous dissents were registered by Joseph Wood Krutch in *The Nation* and Stark Young in the *New Republic*. For Krutch, the entire show—music and staging—was too elaborate; unmoved, he found Mamoulian's contributions mechanical and Gershwin's score deficient in tunefulness and drama. For Young, the opera was monotonous. Of Mamoulian, he wrote: "Where the music grows more beautiful or the drama narrows to greater intensity, this detailed directing, so busy, subdivided and individual, sometimes

---

*"It is hard to remember a production more captivating, more interesting in color and movement, in all respects more satisfying, than that which Rouben Mamoulian and Serge Soudeikin and the rest have contrived. . . . It is one of two or three stagings within my experience which are exciting merely to look at. . . . All [Mamoulian's details] are at once background and story and, in a fashion, music, too." —Richard Lockridge, *New York Sun*. "The direction of Mr. Mamoulian was all his admirers expected of him." —Julian Seaman, *New York Mirror*. "[The Occupational Humoresque] works out thumpingly in the opera, releasing it from the old, traditional forms." —Whitney Bolton, *New York Telegraph*. "The Guild has lured Mr. Mamoulian back to perform his wizardries all over again." —John Anderson, *New York Evening Journal*. "Astonishing and superb, an authentic triumph for Mr. Mamoulian." —Lawrence Gilman, *New York Herald Tribune*. "This man is a genius in whipping up the rhythms of the motley congregation on the stage to fit in both with the story and the music that interprets the story. Every second the stage is alive and organic. . . . The obbligato of stage movement is simply perfect." —Thomas Dash, *Women's Wear Daily*. "Puts the Met to shame." —Arthur Pollack, *Brooklyn Daily Eagle*. "I'm not so sure that it would be especially thrilling without Mr. Mamoulian's imaginative direction, but since *Porgy and Bess* has been Mamoulianated, such speculation doesn't matter." —"Musical Events," *New Yorker*. "For a symphony in stage movement, with colors, actions, music, synthesized as never before in an attempted American opera, it reaches the ultimate in theatrical production." —George Holland, *New York American*. All reviews Oct. 11, 1935, except *Daily Mirror* (Oct. 12), *Stage* (Oct. 1935), and *New Yorker* (Oct. 15).

makes the singing and acting seem to be going on against a background of monkey-cage."[43]

Brooks Atkinson and Olin Downes, writing in tandem for the *New York Times* from their respective drama and music cubicles, filed mixed reports crossing over into one another's terrain. Downes said of the production: "If the Metropolitan chorus could ever put one-half the action into the riot scene in the second act of 'Meistersinger' that the Negro cast put into the fight that followed the craps game, it would be not merely refreshing but miraculous. And when did Isolde wave a scarf more rhythmically from the tower than those who shook feather dusters and sheets from the windows to accompany Porgy's song?" Atkinson saw fit to deliver a lecture flogging Gershwin's recitatives: "Why commonplace remarks that carry no emotion have to be made in a chanting monotone is a problem in art [this reviewer] cannot fathom." Returning to his drama desk, Atkinson added: "Mr. Mamoulian is an excellent director of dramas of ample proportions. He is not subtle, which is a virtue in showmanship. His crowds are arranged in masses that look as solid as a victory at the polls; they move with simple unanimity, and the rhythm is comfortably obvious." But chiefly interesting in Atkinson's review is his comparison to *Porgy* the play.

Let it be said at once that Mr. Gershwin has contributed something glorious to the spirit of the Heywards' community legend. If memory serves, it always lacked glow of personal feeling. . . . The groupings, the mad fantasy of leaping shadows, the panic-stricken singing over a corpse, the evil bulk of the buzzard's flight, the screaming hurricane—these large audible and visible items of showmanship took precedence over the episode of Porgy's romance with Crown's high-steppin' gal. . . .

The pathetic apprehension of the "Where's My Bess" trio and the manly conviction of "I'm on My Way" adds something vital to the story that was missing before. . . .

The fear and the pain go deeper in "Porgy and Bess" than they did in penny plain "Porgy."

That Gershwin brought to *Porgy* a capacity for empathy foreign to Mamoulian is a topic to which we will return.[44]

It was merely logical that the *Times* and several other papers saw fit to send both drama and music experts: operas did not normally take place on Broadway stages; both Gershwin and Mamoulian straddled multiple worlds of theater and music, art and entertainment. Downes appreciated Gershwin's score less than Atkinson. And this proved the norm: New York's music critics were more critical of Gershwin than New York's theater critics. Gershwin, Downes wrote, had underutilized "the resources of the operatic composers." His unformed style oscillated from opera to operetta to Broadway entertainment.

Of the other New York music critics who reviewed *Porgy and Bess* in the daily press, the best-known included Lawrence Gilman, Samuel Chotzinoff, Leonard Liebling, and W. J. Henderson. Gilman wrote for the *Herald Tribune*—a paper as prestigious as the *Times* but more receptive than the *Times* to idiosyncratic opinion. Having earlier found the Concerto in F too tame and insufficiently modern, Gilman called *Porgy and Bess* "by all odds, the most noteworthy thing that [Gershwin] has given us." He also said: "Perhaps it is needlessly Draconian to begrudge Mr. Gershwin the song hits he has scattered through his score . . . yet they mar it. . . . Listening to such surefire rubbish as the duet between Porgy and Bess . . . is to wonder how the composer of the magnificent choral scenes of this opera could stoop to such easy and such needless conquests." Chotzinoff, in the *Post*, found too much recitative in *Porgy and Bess* and not enough dialogue. Liebling, in the *American*, barely caviled: he considered Gershwin's music "appropriate," "important," and "American." Henderson, in the *Sun*, offered a response too significant to summarize—I will return to it below.[45]

The theater critics who adored Mamoulian's staging were on the whole less satisfied with Gershwin's score. The most negative reviews were from the intellectuals. I have already cited Joseph Wood Krutch and Stark Young—whose misgivings were outdone by Paul Rosenfeld's in his *Discoveries of a Music Critic* (1936). In high-toned musical circles, Rosenfeld functioned as a watchdog for modernism. Eyeing "our Broadway paladin," he nervously growled and snarled:

To qualify as a vulgar composer and rank with Chabrier, Albéniz, Glinka, and even with Milhaud and Auric at their best, a musician has to "compose" his material, to sustain and evolve and organize it to a degree sufficient to bring its essences, their relationships, their ideas, to expression. And that Gershwin has accomplished to no satisfactory degree. . . .

Take any one of his ambitious products. It is only very superficially a whole, actually a heap of extremely heterogeneous minor forms and expressions . . . they remain equally disparate in point of style, some of them being popularly American in essence or gaily, brightly Yiddish, and others impressionistic, or vaguely grand-operatic, or reminiscent of the melodramatic emphasis and fioritura of Liszt, or Chopinesque. And they also remain disparate in point of quality, since a number of them have sharpness, jauntiness, dash, indicating a perhaps shallow but distinct vitality, while others are weak, soft, cheap, representing a vitality duller and lower than that at which interest commences. . . .

Porgy and Bess . . . fortifies one's conviction of Gershwin's shortness of the artist's feeling. The score is a loose aggregation. . . . [It] sustains no mood. There is neither a progressive nor an enduring tension in it. . . . Ultimately, . . . the expression lies in conventional patterns, as if the feeling of the composer had been too timid to mold musical forms. . . . Long before the conclusion one feels the music has got one nowhere new and true.[46]

A special precinct of critical response was the black press. In New York's *Amsterdam News*, Carl Diton—a Harlem Renaissance musician of distinction—admired Gershwin's score and expressed "the sincerest hope" that *Porgy and Bess* would "never die." Ralph Matthews, in *Afro-American*, called *Porgy and Bess* a twangy hybrid; he missed Hall Johnson's "sonorous incantations." Hall Johnson himself—whose famous choir purveyed his skilled arrangements of spirituals; who created the score for Marc Connelly's Pulitzer-Prize winning *The Green Pastures* (1930)— reviewed *Porgy and Bess* at length in the January 1936 *Opportunity*, a distinguished "Journal of Negro Life." After attending four performances, he decided "that I do like it and that it is a good show." But he added: "It is only as good as it seems to be because of the intelligent pliability of the Negro cast. While obviously working under strict direction, they are able to infuse enough of their own natural racial qualities into the proceedings to invest them with a convincing semblance of plausibility." Johnson found Gershwin's score "delightful as a musical show," but relatively stiff and artificial. He cited "instances where Mr. Gershwin's music has missed a Negro feeling," and others that "succeeded in catching a real racial strain." And, echoing Stark Young's southern perspective in the *New Republic*, he felt that Mamoulian's ignorance of African-American life hurt the hyperactive production:

> Of what good could be the truest Negro opera idiom if it is to be coupled, as in this case, with a stage-direction which affronts every sensibility of the Negro temperament? Will the time ever come when a colored performer on a Broadway stage can be subtle, quiet or even silent,—just for a moment, and still be interesting? Must the light revues always be hot, fast and *loud*, are the serious pieces always profane, hysterical and *louder*? . . . By now we are fully and painfully aware that in all Negro group-scenes on Broadway there must be much swaying of bodies and brandishing of arms with SHADOW EFFECTS,—though this has not always been so stiffly stylized as in

the present Russian pictorial edition. . . . [The direction] flounders uncertainly between alternating periods of *tableaux-vivants*, Russian ballet, conventional opera and slap-stick vaudeville.*

Rob Roy, in the *Chicago Defender*, wished that J. Rosamond Johnson—for three decades, an established African-American composer—had composed *Porgy and Bess*. As J. Rosamond Johnson in fact took the part of Lawyer Frazier, he obviously knew both Gershwin and his opera at close quarters; at the Boston premiere, he grasped the composer's hand and whispered, "George, you've done it—you're the Abraham Lincoln of Negro music." The most publicized black response came from Duke Ellington, who was interviewed by Edward Morrow in *New Theatre*. Morrow's own accompanying sentiment that "the times are here to debunk such tripe as Gershwin's lampblack Negroisms" was widely attributed to Ellington. Ellington subsequently disassociated himself from the Morrow article, but not without adding that Gershwin's music, though "grand," was "not distinctly or definitely Negroid."[47]

Olin Downes felt the need to write a Sunday *Times* piece, "When Critics Disagree," running October 20—ten days after the Alvin Theatre opening. He observed the irony that music critics had found "less dramatic fitness" in Gershwin's opera than had theater critics. The music critics, Downes continued, felt the need to ask two questions: "Doesn't the play 'Porgy' lose somewhat by being turned into an opera?"; and "Is [*Porgy and Bess*] anyhow an opera in the complete meaning of that term?" Though Downes did not see fit to ponder why music critics should be unhappier with Gershwin than theater critics, the reasons are

---

*Of additional interest in Johnson's review are his thoughts about the proper future of African-American theater. "The next step forward will be the insistence upon *authenticity of style*. . . . There must be born a genuine Negro theatre to which superior training in theatrical technique must be the wise and willing servant of superior familiarity with the new material. . . . It is possible, and not improbable, that an injection of genuine Negro folk-culture may be good for the anaemia of the American theatre. If so, who will prove it? Only we who sowed the seed can know the full and potent secret of the flower. The fact that others try to master it and fail . . . should not fill us with resentment, but with pride and fresh determination." Decades of changing black Broadway fare informed the context of this exhortation.

obvious enough, at least in retrospect. Their world of classical music was the more European; they felt the more encroached upon.

For all his popularity, Gershwin was in his lifetime enveloped in an impenetrable fog of opinion that categorized him as an interloper—ultimately, an outsider, however naturally gifted, to the citadel of high culture; also an outsider, however well-intentioned, to the black experience. It was next to impossible for an American to respond to *Porgy and Bess* without prejudice.

VIRGIL THOMSON AND W. J. HENDERSON

The two most sophisticated initial assessments of Gershwin's opera deserve to be cited in detail. One came from a fellow composer, the other from a music critic with a longer memory than any other observer of the Gershwin phenomenon. Both embraced or tolerated a degree of cultural fluidity their colleagues could only find alienating. The composer was Virgil Thomson, the critic W. J. Henderson.

In 1940, Thomson would succeed Lawrence Gilman as chief music critic of the *New York Herald Tribune*. In 1935, he was an established composer who wrote on the side for other composers in the periodical *Modern Music*. Anomalously, he was an artist-intellectual in good standing who rejected the reigning modernist ideology of complexity. A Francophile, he imbued his compositions with a faux innocence recalling the ironic simplicities of a Satie. He had already produced an important and unclassifiable music theater piece—the 1934 "opera" *Four Saints in Three Acts*, whose black cast sang Gertrude Stein words lubricated with catchy tunes and plain harmonies. He would shortly compose two iconic documentary film scores—for *The Plow that Broke the Plains* (1936) and *The River* (1938)—combining hymns and popular songs with techniques of counterpoint and leitmotif. At all times a caustic enemy of sanctimonious cultural hierarchies, he would famously denounce "music appreciation," with its gaudy appetite for eighteenth- and nineteenth-century European "masterpieces," as a "racket." Thomson's essay "George Gershwin," in the November-December 1935 *Modern Music*, is frequently quoted with scant regard for context. Unlike Rosenfeld and other Olympian Gershwin detractors, he knew what it was to compose and could truly write: "The *Rhapsody in Blue* . . . is the most successful orchestra piece ever launched by any American composer. It is by now standard orchestral repertory all over the world. . . . It is a thoroughly professional job executed by a man who knew how to put over a direct musical idea and who had a direct musical idea to put over." Thomson anointed Gershwin "America's official White Hope"—by which he undoubtedly alluded to a hoped-for synthesis of American popular art and venerable Old World models. In the Concerto in F and *An American in Paris* Thomson discovered "execution not so competent" as in the *Rhapsody*, the latter having adopted a less demanding form. He considered Gershwin's musical materials a "melting pot" too "unsavory" and "impure" to adequately support "serious or direct musical expression."

The negatives in this critique, initially, are not so different from contemporary conventional wisdom. But only Thomson could have added:

> I do not wish to indicate that it is in any way reprehensible of [Gershwin] not to be a serious composer. . . . It was always certain that he was a gifted composer, a charming composer, an exciting and sympathetic composer. His gift and his charm are greater than the gifts or the charms of almost any of the other American composers. And a great gift or great charm is an exciting thing. And a gifted and charming composer who sets himself seriously to learn his business is a sympathetic thing. I think, however, that it is clear by now that Gershwin hasn't learned his business. At least he hasn't learned the business of being a serious composer, which one has always gathered to be the business he wanted to learn.

As for *Porgy and Bess*, it seemed to Thomson "an interesting example of what can be done by talent in spite of a bad set-up"—meaning a story and libretto laden with "fake folklore."

> Gershwin does not even know what an opera is; and yet *Porgy and Bess* is an opera and it has power and vigor. Hence it is a more important event in America's artistic life than anything American the Met has ever done. . . .
>
> There are many things about it that are not to my personal taste. . . . I do, however, like being able to listen to a work for three hours and to be fascinated at every moment. I also like its lack of respectability, the way it can be popular and vulgar and go its way as a real professional piece does without bothering much about the taste-boys. . . .
>
> In a way, [Gershwin] has justified himself as a White Hope. He has written a work that can be performed quite a number of times, that can be listened to with pleasure by quite different kinds of people, and that can be remembered by quite a few of them.[48]

Thomson recognized that by 1935 it was late for a white composer to craft a black folk opera or play—this sort of thing was more the business of the twenties. In this regard (among others), he sized up Gershwin as naïve. Yet Thomson respected Gershwin; his disappointment in *Porgy and Bess* was unfeigned rather than self-satisfied.

If idiosyncrasy was a catalyst for Thomson's complexly sympathetic Gershwin response, Henderson came to Gershwin from a time warp. Born in 1855, he had been, with Henry Edward Krehbiel and James Gibbons Huneker, one of three preeminent practitioners of a turn-of-the-century golden age of New York music criticism. Not only had Henderson attended the Carnegie Hall premiere of Dvořák's *New World* Symphony; his 3,500-word review of that 1893 New York Philharmonic concert remains a supreme specimen of American musical journalism.[49] His clarion thesis, in the *Times*, challenged writers like Boston's Philip Hale, who denigrated African-American musicality and disputed African-American authorship of plantation song. Henderson also wrote: "The American people—or the majority of them—learned to love the songs of the negro slave and to find in them something that belonged to America. If those songs are not national, then there is no such thing as national music." Dvořák himself had led the way when he praised Stephen Foster's minstrel songs for their black folk roots, and predicted that "negro melodies" would engender a noble American music to come. "We Americans," Henderson concluded, "should thank and honor the Bohemian master who has shown us how to build our national school of music."[50]

And Henderson harbored other potent, pertinent memories—of a New York operatic heyday populated with astonishing singing actors and actresses; of the Met's German seasons (1884–91), when fashion-hungry boxholders ceded authority to ardent Wagnerites hungry for intense experience. He lived on and on, a witness to modernist composers estranged from audiences, to audiences enslaved to commercialized snob appeal. A formidable connoisseur of bel canto, he decried the decline of *messa di voce* and kindred vocal refinements. A keen observer of the delayed quest for an American school of symphonies and operas, he decried the Eurocentricity of the Toscanini cult.

Encountering *Porgy and Bess* at the age of seventy-nine, Henderson penned an October 11 review for the *New York Sun* and followed up with a lengthy Sunday piece on December 7. His breadth of perspective was commanding. This was the context he brought to bear on Gershwin's new opera:

When the box office gets control high art goes out of the window. Still more when any species of art becomes a pastime of fashionable Society it will be a toy and nothing more. Fashionable Society is not usually in earnest about anything except amusing itself, and it does not find any amusement in the intellectual effort required to grasp the message of a new art conception. . . .

Now when we remember that an institution like the Metropolitan Opera House is obliged to furnish so much entertainment to smart Society, we can understand why opera, striving to pure art, is likely to experience difficulties. A brilliant success by an opera entirely new in style and construction is almost inconceivable in such conditions. . . .

One cannot wonder that to many composers of real talent the easiest way appears to be the only way, and so they bend themselves to preparing lyric entertainment for casual listeners and make no attempt to scale Olympian heights.

What ought the artist to do?

In Henderson's opinion, Gershwin's response, sidestepping the Met for Broadway, was imperfect but triumphantly sufficient. Composing *Porgy and Bess*, Gershwin was "at his best when he is writing songs with a touch of jazz in them, with ragtime rhythms, harmonies that sting, choruses which echo the 'shout,' the camp meeting, and the spiritual." Gershwin's hit song was "I Got Plenty O' Nuttin'"—but it was not opera. Robbins's wake was excellently done. Gershwin's music perfectly fit the libretto; it gripped and held. The opera was overlong. The weakness of the recitatives was not unique to Gershwin—no American composer had yet found an equivalent for swift Italian patter or French vocal declamation.* Be that as it may, *Porgy and Bess* successfully prioritized text and story. What is more:

Art addresses itself to humanity; it cannot be monastic, nor can the artist live a hermit life. What he has to do is to study his own people and his own time and strive ever to bring his inner life into harmony

---

*Henderson might have discovered what he sought in the songs and stage works of Marc Blitzstein.

with them. George Gershwin has done precisely that. He has not sought to align himself with Wagner or Mozart or Verdi. He has written a message for the people of Broadway, and he has written it brilliantly. It is not grand opera; it is not folk opera; it is not pure Negro, but it is Gershwin talking to the crowd in his own way. And that is a very persuasive way.

The "American school" Dvořák prophesied foresaw symphonies and operas of world import infused with Negro melodies. Henderson lived long enough to audition a single, singular fulfillment. His self-inflicted death—grown too old, he methodically put a bullet to his head on June 5, 1937—spared him the knowledge of Gershwin's own, premature passing.

Amid the buzz and clamor attending the New York premiere of *Porgy and Bess*, Henderson furnished the closest thing to an informed affirmation. No other writer so comprehended Gershwin as a remedial influence on a New World musical topography grown stratified and fractured, crippled by a high/low schism that distorted readings of Gershwin's own achievement. An outsider, the product of another century, Henderson no more understood Gershwin as an interloper than he had so understood Dvořák. His long-range vision told him that Gershwin was in fact a quintessential insider, an iconic American—an insight otherwise vouchsafed to immigrants like Rouben Mamoulian, or to enthralled foreigners whose Gershwin views we will eventually encounter.

THE ACHIEVEMENT

An earlier section of the present chapter revisited the first reviews of *Rhapsody in Blue* and the Concerto in F—New World/Old World syntheses notable for stylistic fluidity and for fluidity of interpretation in performance. *Porgy and Bess* maximized the stakes: Gershwin's polarities now ranged from vaudeville to grand opera, with additional genres, new and old, percolating in between.

Early assessments of the *Rhapsody* and the Concerto were notably patronizing. A decade later, Gershwin the concert composer was less novel, more familiar—and reviews of *Porgy and Bess* acquired a patronizing familiarity accordingly. Tapping George on the shoulder, Brooks Atkinson advised that he think twice about those recitatives. Patting him on the back, Olin Downes counseled a little more technical study. The perennial Gershwin question—"What is it?"—was more insistently asked than ever.

Atkinson and Downes were merely typical for failing to gauge Gershwin's stature, or the future resilience of what he had freshly wrought. That Gershwin might be consciously innovative, rather than naïvely eclectic, remained mainly unthought. That he had achieved a synergistic density of stylistic fusion unprecedented in American musical theater; that—as his opera's singular performance history would illustrate—he had in fact created a *sui generis* integration of opera and entertainment remained unglimpsed. An irony unexplored even by writers like Thomson, who called *Porgy and Bess* the best American opera to date, was that Louis Gruenberg, a pedigreed American composer whose teachers included Ferruccio Busoni in Vienna, had recently written a prominent black opera of some success—*The Emperor Jones*, starring Lawrence Tibbett at the Met in 1933 and 1934—and that Gruenberg's opera, crossing over into the spiritual "Standin' in the Need of Prayer," did not so much as attempt an integrated New World/Old World style. Gruenberg's parlando vocal writing also happens to be less varied or expressive than Gershwin's rebuked recitatives.

The introduction of this book recounted my own pivotal encounter with *Porgy and Bess* in 2005, when I discovered that a Wagnerian deployment of leitmotifs in the final scene consummated the emotional scenario. My modest analysis of how transformations of Porgy's theme insinuated psychological nuances assays a more detailed exploration of Gershwin's craftsmanship than any attempted by some three dozen reviewers and writers in 1935. Incredibly, not until 1984 did Larry Starr become the first Gershwin commentator to explore with any specificity the leitmotifs girding *Porgy and Bess*.[51] Other recent analysts of *Porgy and Bess* have explored the influences of Joseph Schillinger and Alban Berg. Schillinger, with whom Gershwin began studying in 1932, developed an encyclopedic composition method engulfed in mathematics. He used rhythmic patterns to generate melody, counterpoint, and other musical parameters. He devised methods for expanding and contracting themes. He explored polytonality and twelve-tone rows. Such aspects of *Porgy and Bess* as a rhythmic canon, symmetrical chord progressions, and thematic linkages have been traced to Schillinger's teachings. Gershwin himself talked about composing *Porgy and Bess* "with algebraic formulas." Berg—who was obsessed with numbers; whose music abounds in precise complexities of construction—was visited by Gershwin in Vienna in 1928. Gershwin returned home with treasured scores of Berg's *Lyric* Suite and *Wozzeck*. In 1931, he attended the American premiere of *Wozzeck*, with Leopold Stokowski and the Philadelphia Orchestra, and was "thrilled." Jasbo Brown, "Summertime," the craps-game fugue, and "It Ain't Necessarily So" are among the *Porgy and Bess* episodes paralleling features of Berg's opera, which Gershwin undoubtedly studied as a model for constructing and binding musical-dramatic incident. He was equally intent on achieving a succulent modernist dissonance audibly akin to Berg's idiom. Paul Rosenfeld, extolling high modernism, castigating Gershwin, could not possibly have realized that Schillinger and Berg were as pertinent to Gershwin's style and technique as Broadway tunes or Gullah shouts. Doubtless he was equally unaware of Gershwin's eventful personal and professional relationship with Arnold Schoenberg, whom Gershwin first met in Berlin in 1928, having already heard *Pierrot Lunaire* and other nontonal Schoenberg compositions; later, in America, Gershwin helped to underwrite the Kolisch Quartet recordings of Schoenberg's four string quartets.[52]

As composers go, Gershwin was not notably thin-skinned. Still, his immersion in Schillinger, Berg, and Schoenberg, buttressed by the dazzled admiration of his *Porgy* cast and an ample circle of friends, could only have produced a wave of cognitive dissonance in the face of confident reviewers who continued to treat him as a naïf. As countless observers testified, Gershwin appreciated his own importance. Henry Cowell recalled attending *Porgy and Bess* with its composer: "[He] was overcome with joy. He felt with the greatest sincerity that it was the greatest work ever produced in this country."[53] In any event, Gershwin felt the need to defend his offspring in the October 20 Sunday *New York Times*—ten days after the New York opening. He began:

> Since the opening of "Porgy and Bess" I have been asked frequently why it is called a folk opera. The explanation is a simple one. "Porgy and Bess" is a folk tale. Its people naturally would sing folk music. When I first began work on the music I decided against the use of original folk material because I wanted the music to be all of one piece. Therefore I wrote my own spirituals and folksongs. But they are still folk music—and therefore, being in operatic form, "Porgy and Bess" becomes a folk opera.
>
> However, because "Porgy and Bess" deals with Negro life in America it brings to the operatic form elements that have never before appeared in opera and I have adapted my method to utilize the drama, the humor, the superstition, the religious fervor, the dancing and the irrepressible high spirits of the race. If in doing this, I have created a new form, which combines opera with theatre, this new form has come quite naturally out of the material.
>
> The reason I did not submit this work to the usual sponsors of opera in America was that I hoped to have developed something in

American music that would appeal to the many rather than to the cultured few.

Gershwin was unashamed of writing songs for *Porgy and Bess*. "Song hits" may be found in Verdi and Bizet, he wrote. As for his recitatives: "I have tried to make [them] as close to the Negro inflection in speech as possible, and I believe my song-writing apprenticeship has served invaluably in this respect, because the song writers of America have the best conception of how to set words to music so that the music gives added expression to the words." Lightly alluding to his studies with Schillinger and of Berg, he stated: "I have used sustained symphonic music to unify entire scenes, and I prepared myself for that task by further study in counterpoint and modern harmony." Intent upon "American opera," he had set an American story. Also: "An American opera without humor could not possibly run the gamut of American expression. In 'Porgy and Bess' there are ample opportunities for humorous songs and dances. This humor is natural humor—not 'gags' superimposed upon the story but humor flowing from the story itself." That Gershwin's apologia failed to impress Olin Downes would became apparent twenty-one months later when Downes summed up the Gershwin career alongside an obituary notice.

Porgy and Bess likewise confronted Rouben Mamoulian with a mountain of cognitive contradictions. In later years, his memory of the New York reviews would drive Mamoulian to uncharacteristic expletives. "Have you read the [1935] reviews of *Porgy and Bess*?" he asked an interviewer in 1973. "Did you notice how patronizing the critics were to George Gershwin? They kept asking, 'What is this? It's not an opera. It's not this, it's not that.' It took those bastards five years to realize that [it] was the greatest single contribution to the American musical theater." Mamoulian's *Porgy and Bess* scrapbook bulges with notes and telegrams testifying to a rare human experience at odds with issues of genre and technique imposed by querulous writers. The day of the Alvin Theatre premiere, Todd Duncan telegrammed Mamoulian:

> YOUR GENIUS AND ART IS INEVITABLE IN PORGY MAY
> OTHERS GROW THROUGH YOUR TUTELAGE AS I HAVE YOU
> HAVE WORKED HARD TO PLACE THE NEGRO ARTIST ON A
> HIGH ARTISTIC PLANE KNOWING THE INNERMOST AND
> SINCERE FEELING OF OUR GROUP THEY WILL DO THEIR
> UTMOST TO CROWN YOUR EFFORTS WITH OVER WHELMING
> SUCCESS.

Other cast members wrote notes to and about Mamoulian. Ruby Elzy: "I am fortunate, oh so very fortunate, because my life . . . has been touched by your wonderful spirit." John Bubbles: "God didn't give me everything until he gave me to you." Anne Brown: "I can truthfully say that you have helped me to live more beautifully." Georgette Harvey, who sang Maria: "My beloved friend Rouben Mamoulian [is] the source of my inspiration. . . . I shall be eternally grateful for his kindness and ingenious ability to bring out talents in me which I never dreamed existed." In December, two months after *Porgy and Bess* opened, Eva Jessye wrote to report that her celebrated Eva Jessye Choir—the chorus engaged for the show—was being trimmed to economize, that Bubbles was missing cues, that "I Got Plenty O' Nuttin'" stopped the show every night—and that she wanted, please, a signed photograph of Rouben Mamoulian.[54]

Decades later, Mamoulian recalled that when he left New York to return to California:

> the whole cast surprised me at Grand Central Station to see me off. As I started down the ramp, I saw a red runner of carpet leading to the train. I thought I was crazy when I heard a band playing *Porgy and Bess*'s "Orphans' Band" music. They even had the goat and the cart

there. After I had gotten inside, I could see nothing through the large window but a sea of black faces, pressed against the glass and looking at me with such love that, you know, I couldn't help it, I just broke down and cried.

Less than an hour later, on the Twentieth Century Limited, Mamoulian sent a telegram to his cast:

HAVE NO WORDS ONLY A TREMENDOUS FEELING WHICH MADE ME BREAK DOWN AND CRIE [*sic*] LIKE A BABY NEVER HAVE I BEEN SO SAD AND SO HAPPY BLESS YOU ALL YOU SWEET LOVELY AND DEARLY BELOVED FRIENDS.

An hour later, Mamoulian telegrammed again:

DEAR PRECIOUS CHILDREN MY HEART IS SO UNBEARABLY FULL THAT I WANT TO TELL YOU AGAIN AND AGAIN HOW SWEET YOU ARE AND HOW MUCH I LOVE YOU.

Still en route to California, Mamoulian received a telegram signed by "Anne [Brown], Georgette [Harvey], and Ruby [Elzy]." It read:

DEAR MR MAMOULIAN WE ARE STILL WITH YOU AND WE LOVE YOU MORE THAN EVER.

Months later, Duncan wrote to Mamoulian:

I had considered you a great director, a great inspiration. . . . But after your speech Feb. 14 before a crowded house at the Curran Theatre, I see you as a great moving spirit for a minority group—my group, THE NEGRO RACE. . . . I am grateful for your existence and for the forces that brought you to us; all Negroes will be grateful to you and will speak of you in terms of devotion, sincerety [*sic*] and reverence in the next century.[55]

If Gershwin died with the knowledge that *Porgy and Bess* was his peak achievement, *Porgy and Bess* remained unvindicated. The day after his passing, Downes opined in the *Times*:

In some respects, and partly by virtue of the immense amount of publicity he received, his value may have been exaggerated. It remains that [he] gave jazz itself a new importance and consideration as a musical medium, and proved that significant creation was possible in the terms of this popular national idiom.

Gershwin was not the first to realize this possibility. . . . But Gershwin, in the first place, had the popular ear. In the second place, while he never was an intellectual composer, he had an extraordinary musical instinct and capacity for assimilation. . . .

He never passed a certain point as a "serious" composer. It was not in him to do what Dvořák did for Bohemian music, or even for America in the "New World" symphony. . . . Gershwin had too limited technic for that. . . .

The first act of "Of Thee I Sing," and passages from his best light operas will rank much higher than any part of his attempted "folk opera" "Porgy." . . .[56]

A different tune was sung in Los Angeles by foreign-born musicians who, on both sides of the Atlantic, invariably appreciated Gershwin best. Jascha Heifetz, who had hoped for a Gershwin violin concerto, and whose *Porgy and Bess* transcriptions for violin and piano would constitute an inspired tribute, told friends, "We should be ashamed that we didn't appreciate this man more when he was here in our midst." Otto Klemperer, conducting at the Hollywood Bowl Gershwin Memorial Concert, led the Los Angeles Philharmonic in his own telling transcription of Gershwin's Second Prelude, intensely reconceived as a dirge. Arnold Schoenberg, Gershwin's frequent tennis partner, wrote Gershwin eulogies in 1937 and 1938. The second stated: "It seems to me beyond doubt that Gershwin was an innovator." The first read in full:

> George Gershwin was one of these rare kinds of musicians to whom music is not a matter of more or less ability. Music to him was the air he breathed, the food which nourished him, the drink that refreshed him. Music was what made him feel and music was the feeling he expressed.
>
> Directness of this kind is given only to great men and there is no doubt that he was a great composer.
>
> What he was achieved was not only to the benefit of a national American music, but also a contribution to the music of the whole world. In this meaning I want to express the deepest grief for the deplorable loss to music; but may I mention that I lose also a friend whose amiable personality was very dear to me.[57]

One could say that in a sense Mamoulian's appreciation of Gershwin— his kindred cultural fluidity—delayed widespread appreciation of *Porgy and Bess*. Unlike Brooks Atkinson, Virgil Thomson, Samuel Chotzinoff, and countless others, Mamoulian endorsed (albeit with qualifications) Gershwin's operatic use of recitative; he distinguished between discardable "Italianate" recitatives and others he considered organic to Gershwin's score. Gershwin's orbit was Mamoulian's orbit: in Hollywood, Mamoulian had directed Chevalier, Dietrich, and Garbo; he had mounted Turgenev, Eugene O'Neill, and George M. Cohan on Broadway; he had even, in 1930, directed Schoenberg's atonal *Die glückliche Hand* for Stokowski at the Metropolitan Opera House. Gershwin's *sui generis* confluence of high art and high entertainment, intermingled without prejudice, was native to Mamoulian; his way with *Porgy and Bess* sustained a dynamic equilibrium transcending genre. But this shared Gershwin-Mamoulian comfort zone, ahead of its time, was discomfiting to most. Only in 1941 when *Porgy and Bess* was produced by Mamoulian's onetime Theatre Guild assistant Cheryl Crawford did it achieve the recognition denied Gershwin in 1935. Crawford's triumphant revival, running for 286 performances plus a forty-seven-city tour and a return New York engagement, transformed Gershwin's polyvalent opera into a sleek two-and-one-half-hour musical show. With her director, Robert Ross, and Alexander Smallens, who again conducted, Crawford replaced much of Gershwin's recitative with dialogue. The orchestra was reduced to twenty-seven players. The pacing was snappier, the directorial touch lighter, the wartime production less opulent and expensive. The top ticket was lowered to $2.75. Critics who had caviled in 1935 now found *Porgy and Bess* a compelling stage work—but, the composer's intentions notwithstanding, not an opera after all. Overriding Gershwin's cultural fluidity, understating his originality, the production evinced new understanding that was equally a misunderstanding.

Mamoulian, of course, felt that Crawford had betrayed Gershwin, *Porgy and Bess*, and himself. He called the revised tempo of the production "at least three times faster than George intended." He later claimed that Ira Gershwin had agreed that Crawford's *Porgy and Bess* was "lousy," but appreciated "the royalties we're getting."[58] Mamoulian would be aroused to further displeasure by every subsequent staging of Gershwin's magnum opus.

THE RUSSIAN CONNECTION

I conclude this chapter with two further perspectives on *Porgy and Bess*, the first Russian, the second Brechtian.

It did not escape the first chroniclers of *Porgy and Bess* that three of its principal makers were "Russians." Mamoulian, however Armenian, was so identified. Serge Sudeikin, who created the sets and costumes, was born in Smolensk, Alexander Smallens in St. Petersburg.

Smallens presumably came to Gershwin's attention partly via Alexander Steinert, whom Gershwin had engaged as a vocal coach for his opera. Born in Boston to the Steinway Piano family, Steinert was no Russian, but was known to Gershwin as a conductor and coach of the New York-based Russian Opera—for which Smallens led *Boris Godunov* and *Prince Igor* in 1935. To this list of Russian connections one must add the indispensable Joseph Schillinger, born in Kharkov, and Gershwin's psychiatrist Gregory Zilboorg, born in Kiev, who saw Gershwin as often as five times weekly in 1934–1935.

That the Russian-Gershwin connection is not merely anecdotal becomes obvious when one considers that Sudeikin was a leading theatrical designer in tsarist Russia and that he departed for Paris in 1906 at the invitation of Serge Diaghilev.* To Diaghilev's revolutionary Mir Iskusstva movement, Sudeikin contributed colorfully styled sets and costumes; like Mamoulian, he fed on the Russian avant-garde. For Catfish Row, Sudeikin created a three-story façade taller than Cleon Throckmorton's 1927 set, and with double the number of windows and doorways. Serena's room, with its towering shadows, was twice the height of Throckmorton's. Sudeikin's fanciful Kittiwah Island, documented in a color photograph, flaunted tropical pastel shades. Temperamentally, he was as immodest as his designs; Mamoulian had to intervene to keep peace with the Theatre Guild.

And Gershwin himself was of course born to Russian parents. He grew up hearing some Russian at home, and according to Stravinsky retained some Russian in later life. He associated his disconsolate side with his Russian lineage. "Here I am, just a sad Russian again," he would tell Kay Swift. Merle Armitage wrote: "Deep in the being of George

---

*Seven years later, he eloped to Paris with Vera de Bosset, subsequently his wife and later Stravinsky's.

Gershwin was a map of all the human suffering of the world. Anyone who knew him could not have missed that characteristic feature." The Gershwin parental household, though English-speaking, was also Yiddish—a tongue George and Ira retained as adults. Surely the Yiddish Russian shtetl—an intimate community bound by language and ritual—was one ancestor of Catfish Row. And the Yiddish theater, which Gershwin knew from an early age, was culturally fluid, a mélange of teary melodrama and Russian experimental art. Gershwin testified that "Summertime" sounded "cantorial" to his own ears. To ears similarly attuned, "Gone, Gone, Gone" and "It Ain't Necessarily So" are wailing and narrative synagogue chants.[59]

The twentieth-century cultural and political affinities binding Russian Jew and African-American were manifold, complex, and controversial. Jewish entertainers of Gershwin's generation—Al Jolson, Eddie Cantor, George Jessel, George Burns, Sophie Tucker—sang in blackface; they even, in the case of Jolson's "Swanee," sang Gershwin in blackface. *Porgy and Bess*, which Gershwin insisted be sung by African-Americans, stripped the black mask to reveal black skin. That Gershwin—like Stephen Foster in his minstrel songs—sympathized or identified with black Americans did not (as we will see in chapter 4) absolve him from accusations of stereotyping black character and behavior.* If Gershwin therefore became a racial adversary in the fifties and sixties, it remains pertinent that both Jew and black were outsiders mutually participating in a drama of assimilation.

Mamoulian, compared to Gershwin, was a different kind of "Russian"—aristocratic, cosmopolitan, peripatetic—and yet equally a study in rootlessness. That Gershwin was ever in search of himself was not

---

*A concise but acute consideration of this topic may be found in David Schiff's *Rhapsody in Blue* (1997), in which Schiff writes in part: "While blacks might be lower in the social order than Jews, they were also, by being Christian, at once more American and more religious than the immigrant Jews, many of whom had abandoned any religious practice. African-Americans were also more embedded in American history, however tragically, than Jews would ever be. Jewish blackface was thus a complex phase of cultural negotiation which partook of identification and indifference, idealization and condescension, admiration and envy" (p. 98).

least observed by Mamoulian when he wrote: "I think that to know himself was what he wanted most in life. . . . He searched for a solution of himself. . . . He was hoping the psycho-analyst would unravel to him his own mystery."[60] Mamoulian's own search for self would prove a terminal mystery as *Porgy and Bess*—which as he told his beloved black cast made him sadder and happier than he had ever been before—faded into mere memory. Both Gershwin and Mamoulian needed anchoring; both quested for "America" via the self-reflective surfaces of creative art. *Porgy and Bess*, for both, powerfully addressed this need.

Singular documentation of the "Russian connection" to *Porgy and Bess* is furnished by an undated essay, handwritten in Russian, found among Mamoulian's papers when he died.[61] It is titled "Rehearsing Porgy." The unidentified author has access to Mamoulian's rehearsals.* He or she has "spent half my life backstage in theaters." Rouben Mamoulian is adored as a genius. The essay reads in part:

> Greek tragedy, with its chorus, showed the tragedy of human existence, the agony of the soul, true self-awareness. . . . In our time the chorus of the theatre of antiquity was translated into opera. . . . The choruses in Russian operas, let's say of Mussorgsky, are the highest [such] achievements. . . .
>
> If humanity manifests its spiritual power, its inner "I," then most of all it is expressed in choral singing. . . .
>
> All the masterpieces of the operatic genre . . . are built upon so-called folkore, that is to say on folk song. . . .
>
> And so can there be American opera? Where is the folklore? . . . Operas written by Americans make no sense to me. They are neo-Europeans. . . . I am not a specialist on music, but . . . I can state that the opera *Porgy and Bess* makes sense. It is cleverly built on American folklore, i.e. on Negroes. When the choral singing reaches its apo-

---

*Kurt Jensen (author of a forthcoming Mamoulian biography) speculates that the essay was written by Sudeikin.

gee then I no longer perceive nationality. For me, the chorus becomes universal and one cannot but be moved by Gershwin. He was able to achieve in his choruses such anguish of the human soul that folklore becomes universal.

What did I see at these rehearsals? Negroes . . . are playing, arguing, singing, dancing, and enjoying life. But then one strong man, in a white shirt without a jacket, says only one word—"Children"—and all are in their places; this man is clearly adored by all. He never raises his voice and never makes anyone do anything unnecessary. His memory is phenomenal . . . he remembers the coordination of music, drama, lighting, and rhythm. It's as if he had written two contrapuntal operas based on *Porgy and Bess*. . . .

Most likely much has been written about the scene [of Robbins's funeral] . . . an ecstasy of raised hands suddenly reaching from one side, now from another, . . . trembling, like leaves on a tree after a storm . . . with colossal shadows in the room without a ceiling . . . with the wife of the deceased throwing the largest shadow with outstretched arms as the curtain goes down. . . .

There are still people who know how to create theatre. The majority of them are Russians . . . Meyerhold, Diaghilev, Stanislavsky, and finally our American Mamoulian, like a deer leaping from rock to rock. If one were to put into order Mamoulian's rehearsals and note down all that took place, a book about the theory of theater would come into being.

The writer situates *Porgy and Bess* within a Russian operatic tradition privileging the chorus as a folk protagonist, and within a Russian stage tradition vigorously integrating theater and song. Mamoulian himself would tell an interviewer in 1973:

What I'd seen of American burlesque, vaudeville, singing and dancing struck me so forcefully. . . . They have contributed a great deal to this country. . . . And I thought how odd it was that in America there was no indigenous theatrical form. What you had was grand opera and that [is] a European tradition. Viennese operetta is the same. You had the so-called musical comedy. . . . A girl would break into song and deliver it to the audience. Then there would be a dance specialty. It was strung together very loosely. So I thought there was a possibility here of a new style of stage production which would integrate all the elements. That would be a tremendously powerful theatrical medium.[62]

Paul Rosenfeld, a German Jewish intellectual for whom the Russian Jew signified dirt, wrote in 1936: "That [Gershwin's compositions] are characteristic American productions is not to be doubted. Their spirit unfortunately makes them so, since weakness of spirit, possibly as a consequence of the circumstance that the new world attracted the less stable human types, remains an American condition."[63] For the immigrant Mamoulian, as for Gershwin, the New World was itself a necessary stabilizing force. Versed in the theater and its lore, intent upon integrating drama and music, already practiced in staging a variety of operas and operettas in Rochester, he must have puzzled over how best to create an "American" musical theater. It could not have escaped his attention that in *Porgy* and *Porgy and Bess* an African-American chorus recapitulated in eloquence and function the choruses of Aeschylus and Mussorgsky.

Not so many years previous to *Porgy*, Stravinsky had mined shouting and keening peasant wedding ceremonies in pursuit of a twentieth-century national style. Mamoulian and Gershwin mutually discovered in black America the folk roots of an original American genre.

MAMOULIAN AND BRECHT

In Tom Milne's *Rouben Mamoulian* (1969), the author's apologia for one of Mamoulian's most problematic films, *High, Wide, and Handsome* (1937), infers a Brechtian *Verfremdungseffekt* (alienation effect) at work—a conscious strategy to distance the audience and provoke thought. Interviews with Mamoulian disclosed no familiarity with Brecht, and Mamoulian was not a political or confrontational artist. At the same time, Brecht's "epic theater" is not irrelevant to the Mamoulian approach. No less than Brecht, Mamoulian shuns realism and also Germanic *Innigkeit*: interior psychological portraiture does not engage him. His best milieu is stylized ceremony, spectacle, the crowd. He reaches for the elemental and universal. His light or heavy touch imparts moral instruction.

DuBose Heyward populated his novella *Porgy* with a shadowy title character and a supporting cast even less detailed or specific. The inner life of feeling and thought matters little; the community is all or nearly all. Mamoulian transformed *Porgy* the play into a saga no longer local. He also amplified the characters—but more as archetypes than individuals. *Porgy and Bess* is bigger still: an epic. That they sing rather than speak makes everyone more formidable in expression. The juxtaposition with barking white interlopers adds further stature to the human drama of Catfish Row. And yet the dramatist in Gershwin is no O'Neill: the confessional mode is never in play. And the music dramatist in Gershwin, whatever his debt to *Die Meistersinger*, is no Wagner, obsessed with inner life. Porgy is not Hans Sachs; he sings no soliloquies.

Considered as archetypes, the dramatis personae of *Porgy and Bess* are varied and strong. Porgy, a cripple made whole, becomes the community's moral beacon. From the start, his disability and affability command respect. He is a source of enlightenment—"de things dat I prize like the stars in the skies all are free"—even before he experiences love and forgiveness to the full. He righteously slays Crown. His theme, as musically crafted by Gershwin, combines sorrow and strength.* Bess is an addict and knows it: she can resist neither happy dust nor Crown. She loves Porgy for his goodness, yet understands and confides that when Crown calls, "he hypnotize me," "I know I have to go." Striving to redeem her-

---

*See p. 7.

self, she adopts an orphaned baby. Her fickleness and vulnerability are pathetic; she is more a victim than a troublemaker. "Some man always willin' to take care of Bess," she says.* Crown is carnal, Sporting Life satanic, Maria an earth mother, Serena a church lady. To dwell on the nuances of these characters would mainly serve to weaken them.

One man's archetype is another's stereotype—and it is wholly understandable that as times changed, artists and audiences took offense. Porgy's gullibility, Bess's sluttishness, may be read as derogatory African-American imagery; the absence of private thought may be experienced as an intellectual debit. If these impressions were chronic, *Porgy and Bess* would by now have faded as a period piece. In fact, *Porgy and Bess* in many respects resembles a metaphoric religious oratorio or pageant play. As Howard Pollack shrewdly observed in 2006: "The whole opera is like a prayer or rite, each act concluding in a state of communal supplication or exaltation; even the craps game begins with an invocation that reflects on man's transience."

Invoking Brechtian ideals illuminates the impersonal grandeur of *Porgy and Bess*, and also an antipathy to *Innigkeit* common to Mamoulian and Gershwin. At the same time, the appeal to epic theater clarifies a point of difference: unlike Brecht, unlike Mamoulian, Gershwin is an empathetic dramatist; and he empathizes with Porgy. Let us suppose, as a hypothesis, that two Gershwin self-images arising from his search for self-understanding—a search presumably facilitated by Dr. Zilboorg, certainly abetted by the creative act—were of the outsider and of the prepossessing cripple. We know that Isaac Goldberg, among other Gershwin acquaintances, had been urging George to dig deeper—to compose music more personal and profound in sentiment. We know that Gershwin the man was considered—if not "crippled"—fundamentally impenetrable, more questing than fulfilled; that no more than Porgy was he prone to confide his innermost thoughts. Gershwin

---

*James Baldwin felt that Billie Holiday "would have made a splendid, if somewhat overwhelming Bess," "closer to the original, whoever she was, . . . than anyone who has ever played or sung it."

took to Heyward's novella for reasons conscious and not. We know that he associated African-Americans with fluency of song and of songlike speech. We know that the Porgy story appealed for its strength of tragedy and comedy, and for its American setting. But Gershwin was also self-evidently drawn to Porgy the man. His music tells us so.

Porgy's first entrance, in act 1, is accorded an operatic dignity and ceremony befitting royalty. "Here comes Porgy. Open the gate for him," Maria tells Scipio. Gershwin's orchestra responds with an upward flourish capped by a tingling trill. The gate is opened, and a second ascending flourish is supported by a measured descent in the bass to the tonic E major. Gershwin's strings proclaim Porgy's theme above a stately chordal tread. "Here's the ol' crap shark!" sings Jake. "Now we'll have a game!" exclaims Mingo. Porgy's theme, marked by Gershwin "semplice" and "espressivo," saturates the score for several pages as the excitement occasioned by his arrival subsides. Later in the act, at Robbins's wake, it is Porgy who leads the chant: "Gawd got plenty of money for de sinner." The opera's most momentous music commences, in act 3, with Porgy's return from jail. Mingo runs to the gate and shouts, "It's Porgy comin' home!"—and Gershwin recapitulates the musical commotion and ritual of Porgy's first coming. The entire community sings, to Porgy's theme: "Welcome home, Porgy, we're all so glad you is back again." His leavetaking, with its choral apotheosis, is as mythic as that of Tennyson's Arthur or Longfellow's Hiawatha. Gershwin's Porgy, in short, is heroic, and Porgy's drama of self-realization, transcending the defect that makes him exogenous, is complete. Even absent Bess, Gershwin's music says, Porgy is fulfilled.

Nothing that Heyward or Mamoulian contributed to *Porgy* or *Porgy and Bess* supports a central character this commanding. When Brooks Atkinson, comparing opera and play, credited Gershwin with adding a "glow of personal feeling" that "was missing before," he was responding, in part, to Gershwin's personal feeling for Porgy the prepossessing cripple. Heyward eyed Porgy as an appreciative chronicler of a remarkable Gullah subculture. Mamoulian added his share of admiration and respect. But Porgy in 1927 possessed nothing like the grandeur and fluency of utterance conferred by "I Got Plenty O' Nuttin'," "Bess You Is My Woman," "or "Oh Bess, Oh Where's My Bess?" Frank Wilson, the slender, long-faced former postman who starred in the play, may be observed in a major supporting role in the 1933 film version of *The Emperor Jones*—and he is no Todd Duncan.

In fact, Porgy, in *Porgy and Bess*, conflates a variety of Porgys. Initially, in Heyward's novella, he is detached, elusive, inscrutable. In the opera— irritable with children, sexually inexperienced, gullible, fearful—he retains "weak" traits that are arguably residual. That Bess lacks an aria (she must be more than an accessory), that Porgy from the outset is a commanding presence (he needs room to grow) are production challenges arising from the opera's complex ten-year gestation. Mainly, however, the multifarious contributions of its creators serve to gird, amplify, and enrich the final 1935 outcome.

Of course, the contributions of Heyward, Mamoulian, and Gershwin cannot be regarded as equivalent, or equivalently gratifying. Gershwin is the opera's presiding genius. That Mamoulian was artistically the more replaceable, personally the more deracinated, would cause him pain and disappointment in years to come.

CHAPTER 4

PORGY AND BESS AND HOLLYWOOD

STRESSING HIS BROTHER'S evenhanded mastery of genres high and low, Ira once said, "after writing the 'Great American Opera' George wrote some of the best hits he ever did in his life." Ira was referring to *Shall We Dance, A Damsel in Distress*, and *The Goldwyn Follies*, all scored for Hollywood. But in fact, this final Gershwin chapter—he worked in Los Angeles until his sudden terminal illness—tested the limits of cultural fluidity. Hollywood signified an opportunity for maximum earnings, a subsidy for future stage and concert works. But it also signified an artistic opportunity: Gershwin was considering creating a film musical of his own.[1]

Hollywood, however, had grown distrustful of Gershwin. If in New York highbrows patronized him, film producers were afraid Gershwin would only compose highbrow songs. Responding to a telegram saying precisely that, Gershwin replied: INCIDENTAL RUMORS ABOUT HIGHBROW MUSIC RIDICULOUS AM OUT TO WRITE HITS.[2] He secured a lucrative RKO Pictures contract for an Astaire-Rogers musical with an option for a possible second film; subsequently, the second film was clinched, as was a third for Samuel Goldwyn.

Shall We Dance was released in 1937. The film's "best hits," praised by Ira, included "They All Laughed," "Let's Call the Whole Thing Off," and "They Can't Take That Away from Me."[3] The plot, in which a ballet dancer (Fred Astaire) decides it's more fun to dance with a popular star (Ginger Rogers), pokes fun at highbrows. But Gershwin himself (whose film credit is garnished by an orchestral allusion to *Rhapsody in Blue*) pushes the envelope. His lean instrumental cue "Walking the Dog" is a witty self-sufficient concert cameo,[4] a private commentary on overstuffed Hollywood orchestrations. And the film ends with more than ten minutes of continuous music, chiefly comprising a complex dance ensemble incorporating ballet. Gershwin hastily re-created this finale when he discovered what the studio's resident composers had concocted; the heady gusts of Debussy and Ravel that he interpolated suggest possible new compositional directions. After attending a preview of *Shall We Dance*, Gershwin expressed disappointment that it did not take full advantage of the songs.[5] The Gershwins' second RKO film, *A Damsel in Distress* with Astaire and (in a nonsinging, nondancing role) Joan Fontaine, includes "A Foggy Day" and "Nice Work If You Can Get It." But here the integration of music and dance is even more sporadic; the treatment and placement of the songs lacks anything like the "rhythmic" dimension of—to cite the obvious template for a post-*Porgy* integrated Gershwin film musical—*Love Me Tonight*.

Gershwin began work on the *The Goldwyn Follies* before shooting started on *A Damsel in Distress*. Goldwyn had asked him why he didn't write "hit songs you can whistle." Oscar Levant, a close observer of Gershwin in Hollywood, recalled this exchange as "one of the few occasions in my experience [when Gershwin] was genuinely offended." "I had to live for this," Gershwin told S. N. Behrman, "that Sam Goldwyn should say to me: 'Why don't you write hits like Irving Berlin?'" Eager to return to New York even before his illness forced the issue, Gershwin was spared further encounters with Goldwyn. But his death robbed him of the opportunity to collaborate with George Balanchine: Vernon Duke wound up composing the *Romeo and Juliet* and *Water Nymph* ballets Balanchine choreographed for Goldwyn's *Follies*. According to Balanchine's water nymph (and future wife) Vera Zorina, Goldwyn could not grasp that Balanchine "was way ahead of the game in choreographing for the camera and not the theater." That is: Balanchine's differences with Goldwyn, which drove him to a wholly uncharacteristic fury, limned a Hollywood story in parallel with Gershwin's. A master practitioner of cultural fluidity, Balanchine found Hollywood a lucrative but limited creative opportunity.[6]

When Gershwin died on July 11, 1937, the best Hollywood could do was to halt the studios for a minute of silence five days later. The Hollywood Bowl's nationally broadcast Gershwin Memorial Concert the following September grandiloquently embodied the "What is it?" conundrum plaguing Gershwin at the peak of his truncated career. No mourning or celebratory tone was sustained; no coherent musical portrait was secured. The featured speakers included George Jessel, Oscar Hammerstein, Edward G. Robinson, and Mrs. Leiland Atherton Irish, who managed the Los Angeles Philharmonic. The numbers included an eleven-minute symphonic "Anthology" created by the MGM Music Department. This gaudy Gershwin potpourri, for 150 players, attempted a maximum eulogy with maximum scale and glitter; it is the disconnect between Gershwin and Hollywood musically expressed. The evening's piano soloists were Oscar Levant, in a driving performance of the Concerto in F, and José Iturbi, who both played and conducted *Rhapsody in Blue*. The latter stunt, heralded by the radio announcer as an "unusual and difficult task," backfired when soloist and orchestra hectically parted ways. The Metropolitan Opera singers Lily Pons and Gladys Swarthout, both with Hollywood side careers, offered stiff, manicured readings of "Summertime" and "The Man I Love." Al Jolson and Fred Astaire excelled in "Swanee" and "They Can't Take That Away from Me." The artistic high points* were Todd Duncan, Anne Brown, and Ruby Elzy in selections from *Porgy and Bess*, and Otto Klemperer's stirring funeral orchestration of the Second Prelude. Thunderous applause and cheering punctuated the overlong evening.

MAMOULIAN IN DECLINE

I dwell on this final Gershwin-in-Hollywood episode because it resonates with the Hollywood fate of Rouben Mamoulian, a saga fatally including Samuel Goldwyn and *Porgy and Bess* incongruously in tandem.

Mamoulian's Hollywood career peaked early, with *Love Me Tonight* (1932). *Applause* (1929) and *Dr. Jekyll and Mr. Hyde* (1931) are unquestionably distinctive, distinguished achievements; also, like *Love Me Tonight*, they mark significant technical achievements in the use of camera and sound.† The picturesque musical parody *The Gay Desperado* (1936) is another kind of landmark: Mamoulian never shot another scene as divinely cheeky as the hero's gunpoint rendition of Verdi's "Celeste Aida" (undubbed, unabridged) in a provincial Mexican radio studio. Though Mamoulian's motivic, psychological use of Technicolor in *Becky Sharp* (1935) and *Blood and Sand* (1941) was innovative, these films are otherwise disappointing. If in fact virtually every Mamoulian film brandishes Mamoulian touches, the self-evident artistic control he early exercised is afterward only sporadically in evidence.

Mark Spergel, a theater historian who is also a practicing psychoanalyst, interprets Mamoulian's oeuvre autobiographically in his 1993 Mamoulian study *Reinventing Reality*. Unsurprisingly, *Golden Boy* (1939), in Spergel's reading, confides the director's Hollywood sellout. Joe Bonaparte is a gifted concert violinist who abandons music for fame and fortune in the boxing ring: a gaudy hoodlum milieu. Notwith-

---

*See pp. 126–27.
†See pp. 84–88.

standing an obligatory happy ending, Bonaparte wreaks destruction on himself and others. Mamoulian, it will be recalled, was himself once a violinist. *Golden Boy*, Spergel summarizes, suggests a metaphor for Mamoulian's experience of Hollywood as greedy and cannibalistic, a world where artistic sensitivity is wasted on bread and circuses, where artists are exploited by villainous managers.[7] And *Golden Boy* is not the only Mamoulian film fixed on issues of artistic integrity. Though *Queen Christina* (1933), Mamoulian's Garbo film, is an epic based on the abdication of a seventeenth-century Swedish ruler, history fancifully reconstrued here functions as a backcloth. Mamoulian's Christina is a creative spirit whose poetic sensibility conflicts with political realities and responsibilities; following her inner voice, she resigns the throne. In *Blood and Sand*, a painterly Spanish epic, the matador Juan Gallardo sacrifices a supreme natural gift to debauchery and drink.

But these movies themselves "sell out." Garbo's Queen Christina peaks in two Mamoulian set pieces: the scene in which she reveals her tenderness by caressing bedroom objects (with Mamoulian conducting with metronome and baton), and the famous final tableau, an enveloping tabula rasa of the Garbo visage (for which Mamoulian used multiple lenses to pan from a great distance). But the originality of Garbo and Mamoulian is buried beneath the hokum of a lavish MGM costume drama: wooden ceremony, lifeless dialogue, insipid musical opulence. With a modicum of self-knowledge, Mamoulian would have passed on *Golden Boy*, a filmed Clifford Odets play heavy on dialogue and—until Mamoulian gets in the ring for the climactic boxing match—bereft of spectacle. Young William Holden, as Joe, seems helpless, virtually undirected; Lee J. Cobb, as his father, is misdirected and made a cartoon; the backdrop of poverty and crime is sanitized.

Blood and Sand, by comparison, is all about spectacle and *mise en scène*; no less than Robbins's wake, no less than Bonaparte's prizefight, Gallardo's bullfight is an essay in choreographed rhythm and crescendo, lighting and composition; it attains an iconic grandeur. But Mamoulian can do nothing with his textureless gringo stars Tyrone Power and Linda Darnell. His chronic weaknesses—discomfort with intimate verbal exchange; inability to extract the interior life of a character—render him complicit in the Hollywood manicures inflicted on all three films. His originality—a shaping force on *Sister Beatrice, Porgy,* and *Love Me Tonight*—becomes a tangential fascination, an additional source of spectacle.

The film critic Andrew Sarris summarized Mamoulian's decline as that of "an innovator who ran out of innovations."[8] This much-cited assessment is incomplete but just. Unquestionably, Mamoulian needed to be new and different; unquestionably, the early sound years afforded him an opportunity to experiment in film. Especially in *Blood and Sand*, his later experimentation with color—something new, if not as new as sound—produced indelible results. Once seen, the film's poised, statuesque religious canvases, its majesty of chiaroscuro, the crimsons and ochres of its Spanish costumery and earth cannot be erased. But it is not enough. The studio system played a role in suppressing Mamoulian's originality (early on, he self-produced *Jekyll and Hyde, Love Me Tonight,* and the Marlene Dietrich vehicle *Song of Songs*). The Hays Office—Hollywood's moral watchdog—did its share to stifle his penchant for naughty erotic play and outrageous whimsy (in the thirties, his early films were virtually taken out of circulation). The advent of naturalistic "method" acting, after World War II, made Mamoulian's aesthetics old-fashioned. But Mamoulian himself is scarcely blameless. That he frequently called *Sister Beatrice* his highest accomplishment may possibly be understood less as an accurate memory than a cloaked expression of guilt.

Mamoulian's Broadway career proved more resilient—ultimately, his insistence on stylization and "rhythm" better fit the stage than the screen—and yet spiraled toward an equally premature end. Of the seven Broadway productions he directed after *Porgy and Bess*, the signal successes were, of course, *Oklahoma!* (1943) and *Carousel* (1945). Given the reputation of both shows as landmark exercises in "integration," and Mamoulian's long association with integrated musical theater, it is odd that his role is today so little honored. A rare exception is Mark N. Grant's *Rise and Fall of the Broadway Musical* (2004), in which Mamoulian is called "the first important 'total vision' director of Broadway musicals to break the mold of choreographers, designers, and writers staging a musical—arguably, the first director to bring a coherent directorial style to book musicals' direction, and the first to realize that the vulgar, lowly, vaudeville-derived Broadway musical was a theatrical form to which the full resources of high drama could be harnessed." Richard Rodgers, it will be remembered, was Mamoulian's composer for *Love Me Tonight*, in which music was treated as a vital source of organization and continuity from the project's inception. And Oscar Hammerstein had written script and lyrics for *High, Wide, and Handsome*, in which Mamoulian attempted (however unsuccessfully) to embed song in an ambitious morality tale. Writing and speaking about *Oklahoma!* as a breakthrough, Mamoulian, Rodgers and Hammerstein, choreographer Agnes de Mille, and the Theatre Guild all acknowledged the "integration" ideal, but there was never unanimity over the relative importance of the creative partners. Mamoulian took credit for a great many things, including the late and crucial addition of the title-song production number in act 2. In a 2006 interview, Joan Roberts, who played Laurey, remembered Mamoulian as a "magician" and added:

> The amazing impact of the "Oklahoma!" song had to do with Mamoulian's direction. "You are farmers!" he told us. "You are pioneers!" We had this visual ideal when singing that song—that's what made it so great. Mamoulian painted a picture; "You know you belong to the land! And the land you belong to is grand!" We had to *see* the corn. We had to *experience* the wind sweeping down the plain. We had to have a mental image of every lyric we sang. And this was in wartime, of course. No American could have made us prouder to be an American.[9]

According to Joseph Buloff, who played Ali Hakim, Mamoulian was accused by some cast members of revisiting *Porgy and Bess* in whiteface. In fact, many points of resemblance may be adduced: the musical adaptation of a "folk play" (Lynn Riggs's *Green Grow the Lilacs*), the tableaus of community, the carnal villain slain, the redemptive ending. A 1955 Theatre Guild publication went so far as to call *Porgy and Bess* a "forerunner" to *Oklahoma!*[10]

Though *Oklahoma!* strained relations between Mamoulian and his employers, he rejoined the Theatre Guild, Rodgers and Hammerstein, and de Mille for *Carousel*, whose heavy reliance on music approached operatic practice. With its fluid transitions from dialogue to song, *Carousel* in places strikingly evokes *Love Me Tonight*—and Mamoulian said that Rodgers here acknowledged the influence of their earlier film collaboration. Ferenc Molnár, whose *Liliom* was the source of the plot, and who attended *Carousel* in rehearsal, told Mamoulian he handled crowds better than any director he had previously encountered. Mark N. Grant has called Mamoulian's opening waltz sequence—in which a rotating carousel contributes to a surging pantomime of the drama to come—"arguably the greatest scene in [the history of] American musicals."[11]

Whatever the dimensions of Mamoulian's contributions to *Oklahoma!* and *Carousel*, it is easy to imagine how readily the Rodgers and Hammerstein milieu—the vivid postcard characters, the schematic dialogue, the weighty production numbers, the heady doses of morality, and in the case of *Oklahoma!* an epic thrust—suited the Mamoulian touch.[12] When his volatile professional relationship with Rodgers and Hammerstein ended, Mamoulian found himself eagerly partnered by Kurt Weill. Weill, who considered *Love Me Tonight* the finest Hollywood musical, had failed to obtain Mamoulian for the "American opera" *Street Scene* (1946). Directing Weill's *Lost in the Stars* (1949), Mamoulian again worked with a black cast that included Todd Duncan, as well as a narrative black chorus. An artful or overly artful adaptation of Alan Paton's *Cry, the Beloved Country*, it proved a *succès d'estime* running 281 performances. A planned *Huckleberry Finn*, scored by Weill and directed by Mamoulian, was aborted. And Mamoulian's Broadway career was suddenly over.

MAMOULIAN AT WAR

Mamoulian's spats with Rodgers and Hammerstein were symptomatic of a larger problem. Over time, he acquired a reputation for being willful and self-serving. His own accounts of victorious struggles to maintain artistic authority included a well-worn anecdote we have already encountered—that he overcame a Theatre Guild threat to cancel the "Symphony of Noises" in *Porgy*. Mamoulian told countless such stories—that Maurice Chevalier threatened to quit *Love Me Tonight* because he was not consulted on the script; that Garbo insisted she could not convincingly act Queen Christina if she were rehearsed; that Eugene O'Neill maintained that his script for *Marco Millions* could not be touched. These are tales of momentary travail in which Mamoulian invariably massages would-be opponents into acquiescence. Later tales are far more strident. *Porgy and Bess*—its bonded camaraderie of composer, producers, director, and cast—was a charmed exception that proved the rule.

In the case of *Oklahoma!*, open warfare broke out repeatedly. A transcribed phone conversation documents one such occasion: Lawrence Langner of the Guild told Mamoulian he was "fed up with you and your lousy publicity!" Mamoulian's press agent had placed stories about Mamoulian's role in shaping the show. Accusatory letters from Rodgers and Hammerstein ensued. Mamoulian responded in kind, accusing the Theatre Guild's press department of "minimizing" his contribution, "suppressing and distorting facts," etc. He also maintained that de Mille's choreography usurped his role. As late as 1953, he insisted, through an attorney, that the Guild was violating contractual "advertising and billing provisions."[13] All his career, Mamoulian had revised scripts without credit. But for the musicals *Sadie Thompson* (1944) and *Arms and the Girl* (1950), he was listed as coauthor of the book. For Joseph Hayes's *Leaf and Bough* (1949), Mamoulian's name was billed in letters larger than those accorded the young playwright. Issues of authority and authorship increasingly complicated his Broadway career.

In Hollywood, with its moguls, Mamoulian's penchant to revise and rewrite, his aspirations to novelty and distinction, his painstaking insistence on "rhythm," his tendency to work overtime and overbudget were all the more controversial. In 1938 he figured prominently in a successful effort to compel the studios to sign contracts with the Screen Directors Guild. In 1947, he was part of the group that took sides against Cecil B. DeMille's call for the Screen Directors Guild to require a loyalty oath from all members. A taste of things to come was Louis B. Mayer's resentment when Mamoulian lectured him on why *Queen Christina* did not require a less "depressing" ending.

Looking back at the *Oklahoma!* struggles, Rodgers detected in Mamoulian a loss of "the security of command that I had remembered from . . . *Love Me Tonight*. . . . His clashes with Agnes [de Mille] were unquestionably a result of this insecurity, and it was further apparent when he flew into a rage upon discovering that Oscar and I had been shown the costume and set designs before he'd seen them."[14] Far more undermining for Mamoulian were three Hollywood debacles, each ending with his departure from an unfinished film.

Shortly after *Oklahoma!* opened, Twentieth Century–Fox handed Mamoulian the film noir *Laura*. Mamoulian feuded with Otto Preminger, the producer. Darryl Zanuck, the studio head, did not like the rushes. Over lunch, in front of Mamoulian and more than a dozen Fox employees, Zanuck asked Preminger if he thought Mamoulian should be replaced. Preminger said yes. Zanuck told Preminger, "You can start directing." Released in 1944, *Laura* became one of Preminger's signature films. Fifteen years later, Mamoulian was named to direct Elizabeth Taylor in *Cleopatra* for Fox. Walter Wanger, who respected Mamoulian and had worked with him on *Applause* and *Queen Christina*, was the producer; he felt a wide-screen epic spectacle could use the Mamoulian touch. Mamoulian worked on *Cleopatra* for nearly two years. Script troubles plagued the production. There was uncertainty over whether filming could take place on location in Egypt and Italy. Delay followed delay. On January 19, 1961, Mamoulian resigned, claiming *Cleopatra* was no longer the film he had been hired to direct. Nunnally Johnson, one of the writers, weeks later told Groucho Marx:

> I managed the first successful prediction I have made in my whole life. I bet Walter Wanger that [Mamoulian] would never go to bat. All he wants to do is "prepare." A hell of a preparer. Tests, wardrobe, hair, toenails. You give Rouben something to prepare and he's dynamite. . . . If you make him start this picture, I said [to Wanger], he will never forgive you to his dying day. This chap is a natural born martyr.[15]

For reasons of his own, Wanger left a list of Mamoulian sins including:

— General disorder never returning letters . . .
— Denying that he ever changed his mind in front of the entire production staff after he had said one thing and then reverted to another
— Difficulty in getting him to go see plays or actors to read
— Impossible to get him to work under pressure at nights and weekend
— Not wanting to discuss production at mealtimes
— Idiosyncrasies of the great master and repetition of anecdotes concerning his past
— Rudeness to all and infuriated if anything didn't suit him such as an office, his phones not answering, his mail being not properly presented to him

— Never a definite decision but always protecting himself for a change and blame on others, even with people he is close to . . .

— Alibis in connection with what he did shoot

— The continuous meddling with the script and weakening it

— Preaching to everybody at production meetings quoting the value of *Becky Sharp* and other pictures of the past[16]

But the Hollywood debacle that most damaged Mamoulian, directly preceding his *Cleopatra* assignment (and partly explaining its sorry outcome), was losing a film on which he had made substantial headway, and which meant more to him than *Laura* or *Cleopatra* ever could.

GOLDWYN'S VALEDICTORY

Subsequent to its 1935 run at the Alvin Theatre, *Porgy and Bess* remained a controversial and complex product of the American experience. Its exceptional interpretive fluidity was regularly reaffirmed. Its racial content replaced Gershwin's musical aspirations as a central focus of debate.

During the first quarter-century of its performance history, *Porgy and Bess* already embraced a range of genre and style unattained by any previous musical composition for the stage. The magic of Ruby Elzy's "My Man's Gone Now" at the 1937 Hollywood Bowl Memorial Concert was a compound product of classical training and the aching vocal and verbal inflections of a born blues singer. Both of Todd Duncan's recordings of "I'm On My Way" (1937 at the Bowl; 1940 for Decca) document interpolated melodic ornaments—a practice Gershwin sanctioned. In 1942, Avon Long lent his breathy high tenor to *Porgy and Bess* selections with Leo Reisman's jazz orchestra—not only "It Ain't Necessarily So" and "There's A Boat That's Leaving," both of which he had sung on Broadway, but "I Got Plenty O' Nuttin'" and (with Helen Dowdy) "Bess You Is My Woman Now"—Porgy songs charmingly invested with a lilt and bounce. These were all distinguished black artists. But the first sing-

ers to record *Porgy and Bess* numbers were a pair of white Metropolitan Opera principals: Helen Jepson and Lawrence Tibbett, for Victor
in October 1935. Though Duncan and other original cast members
were understandably miffed with RCA Victor, Tibbett's "Oh, Bess, Oh
Where's My Bess?" is a performance for the ages by America's supreme
Verdi baritone; the heft and pathos of this first recorded rendition will
never be surpassed.[17]

In 1944, Jascha Heifetz, denied the Gershwin violin concerto he had
sought, ingeniously recomposed some fifteen minutes of *Porgy and Bess*
for violin and piano; his various recordings of these six pungent cameos
are among the most impressively personal he ever made, Slavic and jazzy
in equal measure. Having commissioned a *Porgy and Bess* "Symphonic
Picture" from Robert Russell Bennett, Fritz Reiner terrifically recorded
it with his Pittsburgh Symphony; the music of the love duet elicits
uncharacteristically tender music-making from this dour conductor. On
the "popular" side, songs from *Porgy and Bess* had by 1960 been recorded
by Bing Crosby, Billie Holiday, Mahalia Jackson, and Frank Sinatra,
among countless others. Charlie Parker recorded "Summertime" with
strings and harp (1949). Miles Davis's *Porgy and Bess*, with orchestrations
by Gil Evans (1958), comprised an integrated thirteen-movement suite
ingeniously variegated in mood and sonority.

Of the post-1935 stagings, we have already encountered Cheryl
Crawford's 1941 revamping of Gershwin's opera as a musical show with
dialogue (and Rouben Mamoulian's predictable response). Notwithstanding the success of Crawford's revival, *Porgy and Bess* was little seen
in the United States in the 1940s and '50s with the singular exception of
a touring production directed by Robert Breen. It was Breen's inspiration to share *Porgy and Bess* with the world—as Cold War propaganda
supported by the United States Department of State, it would both cel-
ebrate an American artistic landmark and present black American artists in black American roles sympathetically portrayed. Between 1952

and 1956, the Breen *Porgy and Bess* toured North and South America, Europe, and the Soviet Union. Breen's casts included Cab Calloway, Leontyne Price, and William Warfield. Some of what Mamoulian and Crawford had cut, including the "Buzzard Song," was restored. The American response was, if anything, even more positive than in 1941.

But because in Europe *Porgy and Bess* was received with less prejudice or preconception, it was in Europe that *Porgy and Bess* was decisively recognized as a major twentieth-century music theater work. At the premieres in Vienna and Berlin, the curtain calls numbered fourteen and twenty-one, respectively. The major critics, including Max Graf and H. H. Stuckenschmidt, did not voice the reservations long associated with Olin Downes, Virgil Thomson, and Paul Rosenfeld. In Paris, Milan, Moscow, and Leningrad, Francis Poulenc, Riccardo Malipiero, Aram Khachaturian, and Dmitri Shostakovich all expressed keen admiration. Brittle hierarchies of taste that had retarded Gershwin's American reputation did not matter to them. As *Porgy og Bess* in blackface, *Porgy and Bess* also enjoyed a brilliant success in Copenhagen in 1943; after the war, it remained a staple of the Royal Danish Opera through 1953.

And so by the time Samuel Goldwyn undertook a Hollywood film version of Gershwin's opera, it was many things to many people, even to many nations. No performance template had congealed—would ever congeal—with regard to venue, vocal style, or abridgment and modification. For Goldwyn himself, *Porgy and Bess* was a valedictory: in a press release announcing that he had obtained screen rights for his favorite show, he also announced that it would be his farewell. Born Shmuel Goldfisz in 1879 to a Chasidic Polish family, Goldwyn had been producing motion pictures since 1913. *Arrowsmith* (1931), *Dodsworth* (1936), *Wuthering Heights* (1939), *The Little Foxes* (1941), and *The Best Years of Our Lives* (1946) were among the most highly regarded of his seventy-nine films. His signature "Goldwynisms" included "A verbal contract isn't worth the paper it's written on"; "Every director bites the hand that lays the golden egg"; and "Go see it and see for yourself why you shouldn't see it." It was also he, it will be recalled, who had once told Gershwin he should write "hits" like Irving Berlin did.

Goldwyn sought a lavish and prestigious Gershwin entertainment emblazoned with his name. Issues of authenticity and musical continuity were not likely to preoccupy him. But Goldwyn was inescapably burdened with issues of race that had not surfaced in 1935. Auditioning for Gershwin in 1935, Todd Duncan had chosen to sing an Italian aria. Anne Brown, at her audition, sang in French and German. When Gershwin asked her for a spiritual, she grew defensive. "George Gershwin simply looked long at me and he said, 'Ah huh, I understand.' And I realized that he *did* understand and then I wanted more than anything else to sing a spiritual for him. How dumb I had been! Wasn't this to be an opera about Negroes? . . . So I sang a spiritual, 'A City Called Heaven.' And when I finished I knew that I had never sung it better nor would I ever sing it better." Though in the thirties some black writers expressed ambivalence toward *Porgy and Bess*, and though Virgil Thomson considered Gershwin's choice of subject matter naïve, these reservations did not resonate with the opera's black cast. By the fifties, however, black artists were less readily susceptible to *Porgy and Bess*.

William Warfield, Robert Breen's most celebrated 1950s Porgy, was an exception: a true believer, he called *Porgy and Bess* "a celebration of our [black] culture, and not an exploitation of it. . . . It ennobled the characters it depicted. . . . Almost without exception the reviewers in Europe recognized *Porgy and Bess* for what it was—a story of triumph, not degradation." But some members of the black press objected more vituperatively to Gershwin's opera than any had in the thirties. An editorial in the *Pittsburgh Courier* perceived "depraved members of the colored minority in America engaged in its stereotyped role . . . a vehicle of shame, sorrow and disgust." James Hicks, in Baltimore's *Afro-American*, called the Breen revival "the most insulting, the most libelous, the most degrading act that could possibly be perpetrated against colored Americans of modern time." And events would shortly prove that prominent black performers had doubts of their own.[18]

Goldwyn was far from the first Hollywood producer to want to make *Porgy and Bess* into a movie. As early as 1937, Gershwin predicted that his opera would eventually be filmed despite trepidations "on account of the colored question."[19] Goldwyn obtained the film rights for $650,000 in 1957—when debate on Gershwin and the colored question was peaking. Hollywood, suddenly a significant battleground in the fight for racial equality, acquired a small number of glamorous black stars of broad appeal. Goldwyn duly offered *Porgy and Bess* to Harry Belafonte and Lena Horne. Both said no. Then he tried Sidney Poitier and Dorothy Dandridge. Though both said yes, Dandridge was unenthusiastic and Poitier never sought the role. Rather, Lillian Schary Small, a sometime associate of Poitier's agent Martin Baum, sought and acquired it for him. Ultimately, Poitier agreed only on condition that he also be cast in a film he coveted—*The Defiant Ones*.[20]

If in retrospect Belafonte and Poitier were equally implausible as Porgy, Goldwyn's choice as director was less plausible still. When Elia Kazan, Frank Capra, and King Vidor turned him down, Goldwyn offered *Porgy and Bess* to Rouben Mamoulian. Mamoulian could only say yes. *Porgy* had made him famous. He esteemed Gershwin as a genius and *Porgy and Bess* as a masterpiece; he knew better than anyone the magnitude of his contributions to both. He had endured the restagings by Crawford and Breen. His own career, in Hollywood and on Broadway, was dipping. Goldwyn, however, equally claimed possession of *Porgy and Bess*. At the age of seventy-seven, he would be confronted with artistic and political challenges different from any he had faced in more than four decades of filmmaking. Finally, the immigrants Mamoulian and Goldwyn were a study in contrasts so extreme—the one a born aristocrat schooled in Russian experimental theater, the other a graduate of the Jewish glove trade—that their formidably unruly egos were, on balance, what they most had in common. The circumstances would precipitate both a firing and an actual fire.

DEBACLE

The conductor-composer André Previn, born in 1929, is a rare surviving Hollywood hand who worked collaboratively with Mamoulian. Before becoming known as a symphonic conductor, Previn was a reckonable Hollywood musical force; between 1946 and 1975, he served as music director, conductor, or composer for more than three dozen films—including Mamoulian's *Silk Stockings*, with songs by Cole Porter, and *Porgy and Bess*, for which he adapted the score and conducted the soundtrack. His four Oscars are for *My Fair Lady, Irma la Douce, Gigi,* and *Porgy and Bess.*

Silk Stockings—which turned out to be Mamoulian's final completed assignment, in Hollywood or on Broadway—was for Mamoulian "just a job," according to Previn. But *Porgy and Bess*, coming next, elicited from Mamoulian the kind of comprehensive attention that had once been his devilish signature. Previn:

> He was very nice to me, a great help. He liked to just sit and tell stories about *Oklahoma!* or *Carousel*. In this capacity, he was wonderful to be with. He was endlessly entertaining. His stories were always really good, fascinating, riveting. And yet he was a kind of loner. His whole way of working was to be in the center; others made circles around him, but he didn't invite them in. I admired him a lot for his willingness to consider new ideas. For instance, I had a far-out idea for "My Man's Gone Now." I asked him, "What if the orchestral interludes got more and more out of tune—a little sharp, a little flat—as a way of intensifying the piece?" Any other director would have said, 'Behave yourself.' But Mamoulian got it. He actually experimented on his

own, with a phonograph, playing with the speed—and then decided no. Ultimately, things happened pretty much his way, or forget it. But he liked novelty, he was open to it.[21]

Mamoulian's preparatory materials for Goldwyn's film document how assiduously he rethought Gershwin's score. In memos to Goldwyn and Previn, he stressed the need to condense without violating the musical structure of the whole. The "sense of time" is different on screen, he said—one minute was equivalent to five minutes on stage. Though he had retained some of Gershwin's recitatives in 1935, he considered them too "operatic" and "European," as well as "too slow," for film. Perusing the vocal score page by page (an 18-page memo), he advocated excising nearly all of the recitatives, but in such a way as to avoid "a film with songs and ensembles interspersed with purely dialogue scenes." As had Cheryl Crawford, he replaced sung with spoken speech. For the most part, he here retained Gershwin's accompaniments; in some places, he recommended silencing the orchestra. There were also episodes that he wanted musically elongated. He incorporated his "Occupational Humoresque" and the Orphanage Band—ingredients unseen and unheard since 1935. He recommended eliminating the "Buzzard Song." He considered trimming "Oh Bess, Oh Where's My Bess?" as in 1935, but ultimately opted to keep the entire song, albeit as a Porgy aria rather than the trio Gershwin composed for Porgy, Maria, and Serena. To close, he wanted to add an extra repetition of "Oh Lord, I'm On My Way," transposed upward.

To write the script, Goldwyn had engaged N. Richard Nash, whose acclaimed Broadway output included *The Rainmaker* (1954). Nash's first draft attempted various brave departures from Heyward's libretto. Mamoulian's feedback, in a memo, was irritable. "Porgy has become a saccharine 'orphan in the storm' figure, so very sorry for himself. . . . Bess also sentimentalized. . . . Maria is completely false and anachronistic in the scene with the Detective—she should never talk [back] to him like that—nor would he stand for it for a minute. . . . Additions and extensions are not integrated into the musical structure." As the script moved through five drafts, Goldwyn, too, had much to contribute, jostling with Mamoulian for authority over Nash. And Mamoulian minutely supervised Oliver Smith's Catfish Row set design. He acknowledged the need for something larger than a stage set, but "within proper bounds so that it is not open to the usual reproach that Hollywood automatically magnifies and glamorizes everything it touches. While stylized, the set should still convey the illusion of reality and authenticity." Mamoulian found Smith's initial design "too grand in feeling, too large in its dimensions." He insisted that the set be so proportioned that a Todd-AO widescreen long shot would encompass its entire back wall and height. He wanted stylized proportions, with lower ceilings for the higher floors, and windows and doors "more closely spaced than in real life." The "basic impression," he instructed, should be an "isolated community," a "courtyard" rather than a "small town square." He scrutinized colors, props, surfaces.[22]

By midsummer, the set was ready, as were the costumes. Hermes Pan had completed creating the necessary choreography. Dialogue rehearsals had finished. And the bulk of the score had been recorded by Previn. All the singing was to be dubbed. Sammy Davis, Jr. (Sporting Life), Brock Peters (Crown), and Pearl Bailey (Maria) dubbed their own voices. Porgy and Bess were Robert McFerrin and Adele Addison. Serena was Inez Matthews. Louie Jean Norman (a white soprano nominated by Previn) sang "Summertime" for Diahann Carroll, playing Clara. As a guide to the conductor, Mamoulian had determined in detail what gestures and movements the singing would accompany. Previn was impressed. He recalls no evidence of the crippling problems Mamoulian would impose on *Cleopatra*.

Shadowing these painstaking plans was an ominous undercurrent aggravated by Goldwyn's publicized difficulties in finding black actors for black roles. Both the National Association for the Advancement of

Colored People and the Council for the Improvement of Negro Theatre Arts had urged black performers to boycott the film. An advertisement placed by the latter organization in *The Hollywood Reporter* read: "Dorothy and DuBose Heyward used the race situation in the South to write a lot of allegories in which Negroes were violent or gentle, humble or conniving, and given to erupting with all sorts of goings on after their day's work in the white folks' kitchen or the white folks' yard was over, like sniffing happy dust, careless love, crapshooting, drinking, topping it all off with knife play." When a 4 A.M. fire destroyed Goldwyn's Catfish Row on July 2, 1958, arson was instantly suspected. Filming had been scheduled to begin later the same day. Hollywood's second-largest sound stage lay in ruins. The front page of the *Los Angeles Evening Mirror News* screamed:

> $5 MILLION FILM FIRE;
> HINT RACE ROW ARSON
>
> A mystery flash fire early today destroyed Stage 8 housing the controversial "Porgy and Bess" sets on the Goldwyn studios lot. . . . Arson squad detectives were investigating reports that protests against production of "Porgy and Bess" . . . had been received by the studio . . . minority groups had been bitter over the studio's plans to produce the Gershwin musical.[23]

Goldwyn soldiered on, quickly re-creating the costumes and set. Mamoulian, in new production notes, seized this opportunity to make the windows wider, giving more "elbow room" to the actors therein. He wanted shutters with "more color differentiation between shutters and walls." He wanted a courtyard surface "more uneven and more variegated in color." He wanted Porgy's room larger and with a higher ceiling. Previn considered the result "the ultimate theatrical set. The amount of detail was indescribable Mamoulian even argued about the door handles."

It was on July 27—twenty-five days after the fire—that Rouben Mamoulian was publicly terminated by Samuel Goldwyn. Goldwyn issued a press release avowing "I have the greatest respect for Rouben Mamoulian, but he and I could not see eye to eye on various matters." Goldwyn also announced that Otto Preminger would "direct 'Porgy and Bess' when production is resumed." In response, Mamoulian issued a press release of his own, beginning:

> Mr. Goldwyn's bland statement masks a story of deceit and calumny. In a suit, which I propose to file against Mr. Goldwyn, it will be necessary at long last to expose his publicity greed, his professional hypocrisy and selfishness.
>
> In the eight months that I have been working on "Porgy and Bess" for the screen . . . there has not been one iota of dissension between me and Mr. Goldwyn concerning "Porgy and Bess."
>
> There have been, however, other dissensions on his part unrelated to the production which were trespasses upon my private and professional life.

Goldwyn, Mamoulian told the press, insisted on being identified "as the sole creator of 'Porgy and Bess.'" He had demanded that Mamoulian discharge his press agent, Russell Birdwell. He had threatened to ruin Mamoulian "economically and professionally."[24]

In a subsequent deposition, Mamoulian alleged an excruciating back story. He had been summoned to Goldwyn's office on June 6. Goldwyn screamed at him for some fifteen or twenty minutes, shaking his fists and pointing his finger. When Mamoulian inquired "what was eating him," Goldwyn replied: "I'm glad you asked me this question. I will tell you why—you have been talking to the press, and you have engaged Russell Birdwell as your press agent. I want to you fire him immediately." Mamoulian told Goldwyn he had no more right "to tell me to fire Mr. Birdwell . . . than he had the right to ask me to fire my gardener or housekeeper." Goldwyn, Mamoulian's deposition continued, replied that all publicity would emanate from Goldwyn himself, as the film's "sole creator"—and that "I better give in to him or else!" Mamoulian then walked out on Goldwyn. There was a second such meeting twenty-four days later. This time Goldwyn had Mamoulian sit on a couch and began, "You know I love you, don't you, Rouben?" He proceeded to extol Mamoulian, who found himself "on the verge of hugging [Goldwyn] and believing what he said." Then Goldwyn explained his maxim "to love each other, to love man, to be decent and kind to everybody." "He asked me if I ever heard him boast about himself or his achievements or his pictures. . . . I sat there spellbound, fascinated, in a kind of horrible way, not believing my eyes and ears." Now Goldwyn reminded Mamoulian of the fabulous wealth and power he had amassed. He said he had recently met with the President of the United States, who had talked to him "like he was a carpenter . . . because he was talking to me, and I am a very important, powerful man." Eventually, Goldywn told Mamoulian: "The point is: Do you realize what it will mean if I take you off 'Porgy and Bess'? It will have world-wide publicity. It will ruin your career . . . you will never work again." And he again demanded that Mamoulian fire Birdwell. Mamoulian again walked out on Goldwyn. Mamoulian continued to give interviews to the press, insisting his prerogative to do so as long as the subject matter was unrelated to his work for Goldwyn. On July 9 he was invited to dinner at the Goldwyns' house. "Mr. and Mrs. Goldwyn behaved like two very good hosts, most cordial and friendly." He learned of his dismissal eighteen days later.[25]

Mamoulian's ensuing battle with Goldwyn[26]—in the course of which Mamoulian's account of his jousts with Goldwyn was never challenged—was fought in public. The inordinate vehemence and tenacity of Mamoulian's efforts calibrated the personal and professional stakes at hand. Mamoulian felt betrayed by Hollywood itself. And he had resolved to do something about it. Directors must not serve at the whim of philistine moguls. Studio heads must be held accountable for their behavior. Goldwyn had fired Mamoulian without cause, assuming that paying the balance of Mamoulian's salary—which he promptly did—would satisfy his contractual obligations. Goldwyn had hired Preminger at a salary twice Mamoulian's, Preminger had previously displaced Mamoulian on *Laura*, Preminger had no experience with *Porgy and Bess*, Preminger did not remotely command Mamoulian's musical sophistication—it was just too much.

The Screen Directors Guild quickly entered the dispute in a mediating capacity. Mamoulian pled his case in detail. He also stated: "I wouldn't have bothered you if I did not have a deep feeling that this thing in which I am the focal point is of great importance to the whole Guild. I think it is important to the whole industry. I don't think it is stretching the truth to say I think it is important to our national life—whether we still have a democracy or whether we have a dictatorship." He added: "I feel what is right is right and I will fight for it if I have to die for it. I am not going to buckle down to this toy dictator." Goldwyn refused to talk to the Screen Directors Guild unless he were interviewed in his own office. No such interview took place. But Mamoulian was overeager. He called a press conference and produced Leigh Whipper, the Crab Man of his 1935 *Porgy and Bess*, now reengaged for Goldwyn's film. Whipper announced he was quitting the production and continued: "I believe that the proposed *Porgy and Bess* is now in hands unsympathetic to my people." This miscalculation was fundamental and inexplicable: all of Hollywood realized that Preminger was a pioneering advocate for blacks in film. He had directed a distinguished black cast in *Carmen Jones* (1954). As many observed as pertinent, Dorothy Dandridge, his Carmen, was at one time his girlfriend. Through his attorney, he demanded that disciplinary action be taken against Mamoulian for libel.[27]

Meanwhile, Mamoulian's agent, Irving Lazar, had been urging his client to back down and make peace with Goldwyn. When Mamoulian publicly refused, Lazar, in Paris, added an extraordinary cable communication to what was already a rollicking Hollywood sideshow. "It had been my intention not to make any statement with reference to the Mamoulian Goldwyn controversy until I returned to California," Lazar wrote on August 10. "However since Mamoulian has stated publicly facts which are contradictory to the actual events and stated that I was derelict in my obligations to him I feel that I cannot wait until I return." Lazar proceeded to dispute Mamoulian's claim that he only learned he was fired by reading a newspaper. Rather, according to Lazar, Goldwyn's announcement ("I have the greatest respect for Rouben Mamoulian, . . .") had been mutually drafted by Mamoulian, Goldwyn, and Birdwell—albeit without the half-sentence naming Preminger to take Mamoulian's place. Though the Screen Directors Guild formally determined that Mamoulian's dismissal was insupportable, and that SDG members were not to work for Goldwyn, the old man was finished making movies anyway. Ringside sentiment now in fact shifted in Goldwyn's favor. And, for Mamoulian, there was worse to come.[28]

On February 2, with the release of *Porgy and Bess* months away, Mamoulian made it known to the SDG that he protested Goldwyn's intention to give Preminger sole credit for directing *Porgy and Bess*. Instead, he wanted an onscreen credit reading "directed by Rouben Mamoulian and Otto Preminger"—with "Mamoulian" coming first. He cited the eight and a half months he had dedicated to the film, plus "all the knowledge and experience accumulated in 30 years of working intermittently on that subject on stage." He said he had cast all the principal roles as well as the chorus; collaborated on Nash's script through five versions; "single-handedly" compressed the musical score (and was "repeatedly congratulated" by Previn and Goldwyn for this work); offered advice and expertise on the film's sets, costumes, and props; directed two and a half months of rehearsals; and supervised recordings of approximately eighty minutes of Gershwin's score. Behind the scenes, Mamoulian's colleagues urged him to drop this chimerical request, but he persevered. Hearings were duly convened by the Directors Guild. Preminger testified that all of Mamoulian's preparatory work had been modified or discarded; only the cast remained. Preminger also claimed that Previn denied having worked with Mamoulian on the recording sessions—which were, he further claimed, in any case unusable.[29]

On February 10, Mamoulian received a telegram from Joseph Young-erman, executive secretary of the SDG. It read in full:

DEAR ROUBEN THE BOARD GAVE OUT THE FOLLOWING
STATEMENT "THE BOARD OF DIRECTORS LAST NIGHT
UNANIMOUSLY DETERMINED THAT SOLE DIRECTORIAL
CREDITS FOR 'PORGY AND BESS' SHOULD BE GIVEN TO OTTO
PREMINGER" REGARDS JOE

Eight days later, Mamoulian wrote back: "Now that the determination has been made, I would much appreciate, as a member of the SDG, if you would kindly inform me, for my enlightenment, as to what were the reasons upon which your decision was based." He received in reply a letter from George Stevens, writing as vice president of the Directors Guild, explaining that "the Board felt, basically, there must be some point of reference to use in determining whether a Director is entitled to credit on a film. After prolonged discussion, the concensus [sic] of the Board was that at the very minimum, a Director must have directed scenes which appear on the screen."[30]

However Mamoulian may have processed this communication, and continuing coverage of his Goldwyn debacle in the press, his Holly-wood reputation lay tattered. Not only had he misplayed his hand; ultimately, his behavior disclosed a distressed loss of contact with reality.

PREMINGER'S FILM

Remembering when Preminger took over from Mamoulian, Previn reflects: "You cannot think of two more disparate directors. It was like a skit from *Saturday Night Live*. Otto's treatment of the actors was cruel, just dreadful. As for the music, I don't think anybody decided anything. Goldwyn and Preminger wanted to dub Diahann Carroll as Clara. They wanted a trained soprano. But Diahann could have sung 'Summertime.' No one understood the 'Occupational Humoresque'—they all thought it was just a sound effect. I thought the film got further and further away from Gershwin; it made me nervous. Goldwyn's attitude was 'it's my studio.' And it's true, he signed the checks. It really was his money." Goldwyn, succumbing to the Red Scare, told Previn he would be fired if any Communists were discovered in his orchestra. Preminger and Goldwyn held daily shouting matches about which Preminger later boasted: "People used to gather under the open window of my office to hear me bellow at him over the telephone."[31]

On the set, Pearl Bailey refused to wear a bandana or act in bare feet. Poitier resisted the script's dialect, preserving something like the clipped, suave articulation of his characteristic screen persona. At a moment when Poitier was a leading force in achieving new screen roles for black actors, *Porgy*'s dramatis personae seemed unacceptably "stereotypical" to the black playwright Lorraine Hansberry. Speaking on television—and quoted in *Variety*—she argued: "Over a period of time, [we] have apparently decided that within American life [there is] one great repository where we're going to focus and imagine sensuality and exaggerate sexuality . . . and this great image is the American Negro."[32]

Meanwhile, on February 16, 1959, a smiling Sam Goldwyn was treated to a lavish encomium in *Life* magazine. Calling Gershwin the "greatest American composer" and *Porgy and Bess* "the greatest play . . . in the history of American musical theater," Goldwyn said: "They couldn't afford to do in the theater what I'm doing." He had been "stunned" by his casting troubles. The article matter-of-factly rehearsed the dismissal of Mamoulian and its notorious aftermath with the evasive comment: "Trouble between Goldwyn and Mamoulian had been building up for some time." When the finished film was privately screened at the studio, Goldwyn felt fulfilled. Previn remembers: "One thing you can say about

Goldwyn: he adored his movies. And when that screening ended—Otto was not there, by the way—old man Goldwyn was weeping. He put his arm around me and said, 'You should be god-damn proud, kid. You should never do another thing in your life.' On the other hand, when I wanted to borrow some of my orchestrations to do a *Porgy* concert, he said no."[33]

"Samuel Goldwyn's *Porgy and Bess*"[34] opened at Broadway's Warner Theatre on June 24, 1959. Goldwyn initially offered it for reserved-seat runs in opulent movie palaces in major cities. The critical reception was exceptionally mixed—a gauge of mixed ingredients that included Gershwin's unstable reputation, confusion over genre, and sensitivity to race. Bosley Crowther, in the *New York Times*, found *Porgy and Bess* "stunning, exciting, and moving"—"it bids fair to be as much a classic on the screen as it is on the stage." Richard L. Coe, in the *Washington Post*, wrote: "Since Goldwyn chooses to call this 'Samuel Goldwyn's,' he can have it." Coe was displeased with the dubbing, the static direction, the "obviously theatrical" set and neat costumes. *Time* magazine was unhappy with Gershwin, Goldwyn, and Preminger in equal measure. *Ebony* magazine ran an article titled "Why Negroes Don't Like *Porgy and Bess*."

> We do not want to see six-foot Sidney Poitier on his knees crying for a slit-skirted wench who did him wrong. We do not want the wench to be beautiful Dorothy Dandridge who sniffs "happy dust" and drinks liquor from a bottle at the rim of an alley crap game. . . . We do not like to hear our intelligent (Porgy has the highest per cent of college degrees ever recorded by a movie) stars speak in dialect, [to] see them reduced to the level of Catfish Row when they have already risen to the heights of La Scala. We do not want to see them crawl even in make-believe dust after they have walked with their heads in the clouds.

Dorothy Heyward, age sixty-nine, was quoted by United Press International: "I have no quarrel with either Mr. Goldwyn or Mr. Preminger, who did a good workmanlike job, but there were certain Mamoulian touches that I so liked in the original play and the original stage musical version that are not in the film. I do miss them." *Porgy and Bess* was only shown briefly in general release. It earned back half its cost. In 1972, when his father's lease on the rights expired, Samuel Goldwyn, Jr., requested permission from the Gershwin Estate to rerelease *Porgy and Bess* and was turned down. Since then, all prints of the original six-track stereophonic print seem to have vanished. An uncut version may be viewed on a television monitor at the Library of Congress.[35]

To watch Samuel Goldwyn's *Porgy and Bess* through the eyes of Rouben Mamoulian—to encounter it today in the context of the present book—is an excruciating experience.* Goldwyn and Preminger violate the realms Mamoulian owned: music and sound. This *Porgy and Bess* commences with an elegant blue curtain and an extended overture. The curtain rises to credits—and a second, shorter overture. The trouble with both overtures is that they are perfectly competent tune medleys, lushly scored for an 80-piece orchestra. Gershwin's *Porgy and Bess* eschews any overture; it sends the message: my *Porgy and Bess* is *sui generis*. Goldwyn's glossy *Porgy and Bess* overtures[36] send a different message: my *Porgy and Bess* is conventional—it's a show, and as glamorous as possible. Next comes "Summertime," with Louie Jean Norman singing through the lips of Diahann Carroll. At the beginning of *Love Me Tonight*, as we have observed, Mamoulian subtly increases the loudness of a hammer blow when the camera moves closer. At the beginning of Goldwyn's *Porgy and Bess*, Carroll moves near or far, even turns her back on us, and the volume knob does not budge. She "sings" her long high B directly into the ear of her husband while vigorously handing him their baby—and (of course) he does not flinch. This crudity of sound design is a constant feature. The dubbing is lamentable. Not only is the synchronization of music and image rarely credible; Poitier's soft-grained

---

*According to his diary, Mamoulian first saw the Preminger film on June 20, 1974, on Australian television—and found it an "absolute horror." (I am indebted to Kurt Jensen for this information.)

high baritone is not remotely a match of Robert McFerrin's throaty bass-baritone. Poitier, on the set, confided to Previn that he had no ear for music;[37] feigning song, this distinguished actor is clueless. As he more "sings" than speaks, we are confronted with the enigma of two Porgies, one intermittently inhabiting the other.

The score as first edited by Mamoulian for Previn is used to a degree. Many abridgments, many instructions regarding the replacement of recitatives, are retained. But Mamoulian's treatment would have created a much longer film—his trimmed numbers are therefore trimmed some more. The results are not always happy—at one minute, 45 seconds, the "Occupational Humoresque" (for which Previn hired more than a dozen additional percussionists) is not worth the trouble. Mamoulian's extra reprise of "Oh, Lord, I'm On My Way" is kept—Previn duly modulates from D major to F. In the orchestra, a lot of music is recomposed, even newly composed.

Though Preminger had earlier directed a musical film—*Carmen Jones*—there is no evidence of special skill in this department. Staging songs and choruses, he rarely volunteers a fresh idea, and some ideas are mistakes. In the opera *Porgy and Bess*, the huddled choristers singing "Dere's Somebody Knockin' At My Door" imagine an apocalyptic visitor inflicted by the raging storm. But Preminger has already shown us that it is merely Crown who is knocking. The operatic potency of the moment is canceled; it becomes yet another entertainment.

Mamoulian, in his memos to Goldwyn, worried that Porgy would seem "saccharine" and Bess "sentimental," that Oliver Smith's Catfish Row would seem "glamorous," "too grand." In his absence, these prophecies came true. So sanitized is Goldwyn's *Porgy and Bess* that we feel we are witnessing affluent African-Americans inhabiting a movie set. Bess is not "getting old now." Porgy is soft-spoken and suave; his mature flash of anger at a white detective is pure Poitier. Neither character evolves. Neither embodies the resonant archetypes secured by Mamoulian in 1927 and 1935.

Mamoulian wanted a main set he could frame in a single long shot. He individually auditioned the members of the chorus, so he could utilize them as individuals, or en masse in elaborately detailed tableaus. He enlarged Smith's windows in order to furnish more elbow room for the inhabitants as they reacted to courtyard events below. His entire modus operandi would have fostered a nonrealistic aesthetic—an aesthetic suited to Smith's beautifully synthetic Catfish Row. But Preminger's Catfish Row community is as aimless and passive as Mamoulian's had been active, expressive, and "stylized." As employed by Preminger, the calculated artifice of Mamoulian's set becomes a problem.

On its own terms—standard Hollywood terms—Samuel Goldwyn's *Porgy and Bess* is a reasonable confection. The tunes are great. The score is handsomely sung and conducted. Poitier is a strong if incongruous presence. The décor and costumes are pleasing. Preminger's eschewal of close-ups supports the wide-screen visual aesthetic. Though critics of the film complained that Porgy, Bess, Sporting Life, and Crown are stereotypes, a greater problem is that Goldwyn's *Porgy and Bess* is itself a Hollywood stereotype reinforcing a Gershwin stereotype. Shallow entertainment masquerading as high art, it makes insidiously plausible the view that Gershwin merchandised ersatz majesty and tragedy, that he was a tunesmith tackling more than he could handle.

FORCED RETIREMENT

How Mamoulian managed to survive his Goldwyn debacle is a question whose answer—if it can be called that—was his impossible deportment attempting *Cleopatra. Porgy and Bess*, which had made him, had also ruined him. He never again directed a play or a film to fruition.

Over the course of nearly three subsequent decades, Mamoulian wrote a book for children, *Abigayil: The Story of the Cat at the Manger* (1964) and a version of *Hamlet* in modern English (1965). He occupied himself with copious personal reflections, typically titled "Jottings" or "Notes from a Desk Pad." His *Hamlet* received a single production, in 1966, in Lexington, Kentucky; he did not direct. In 1980 he was inducted into the Broadway Hall of Fame. Three years later, he received the D. W. Griffith Award for Lifetime Achievement from the Directors Guild of America. Though he never formally retired, his withdrawal from professional responsibilities was complete. Whether or not he was blacklisted, as some maintain, he emerged a pariah from his *Porgy and Bess* and *Cleopatra* wars. Previn remembers a dinner party at the Mamoulians': "George Sidney of the Director's Guild was there with his wife, Lillian Burns, an acting coach at MGM who was as loony as they come. Mamoulian remarked that he could never work for Samuel Goldwyn again. Lillian exploded, it was a moment out of *Electra*—'How dare you! How can you insult Sam Goldwyn!' Rouben tried to change the subject but she couldn't be stopped. 'He's a great man and you're not! George, we're leaving.' And they left."[38]

A typical "late Mamoulian" interview—by Philip K. Scheuer in the April 5, 1970, *Los Angeles Times*—paid respect to an eminence grise. It rehearsed his catalogue of innovations, beginning with *Applause*. "A perfectionist of what is now known, unhappily, as the old school, [Mamoulian] says unequivocably, 'If I couldn't have full authority I would resign. I stand by everything I've ever done—credit or criticism, it was mine. I can't blame the producer, the actor or anyone else.'" Mamoulian's lifelong credo remained intact:

We make a distinction between the [art and entertainment]. Ridiculous! If it's not entertainment it must be very poor art. In the whole of the arts, what have been greater "box office" than Shakespeare, Michelangelo, Da Vinci, all the great composers? For me, at the age of 18 I had a sort of artistic philosophy, art for art's sake. I outlived it by the time was I was 19. Art is for life's sake! The first always results in artificial productions—although one may now and then catch on as a fad. With a very high rate of mortality; after a few years it's dead as a doornail. The goal is to add to the beauty and dignity of man.

If we agree that the world is in such a total mess—absolutely appalling—then I say of those who are engaged in any art, especially the profession of movie-making, that it certainly puts an obligation on them. It's the only art mankind invented that is 60 years old—as against thousands for others. . . .

With the arts we still have a hope. When they fail we have great reason to worry, not only for the state of the nation but for the state of the world.

The stories Mamoulian told Scheuer were the stories he had always told—of successfully cajoling actors and technicians, of combating Hollywood philistines. Meanwhile, in hundreds of pages of Jottings, he excoriated "new permissiveness" in art and society—a decline in moral standards and social integration. He felt estranged from naturalism and nudity in American cinema—and equally from the French "New Wave." He insisted that art uplift.

The private "Notes from a Desk Pad" that Mamoulian amassed reprised these themes in the context of detailed recollections of his early Hollywood output, beginning with *Applause*. He extensively reported the banalities of television (but was evidently watching a lot of it). He apparently envisioned turning his Notes into a book (and prepared a detailed title page for this implausible project). He also signed a contract with Knopf to write an autobiography. Meanwhile, his aged parents died—in 1966 and 1972—and his wife Azadia declined into violent alcoholism and dementia. Though Azadia's behavior precluded keeping domestic help in their Beverly Hills home, he resisted institutionalizing her. When in 1975 she was away, he wrote a poem:

> We miss you so, our red-haired beauty,
> And not just out of sense of duty,
> But out of fondest love for you.
> Your absence makes us feel so blue!
> From day to day we're getting thinner,

Because we hardly touch our dinner.
We look and sniff, but do not eat,
That goes for crispies and for meat.
Without you every food tastes sour.
And so we pray from hour to hour
With all our hearts to the Power above
To heal and bless our sweet dear love
And bring her home, so that we may
Enjoy our meals again and play.[39]

Azadia's role in Mamoulian's own decline is ponderable; subsequent to their marriage, in 1947, his output plummeted. A painter, Azadia was born in Washington, D.C., to great wealth. She did not mingle with Mamoulian's Armenian acquaintances in Los Angeles; they agreed with his mother that she was an unfortunate influence. According to the Los Angeles Archbishop Vatché Hovsepian: "As I observed his conversations with his wife, he was always careful and hesitant. She was like a spoiled woman, controlling his life. Mamoulian himself was very calm; he generated warmth. I would say he became an increasingly passive person. He talked about Elizabeth Taylor missing rehearsals for *Cleopatra*. Mainly, he would talk about *Porgy and Bess*." The theater historian Miles Kreuger, who knew Mamoulian in the years of Azadia's infirmity, recalls:

Rouben and Azadia were inseparable. She barely knew how to boil an egg, you know. She used to say: "When I was growing up, we were told never to learn to do anything." They had a big house on Schuyler Road, a ranch house surprisingly without style, without elegance. One day when I visited Rouben—we were sitting in a dark dining room; he didn't even turn the lights on—he said to me, "There's no food in the house." He gave me a one hundred dollar bill and asked me to go to Hamburger Hamlet and get some hamburgers and salad. On another occasion, he asked me "Do you think Azadia is suffering from that terrible disease?" I said, "Do you mean Alzheimer's? I suspect it's very likely; you have to take her to a specialist. I think her condition is destroying your life. Maybe you should consider moving her into a special home of some kind." But he wouldn't consider that.[40]

When in 1986 Mamoulian's health precluded his attendance at a fiftieth-anniversary celebration of the Directors Guild, he appeared on camera to address the gathering. Disheveled and gaunt, yet worldly and charming, he extemporized a lecture on cinema as "the most universal, most powerful medium in the world," "an international human language."

> At this time when the world is so fragmented, in such a sad state . . . we don't do enough films that can carry a message that can balance all this horror that is going on. . . . I don't mean . . . sissy films and funny entertainment. Because for me all real art is entertainment—while not all entertainment is art.[41]

Mamoulian died a year later at the age of ninety, a victim of spreading prostate cancer. The house was overrun with the Mamoulians' cats—more than forty of them. Feces and urine had destroyed the furnishings. That Mamoulian died intestate was final testimony to his flight from reality. The *New York Times* obituary was perfunctory.

PORGY AND BESS RESURGENT

Porgy and Bess enjoyed a happier post-Goldwyn fate. Though the New York City Opera mounted *Porgy and Bess* in 1962 and 1963, Gershwin's opera remained little seen. The music historian Richard Crawford, surveying the controversial history of *Porgy and Bess* among African-Americans as of 1972, reported, "Its survival as an opera may be jeopardized for reasons only partly related to the music." But *Porgy and Bess* was (as ever) successful overseas, including productions in New Zealand, Estonia, and Tel Aviv. Götz Friedrich—a leading figure abroad—directed *Porgy and Bess* in 1970 for East Berlin's Komische Oper; calling it "absolutely one of [my] favorite operas," he remounted *Porgy* in West Berlin in 1988 and thereafter.[42] A landmark American concert performance, signaling a sea change, was Loren Maazel's with the Cleveland Orchestra in 1976, followed the same year by a Houston Grand Opera production that would tour triumphantly through 1987; the venues included a Broadway theater and Radio City Music Hall.[43] In 1985, *Porgy and Bess* made its Metropolitan Opera debut under James Levine. The Cleveland, Houston, and Met productions all argued—with variable success—for an uncut or nearly uncut presentation, and so did Trevor Nunn's 1986 Glyndebourne production, conducted by Simon Rattle. *Porgy and Bess* suddenly enjoyed an unprecedented operatic pedigree—and so, concomitantly, did George Gershwin. Between 1995 and 2008, opera companies in Chicago, Dallas, Denver, Houston, Los Angeles, New York, San Diego, San Francisco, Seattle, and Washington, D.C., offered new stagings incorporating various abridgments. Nunn's 2006 London version employed dialogue and a new orchestration. So did Diane Paulus's controversial 2011 American Repertory Theater production, which moved on to Broadway from Cambridge.[44] Concurrently, *Rhapsody in Blue*, the Concerto in F, and *An American in Paris*—long ghettoized as pops pieces—entered the mainstream American symphonic repertoire.*

---

*In 1997, 2005, and 2005, the Boston Symphony Orchestra performed *Rhapsody in Blue*, *An American in Paris*, and the Piano Concerto in F, respectively—the first time any of these works had turned up on a Boston Symphony subscription program (rather than being presented by the Boston Pops). Jean-Yves Thibaudet, the soloist in the concerto, was incredulous when informed that his Boston performances were a landmark event. He added: "I was also told that in San Francisco I will be giving the first Concerto in F on subscription in 56 years. I thought they were joking." Among French pianists, Philippe Entremont, Pascal Rogé, and Hélène Grimaud are also Gershwin players. When Alexander Toradze defected to the United States from the Soviet Union in 1983, two American managers advised him not to perform the Concerto in F lest it harm his professional standing. Toradze commented, "In Russia, if you could improvise and play Gershwin, your reputation went up, not down." Nowadays, however, American-born conductors program Gershwin on subscrip-

In short, by the time Rouben Mamoulian died, Gershwin's cultural fluidity was honored as never before. His works for the concert hall and opera house have now acquired a vigorous multiple life. Enthusiastic Gershwin scholarship grows apace. It is no longer necessary to resort to a British writer—Wilfrid Mellers, in his *Music in a New Found Land* (1964)—to savor a clarion appreciation of *Porgy and Bess* that says things that were not said in 1935, and which were not previously said by an American:

> Its impact increases, rather than diminishes, with the passage of years. . . . What matters is that the moments of feeling should all be musically true. In this, Gershwin never lets us down. . . . There are greater twentieth-century operas: but not one which offers more of the qualities that opera used to have in its heyday, and must have again if it is to survive. Gershwin's *Porgy*, like the operas of Mozart or Verdi, is at once a social act, an entertainment, and a human experience with unexpectedly disturbing implications.

Meanwhile, the discourse on Porgy and race long ago peaked with Harold Cruse's *Crisis of the Negro Intellectual* (1967), which urged black Americans to seize control of their cultural identity. *Porgy and Bess*, Cruse wrote,

> must be criticized from the Negro point of view as the most perfect symbol of the Negro creative artist's cultural denial, degradation, exclusion, exploitation and acceptance of white paternity. . . . Negroes had no part in writing, directing, producing, or staging this folk-opera about Negroes. . . . [It] should be forever banned by all Negro performers in the United States. . . . If white producers want to stage this

---

tion with impunity. See Joseph Horowitz, "An Upstart Named Gershwin Gets His Shot," *New York Times*, Oct. 2, 2005.

folk-opera it should be performed by white performers made up in blackface, because it is distorted imitation all the way through.

No one any longer instructs black Americans to boycott *Porgy and Bess*.[45]

Gershwin chose to compose a black opera because he admired the African-American capacity for song and songful speech, and because he associated black self-expression with elemental feeling. Mamoulian appreciated the unmediated self-expression of his black singing actors; he therefore called them "children." These attitudes would of course not be acceptable today. But it remains pertinent that the blacks portrayed by Gershwin were from another, simpler time and place— which supported the extrapolation of archetypes. Neither Gershwin nor Mamoulian sought an "authentic" ethnographic rendering, after Heyward's novella. Rather, for them Porgy and Bess were elemental metaphors for humankind, buttressed by a milieu of heightened feeling and community. For Jack O'Brien, directing the Houston production, *Porgy and Bess* "was not a put-down of blacks, written by whites, but a moving story about people who happen to be black. I was determined to tell the truth about the show as I felt it, in terms of how it dealt with love, jealousy, death and adversity. What a revelation! The company went with me all the way."[46] Mellers is surely correct in inferring that Gershwin identified with Porgy, in asserting that Porgy (the character) is epic, that the ceremony of Robbins's funeral is "epic and communal." Once established, the pronounced universality of *Porgy and Bess* makes irrelevant the absence of explicit social analysis. It is about all of us.

POSTSCRIPT: CARMEN

A buried history—a series of unfulfilled expectations—fashions a tantalizing coda to the saga of Mamoulian and *Porgy and Bess*.

In fall 1950, Rudolf Bing took over the Metropolitan Opera intent on a housecleaning. Among other things, Bing was eager to do something about the way operas looked—a factor that had utterly distinguished *Porgy and Bess* from the Met in 1935. He resolved to engage important stage directors—and so Margaret Webster directed *Don Carlo* and *Aïda*, Tyrone Guthrie directed *Carmen*, Peter Brooks directed *Faust*, Garson Kanin directed *Die Fledermaus*, Alfred Lunt directed *Così fan tutte*, and Cyril Ritchard directed (and starred in) *La Périchole*. What is more, *Fledermaus*, *Così*, and *Périchole* were all done in English. But the director Bing most wanted was—a logical choice—Rouben Mamoulian.

Bing first wrote to Mamoulian on January 16, 1950, "extremely anxious to have you direct at the Met." He offered Mamoulian the new production that would inaugurate his regime—*Don Carlo*, a late Verdi masterpiece unseen in New York since 1922. He also offered Mamoulian *Die Fledermaus, Carmen*, or *La bohème*. On February 9, Bing wrote to Mamoulian again. Referring to *Don Carlo*, he said, "I want you to help me in making operatic history. . . . It would be disastrously disappointing if you had to let me down. . . . I am perfectly willing to give you first refusal of stage directing *Carmen* or any other work to be agreed upon in a subsequent season."[47]

Mamoulian's response was complex. He wrote back that he was reluctant to make commitments far in advance—he wanted to keep open his options in Hollywood and on Broadway. To others, he said he did not want to work at the Met—that he would have insufficient rehearsal, that the chorus could not act, and neither could the principal singers. He was also—as he told Bing—engaged in a Broadway *Huckleberry Finn* with Kurt Weill and Maxwell Anderson. Meanwhile, someone—Mamoulian himself, it was thought—leaked a story to the *Times* that Mamoulian would in fact direct *Don Carlo* for Bing. Weill and Anderson responded with consternation.

Bing's next letter to Mamoulian—dated February 22, 1950—began with a diatribe:

Dear Mr. Mamoulian:

I gather there is no change in the selfish, unreasonable and inconsiderate attitude of your friends which has forced you to a decision, which, considering the whole development of this affair, must now be looked upon as pretty unfair on me. However, let us not go over the past, and I shall be glad if you would very kindly at your earliest convenience, return to me the score and the translation of Don Carlos.

Mamoulian had evidently fingered Weill and Anderson in a phone conversation the previous Monday. Bing now pressed for *Die Fledermaus*—in English, with a "lovely cast" including Ljuba Welitsch as Rosalinda and Jarmila Novotna as Orlovsky: singers of formidable dramatic presence. Rolf Gerard would do sets and costumes. Fritz Reiner would conduct. "You know the work, and so there cannot be any difficulty of your getting familiar with it; it also meets your point that here is a well-known traditional classical operetta which can be done in a new way, and at the same time distinguished from its Broadway debasement.[48] Also, it will be done in English." This was an offer both shrewd and plausible, an assignment tailored to the director of *Love Me Tonight*. Nothing came of it.[49]

Kurt Weill died suddenly on April 3, 1950. Weeks later, Anderson and Mamoulian, having heard of a planned *Huckleberry Finn* MGM film musical that would compete with a *Huckleberry Finn* show, abandoned their Mark Twain project. Bing now offered Mamoulian *Pagliacci* and *Cavalleria rusticana, Rigoletto, Aïda*—anything. On May 15, 1950, he wrote to Mamoulian: "I am very sorry that Kurt Weill's tragic death makes the collapse of our negotiations appear even less necessary than I always thought it was. However, this cannot now be helped but you always said that you would like before anything else, to stage an opera of the good old stock repertory in order to be able to show more clearly what can be done with one or the other of the hackneyed works. This is exactly what I want to do. . . ." Finally, on February 10, 1951, Bing fixed his sights on

Carmen, for January 1952 with Risë Stevens and Richard Tucker in the leads, and Reiner in the pit. Mamoulian replied six days later:

> As fate would have it, only a few days ago I embarked upon two projects which . . . will keep me occupied for the whole next season. This makes the January "Carmen" at the Met impossible for me.
>
> I regret very much to miss this opportunity and pleasure of working with you. . . .
>
> I still hope that at some future time it will be possible for us to work together. I am in deepest sympathy with what you are trying to do and I admire the courage and determination with which you are cutting windows in the old Opera House and letting in some fresh air.[50]

Was Mamoulian actually interested in working at the Met? Dramatically, Tucker was self-evidently an impossible Don José. And, for Mamoulian, Stevens was an unacceptable Carmen. We happen to know this, because Mamoulian was intending to create his own film version of *Carmen*—in English, with dialogue—and to follow that with *Carmen* on Broadway. And he explicitly did not want Risë Stevens in the title role. Mamoulian's *Carmen* was in fact the future project he most mentioned in interviews in the fifties, sixties, and seventies. At one point, the *Hollywood Reporter* said it was scheduled for shooting in Spain. That it was for Mamoulian a labor of love cannot be doubted. He made his own preliminary English translation of the libretto. With Anderson, he created a shooting script cued to Bizet's score. In 1953, as a birthday present, Azadia presented her husband with his own *Carmen* script, typed in black (song) and red (dialogue), and bound in red leather.[51]

Even if George Gershwin had never mentioned *Carmen* as a model for working "song hits" into *Porgy and Bess*, even if Gershwin had never called *Carmen* and *Boris Godunov* the operas he most admired, that Mamoulian's *Carmen* project was partly *Porgy* progeny would be obvious. The two stories are cognates: Porgy the vulnerable José, Car-

men the temptress Bess, Crown the fighter Escamillo who lures the
girl away. Gershwin's outcast Gullahs are Bizet's Gypsies, the spirituals
girding their songs are in *Carmen* flamenco song and dance. Three other
factors potently supported Mamoulian's *Carmen* vision. First, there was
the memory of opera in English in Rochester, and on Broadway in 1935.
Second, there was his Hollywood Spanish epic, *Blood and Sand*, a bullring tragedy powered by destructive sexuality. Third, there was the sudden burst of Broadway opera—a decade after *Porgy and Bess*, Broadway
theaters hosted operas by Marc Blitzstein (*Regina*, 1948), Weill (*Street
Scene*, 1946), and Gian Carlo Menotti (*The Medium* and *The Telephone*,
1947; *The Consul*, 1950; *The Saint of Bleecker Street*, 1954), not to mention
Oscar Hammerstein's own Bizet adaptation: *Carmen Jones* (1943).

What Gershwin appreciated, citing those "song hits," was that *Carmen* blended art and entertainment. What Leonard Bernstein stressed,
dissecting *Carmen* on American television in 1962 and conducting it at
the Met in 1972, was that *Carmen* originated as an *opéra comique* with dialogue; only after Bizet's death did Ernest Guiraud add the recitatives that
everywhere transformed *Carmen* into grand opera. Bernstein argued
that *Carmen*, in effect, was a hybrid between opera and something like
American musical theater. But Mamoulian appreciated this years before.
In correspondence, he referred to his intention to interpolate not the
original French dialogue of Henri Meilhac and Ludovic Halévy, but
English-language dialogue of his own invention. When in August 1966
Walter Felsenstein produced *Carmen* at his East Berlin Komische Oper
with the dialogue restored and the recitatives removed, a friend sent
Mamoulian documentation with a note: "You were absolutely right
about the recitatives."[52]

Mamoulian left contradictory memos about casting his *Carmen*
film.[53] He did and did not resolve to avoid dubbing. He considered both
singers and actors. His prospective Carmens included Kathryn Gray-
son, Ann Blyth, Lana Turner, Jennifer Jones, Susan Hayward, and Gina

Lollabrigida, as well as a pair of alluring opera singers: Anna Moffo and Joanna Simon. (Through her agent, Risë Stevens contacted Mamoulian craving the part even though she knew he had not wanted her at the Met.)[54] Mamoulian's hypothetical Don Josés included Mario Lanza, Marlon Brando, and Ramón Vinay. He listed Howard Keel and George London among possible Escamillos. Vinay and London were demonic singing actors. Mainly, however, Mamoulian's glamour lists do not inspire confidence. And neither, alas, does the screenplay. And yet—as so often with Mamoulian—it bristles with points of fascination.

Mamoulian specialized in beginnings—*Applause, Jekyll and Hyde*, and *Love Me Tonight* are spectacular early examples; on stage, *Carousel* had its mimed merry-go-round tableau. Goldwyn and Preminger neutralized the opening of *Porgy and Bess* with an interpolated overture and curtain; Mamoulian retains Bizet's Prelude but *removes* the curtain: his screenplay interpolates a pantomimed minidrama. The orchestra's pounding castanet rhythm translates as pounding Spanish hoofbeats: a horse and rider gallop across the horizon. To keep the rhythm going, Mamoulian cancels Bizet's striding toreador song. The rider is Carmen: a distant red shirt and billowing black hair, her approach intensified by Bizet's crescendo to fortissimo. Where Bizet cuts to his sinister, sinuous fate theme, Mamoulian cuts to Carmen's destination—the interior of a cigarette factory in Seville: "It is a large hall, with many windows, filled with rows of long, narrow tables at which the FACTORY GIRLS are sitting, making cigars," says the scenario. "Some of them smoke while they work. Because of the heat, the GIRLS are in various states of undress." As the fate theme begins its menacing ascent, Carmen enters the room. "She has a beauty that is strange and wild. . . . Her eyes, especially, have an expression both voluptuous and savage, which is hardly ever found in any human eyes—somewhat like those of a cat stalking a sparrow." The Prelude now rapidly begins to crest. Over the music, one of the girls—Juanita—teases: "Late again! Did you fly in on a broom, Duchess?"

CARMEN, her eyes flaring, picks up a cigar knife off the table and
sends it through the air. It plunges into the table-top right in front
of JUANITA, who jumps with a horrified scream. CARMEN, with
both hands on her hips, laughs loudly.
CARMEN: Look at her! Frightened as a monkey! . . . But remember,
Juanita—next time I may not want to miss!"

A triple-*forte* chord—the Prelude's slashing terminus—punctuates Carmen's threat. The frisson of this singular sequence (Bizet is not here
portraying a cigarette factory) arises from the startling juxtaposition of
perfunctory manual labor with looming mystery, of the scanning camera with the smoky room, the erotic girls, and the snake-in-the-grass
encroachment of Bizet's dark, gliding tune.

It is scarcely surprising that what most excites Mamoulian's creativity, adapting *Carmen*, is the music Bizet's orchestra plays with the curtain
down: the Prelude and the entr'actes to acts 2, 3, and 4—all famous
excerpts. His brazen imposition of pantomimes of his own invention
is here unobstructed by singing or speaking.[55] Whatever one makes
of these ingenious revisions—however they might have played out on
film—the attempt to transform the medium of *Carmen* from opera to
cinema is appropriate: no staging could accommodate Mamoulian's
edits and zooms, the galloping horse, the bullring. Another Mamoulian
touch: cueing on a detail from Prosper Mérimée's *Carmen* (the source
for Bizet's opera)—"she clacked her castanets as she always did when
she wanted to banish some disturbing idea"—Mamoulian has his Carmen perform a "castanet soliloquy." How effectively do Mamoulian and
Anderson translate the French libretto? Here is the beginning of the
Toreodor Song:

Brothers all,
This pledge you give to me
I give to you,

I pledge it back to you!
We're all Toreros,
We're all Toreros!
We take pleasure in the fight,
There's no greater delight!

If this rendering seems less than inspired, the script's clumsy dialogue is the more problematic: less schematized than in the original version of Bizet's opera, but falling short of natural speech. What is more, the Mamoulian touches I have mentioned exhaust his creative interventions; for the most part, the script closely follows the opera.

Carlos Saura, in his flamenco film version of *Carmen* (1983), resituates the action in a rehearsal studio and reassigns the plot to dancers embodying a real-life version of the story they are preparing to enact. Ingmar Bergman, in his cinematic *The Magic Flute* (1975), putatively documents a specific performance in a specific Swedish theater, including glimpses of the audience and of the singers backstage; Sarastro studies *Parsifal* and has a hole in one of his gloves. These films, whatever else may be said of them, are filmic. Its novel moments notwithstanding, Mamoulian's *Carmen* is disappointingly conventional by comparison: it does not fundamentally tackle the challenge of transforming a sung stage work into a movie. Though Mamoulian complained he could never find a Carmen for *Carmen*, the pattern of paralysis afflicting *Cleopatra* in 1961 cannot be irrelevant. Mamoulian's Hollywood *Carmen*, and its planned Broadway sequel, must have seemed potentially restorative, counteracting Mamoulian's dismissal from the filmed opera *Porgy and Bess*, reconnecting with the Broadway opera *Porgy and Bess*. But the experimental Mamoulian of *Love Me Tonight* and *Porgy* is here barely a memory.

Could Mamoulian have restarted his career? In the opinion of Miles Kreuger: "Though he would remember one achievement or another, in private conversation he would confide his longstanding frustrations with Hollywood. And he was drifting into a new chapter of his life, traveling,

accepting speaking engagements. Mamoulian led a very ordered life—
nothing ever changed; he had his routines. Did he any longer really want
to work? I would say that he probably wasn't up to it, emotionally."[56]
What was the extent of Mamoulian's "longstanding frustrations" with
Hollywood, which never surface in any of his public utterances? Here is
a private diary entry, from 1940:

> *The Tragedy of the Screen Director, as an Artist*
> All other artist [sic] are allowed to do their ultimate in creation. No
> one and nothing can stop them from executing their highest concep-
> tions in Art no matter how advanced, prophetic or extravagant it may
> be. Mussorgsky could write his music; though "B.G." [*Boris Godunov*]
> was taken off the stage and the rest of his work was never played and
> he died in poverty—still, he put it all down on paper, and today it
> lives. . . . Not so with a screen director. He needs big sums of money
> and he must please millions. His ultimate, which could be appreciated
> by many, even though not by millions, has to remain within his soul
> and his brain. . . .

Four pages later comes a bitter list of preposterous "Harry Cohn Pearls"
including: "Lorna [the Barbara Stanwyck character in *Golden Boy*,
directed by Mamoulian for Cohn] goes back to the man because he
needs her—just like Joan of Arc. We want a Joan of Arc character."[57]

POSTMORTEM: PSYCHOPATHOLOGY?

In its various aspects, Mamoulian's steep downfall was equally personal
and professional, a downward spiral in which his controlling alcoholic
wife and the Goldwyn debacle were especially lurid components. In
his Mamoulian study *Reinventing Reality*, Mark Spergel adduces a further psychoanalytic explanation of Mamoulian's decline. In Spergel's
view, the immigrant Mamoulian was ensnared abroad in the myth of a

"golden childhood" at home. His mother—as self-revealed in an autobi-
ographical diary handwritten in the 1960s—was "utterly self-obsessed,"
"decidedly narcissistic." Her influence on her son's career "was probably
greater than [that of] any other single factor." Spergel continues:

> She devotes much of the diary to her "beloved Rouben," whose mar-
> riage late in life she calls a tragic mistake. Because of his "monstrous"
> wife, she . . . sees her son for only a few minutes at a time on rare
> occasions. . . . Of her many years in Hollywood with her husband and
> son she says, "Beautiful America took away all noble feelings, feelings
> of closeness and human moods. They only dream about dollars and
> their own interests. . . . I think that neither my husband nor my son
> understand or know me."[58]

Virginia Mamoulian and her husband joined Rouben on his film sets,
and at parties and receptions. Rouben, in turn, idealized his early years,
preceding the displacement of exile. His emotional disconnection was
such that he never processed the sordid death of his impoverished
sister, who married early, moved to London, had a child, and died of
tuberculosis.

For Spergel, Mamoulian's aesthetic of "stylization," in film and theater, gauges repression of feeling. It also registers his fear of social disin-
tegration, and of the bestial subcurrents of human nature.

> Mamoulian's decision to become a director reveals an interest in and
> a need to control the mise-en-scène of life through art. Mamoulian
> wrote: "The World is like a hit play—the longer it runs, the more it
> deteriorates . . . the world needs the Director's intervention, without
> which it is doomed to failure." The "Director" Mamoulian refers to in
> this instance is God; the parallel speaks for itself. He clearly felt a need
> to control, to be controlling. . . .
> When Mamoulian abandoned Europe for America, he retained an

old world social order of master and servant as his modus operandus [*sic*] in dealing with the world. He directed his actors with a baton and a whistle. . . . When his artistic vision was inspired, their submission yielded brilliant results. When his vision was less than inspired, their performances were sterile.

Aestheticizing life, Mamoulian distanced himself from temporal realities. His insistence on the universal and sanguine signified a flight from political engagement.

> Mamoulian's "art for life's sake" is a noble, if not grandiose, sentiment. But it denies the true function of art to go beyond the obvious—to stir, provoke, and question. . . .
>
> Mamoulian's unwillingness to confront reality took a tragic toll in his own life. Mamoulian wrote, "To make your *life* a true work of art is the highest achievement *man* can aspire to." His own life was no less filled with the same kind of denial as his work. His existence on Schuyler Road, high up in Beverly Hills, afforded him an Eden within which to retreat unbothered by the pain and brutality of the outside world. . . .
>
> To the end, his life and art were inseparable. In August, 1968, he wrote, "If 'all the world's a stage' then the important thing in life is to give a good performance, regardless of the quality of the play you are in." Appearance was all. His need to control his life and the world through art rendered him inflexible when that life and that world became inconsistent with his aesthetic vision.[59]

To Spergel's analysis of Mamoulian's drive to control one must add that Mamoulian's access to the epic and ironic is partly indebted to his remote perspective, and that there is more than one "true function of art." A simpler summary of Mamoulian's eventual failure to thrive would be that the Mamoulian odyssey suggests a traveler's restlessness or fatigue. Schooled in experimental Russian theater, he was an impatient innovator for whom the New World meant new opportunities—until those opportunities, or Mamoulian himself, dried up.

Certainly, Mamoulian traveled a long road. The charming or aloof young "genius" was, like his 1931 creation Dr. Jekyll (the character Mamoulian's camera eye cleverly inhabits), consumed by a fever to experiment.[60] Later, Mamoulian was no longer subversive; rather, he proudly but fitfully remembered his former creative self. Mamoulian had to somehow acknowledge or rationalize this disconnection. That he also had to endure a new aesthetic *Zeitgeist* hostile to "stylization," that he encountered in Hollywood norms of mass production that contradicted the heady early years of sound film, were equally undeniable factors in his wayward journey.

A chronic Mamoulian complaint was that the silent cinema had attained high artistic distinction just before the advent of sound, and that the sound film had failed to evolve commensurately into a consummated artform. In a published article postdating his active career, he called upon the Hollywood studios to jointly fund an experimental research laboratory:

> All big business spends millions of dollars on experimental laboratories dedicated to the betterment of their product. . . . It seems incredible that one of the biggest industries of the world and certainly the mightiest medium of entertainment, communication and art has not a single "laboratory" dedicated to the creative elements that make up the very foundation upon which the whole colossal structure is built.[61]

Obviously, Rochester had been such a laboratory: the talent at Mamoulian's disposal, the resources, the lavish George Eastman subsidies, created an experimental environment he never again enjoyed. This loss of opportunity linked to a condition of dependency: as a director, Mamoulian could rise no higher than what his collaborators inspired or allowed.

Paul Horgan, Rodgers and Hart, Rodgers and Hammerstein, and Kurt Weill were among his distinguished collaborators before he discovered himself a partner to "Samuel Goldwyn's *Porgy and Bess*."

George Gershwin was in a different league—and Mamoulian knew it. In Rochester, Mamoulian had idealized the actor who spontaneously "burns," who "inflames himself"—a Chaliapin or Duse "endowed by nature with a boundless creative energy," who "lives" onstage rather than "performs." Gershwin was of course an unmediated creative force of this type; Schoenberg said as much when, paying tribute to Gershwin, he wrote that "an artist is to me like an apple tree: When his time comes, whether he wants it or not, he bursts into bloom and starts to produce apples." And Schoenberg added, "It seems to me beyond doubt that Gershwin was an innovator." Composing was for Gershwin organic, serendipitously experimental; he discovered new genres without looking. Mamoulian was not a submissive personality; eyeing colleagues and peers, he would say, "I know better." His reverence for Gershwin, his way of writing and speaking about him, was singular. "Sometimes a great artist can be a small person, but George was great in every way," Mamoulian told a radio interviewer in 1938. "Everybody who knew him knew this."[62]

What was Mamoulian's *Porgy and Bess* like? We cannot really know. Had it been preserved on film, perhaps we would today find it impressively creative; perhaps we would find it disappointingly manipulative. Certainly, it differed very substantially from any subsequent *Porgy and Bess*. What if someone else—say, John Houseman, DuBose Heyward's choice—had directed *Porgy and Bess* in 1935? This question we can answer. The epic dimension Mamoulian brought to Heyward's Catfish Row tale was a dimension previously unknown to Gershwin. Mamoulian and Gershwin amplified one another; something unanticipated, even unprecedented, resulted. Emboldened by ignorance, admiration, and self-esteem, Mamoulian took a story about Gullah life and turned it into a parable about the human condition. Within the black community,

Gershwin's contribution to *Porgy and Bess* was variously judged progressive or naïve. Mamoulian's naïvete, which even decades later he neither understood nor acknowledged, was certainly greater than Gershwin's.

This is not the only perspective framing Mamoulian as an artist who long outlived his moment. Though his film career began with the advent of sound, the sounds with which he was happiest were music and noise, never speech. The filmmaker in Mamoulian was paradoxically grounded in the classic silent movies he studied and restudied in Rochester, in the work of directors like F. W. Murnau, whose *Last Laugh* he adored, whose restless experimentation with lighting, framing, and camera movement became for Mamoulian points of departure. The further evolution of the sound film into new realms of naturalism increasingly stranded Mamoulian's silent-film artistry. As a stage director, too, he belonged to an earlier milieu, one privileging ritual and spectacle; Max Reinhardt's Hollywood fate—to make a single 1935 Warner Brothers film; to never fit in—is not wholly irrelevant to Mamoulian's more gradual tumble into obscurity.

But Mamoulian was equally a harbinger. Like Gershwin's, his embrace of cultural fluidity was decades ahead of its time. Gershwin's level espousal of art and entertainment—his refusal to honor the dictates of modernist fashion and taste—vexed or antagonized his loud American critics. In classical music circles, his swift transition to the concert hall and opera house was read as an assault; it equally bred mistrust in Hollywood. Mamoulian, in Rochester, pursued a short-lived opera-in-English strategy promising democratized audiences. In Hollywood, he concocted an operetta film subverting operetta, and had Dr. Jekyll play Bach on the organ. This mutual espousal of art and entertainment petered out with an abortive *Carmen* in which art and entertainment, opera and Hollywood, Old World and New failed to inspire one another. Both Gershwin and Mamoulian sized up the Metropolitan Opera, with its stodgy European pedigree, as impossibly old-fashioned. But their *Porgy and Bess* proved too operatic for Broadway. In Hollywood, both terminally encountered the mistrust and incomprehension of Samuel Goldwyn, whose muddled aspiration to produce "high-class" screen entertainment caricatured the cultural synthesis Gershwin and Mamoulian prematurely embodied. The plush blue curtain with which Goldwyn sought to elevate *Porgy and Bess* mocked cultural fluidity as kitsch.

FINIS

After World War I, the democratization of learning and the arts was a striking feature of American life. The "new middle classes," with money to spend, flocked to movies, museums, and concerts. The Book of the Month Club, founded in 1926, was the most visible manifestation of a "great books" mentality urging Americans to elevate their reading habits. On the radio, NBC's *University of Chicago Round Table* and CBS's *American School of the Air* were flagship efforts. Popularizers like Will Durant, Hendrik van Loon, and Yale's William ("Billy") Phelps were themselves popular.[63]

This sudden influx of new readers and listeners might have been expected to loosen the grip of cultural pedigree and status. The opposite occurred. Instead of fostering fluidity, the new cultural landscape got stuck in the middle. Dwight Macdonald, in a famous 1960 essay, called the outcome "midcult."[64] "It pretends to respect the standards of high culture while in fact it waters them down and vulgarizes them," he wrote. Ostensibly raising mass culture, midcult corrupted—packaged and petrified—high culture; it traded on snob appeal. Macdonald's examples included the Book of the Month Club, Ernest Hemingway's *The Old Man and the Sea*, and Thornton Wilder's *Our Town*. "Samuel Goldwyn's *Porgy and Bess*" aspired to midcult.

In American classical music, midcult was the "music appreciation" movement, which merchandized a static canon of masterpieces. The major practitioner was the National Broadcasting Company, which published *The Victor Book of the Symphony*, the *Victor Book of Concertos*, *The Victor Book of the Opera*, *What We Hear in Music*, *Music Appreciation for Children*, and at least five other titles, and which created its own NBC Symphony. NBC's RCA Victor recordings enjoyed a sixfold sales increase during the 1930s, with symphonic releases leading the way.[65] At NBC and elsewhere, the music appreciators clung to pedigreed eighteenth- and nineteenth-century European composers. Meanwhile, Aaron Copland's *Our New Music* (1941) likewise ignored both Gershwin and jazz—the new American music perceived abroad as America's vital musical mainstream. This high-low schism, bridged in Europe by Weill, Milhaud, Ravel, and other outspoken jazz admirers, crippled American musical creativity at the high end of the status spectrum. American classical music never acquired a native canon. The core repertoire of American orchestras and opera companies remained resolutely European.

Mamoulian added to *Porgy* and *Porgy and Bess* a redemptive ending powered by Porgy. Gershwin, however incidentally, potentially powered a larger redemption project. He was by far the likeliest candidate to have fostered the "American school" once foretold by Dvořák, to have fashioned an American concert idiom evenhandedly infusing high culture with polyglot democratic strains, with jazz, Hollywood, and Broadway. Just as his Concerto in F had begotten Ravel's jazzy Piano Concerto in G, *Porgy and Bess* might have spawned a species of American folk opera transcending such lesser achievements as Kurt Weill's *Down in the Valley* or Carlisle Floyd's *Susannah*—so long as Gershwin was there to take command.

Decades after Gershwin's death, the high-low schism splitting American music began to dissipate. Today, no one could possibly embrace the music appreciation bibles. *Rhapsody in Blue* and the Concerto in F are purveyed on subscription by the Boston and Chicago Symphony orchestras as never before. The Metropolitan Opera has mounted *Porgy and Bess*. The Houston Grand Opera has taken it to Radio City. Cultural fluidity, once a threat, is now a norm.

What if Gershwin had lived as long as his contemporary Copland, and died in 1990? However unanswerable, the question is inescapable. He would have inhabited cultural decades of wartime patriotism, high modernism, postmodernism. His input, his influence, could only have been profound. Could Gershwin have rescued Mamoulian? At the very least, their paths would surely have recrossed, in Hollywood or on Broadway.

Contradicting DuBose Heyward, Rouben Mamoulian ended *Porgy and Bess* on an upbeat:

> Oh Lord,
> I'm on my way
> I'm on my way
> To a Heav'nly Land

But George Gershwin's end was tragic, and Mamoulian pathetically endured a lingering artistic demise. Of all the potential opportunities snuffed out by Gershwin's fatal brain tumor—the string quartet he had begun, the Abraham Lincoln cantata he had mentioned, the violin concerto Heifetz had requested—the most tantalizing was a heavenly land of American musical theater forever lost.

APPENDICES

⚜

A *Porgy* (1927): "Symphony of Noises" by Rouben Mamoulian

B Synopsis of *Porgy and Bess*

C Four Versions of the Ending
   1. DuBose Heyward's Novella *Porgy* (1925)
   2. The Published Script for *Porgy*, by DuBose and Dorothy Heyward (1927)
   3. *Porgy* Script as Amended in Rouben Mamoulian's Hand (1927)
   4. *Porgy and Bess* (1935) by George Gershwin (music), DuBose Heyward (libretto), and Heyward with Ira Gershwin (lyrics)

APPENDIX A

PORGY (1927): "SYMPHONY OF NOISES"
(ACT 3, SCENE 2)
BY ROUBEN MAMOULIAN

This interlude, created by Mamoulian, was recapitulated as the "Occupational Humoresque" in Porgy and Bess. *The following text may be found in the Rouben Mamoulian Archive, Library of Congress, box 115, folder 7. Mamoulian's "R," "L," and "C" mean right, left, and center; "RC" is right center.*

(The stage is empty except for one Negro asleep at foot of steps. Gradually noises off stage start and grow in volume until in about two minutes the court is alive with noise and people. The windows open as follows.)*

1—Johnson—Top floor left
2—Musa—Second floor R2

---

*Mamoulian identifies the participants by name of character (Lily, Maria, Mingo, Scipio, Serena), or—in the case of choristers and children—by first or last name or performer. The participating choristers are Frank Allen, Clarissa Blue, Marguerite Booth, Richard Bruce, Lillian Cowan, Dorothy Embry, Catherine Francis, Rosa Johnson, Edward Perry, Marie Remsen, Charles Taylor, Philip Thomas, and Musa Williams, plus the children Sylvia Harrigan, and Eddie and Ruth Williams.

3—Blue at Serena's [window]—Over steps center R. back. Both C. Top floor left

4—Remsen—Second floor left over arch

5—Francis—Door second floor left

Then the rest open at once.

Start on $\frac{4}{4}$ count.

Curtain up on 3rd full count of 3rd measure.

1 beat—pound of iron

2

3—snore

4

1—pound iron

2—sweep

3—snore

4—sweep

1—iron

2—sweep

3—snore

4—sweep

1—pound

2—sweep

3—snore

4—sweep. Kid [Eddie] comes from Serena's room to Lillian

Eddie: Can I have a piece of candy?

2—sweep

Lillian: It's too early for candy. (Kid goes up stairs)

3—snore. Embry enters from Arch L. cross to C.
4—sweep. Musa and Johnson open window.

1—pound
2—sweep, pan. Embry drops bucket[,] wakes Taylor, they argue. She
   goes to Maria.
3—bottle, Lily Holmes enters and goes to tub under stair. Maria comes
   on stage after Embry enters her shop

Maria: Good morning, Musa

(Annie opens windows. Lily enters and goes to tub.)

4—sweep, Wilson enters gate with bundle, crosses to arch.

1—pound
2—sweep—pan
3—snore—bottle noise
4—sweep—pan clash.

1—pound. Blue slams door. Beat carpet on first and second beat until
   children come out.
2—sawing—Johnson snaps rug—pan clash
3—sawing—pan—Musa and Johnson snip—rug
4—sawing—Johnson snaps rug

(When Blue starts beating rug Maria sharpens knife on 3rd and 4th beat
or each count until Embry comes out with her pail, crosses L. exits and

hurries back on for Porgy's entrance. The children enter on Embry's entrance)

Eddie (come from Serena's): Can I go out?

(Mingo comes from Lily's door and comes down to Maria's.)

Ruth (comes from arch left): Me too.

Mingo: Got any shark steak Maria? (Mingo goes over L. [to] talk to Perry)

Sylvia (comes on with Ruth): I want to play.

(Scipio and four small boys from the band enter from Lily's door. And all play tag and where the pounding increases their voices rise with it until the patrol bell sounds—they quiet down then)

(They enter and play. Allen from left arch enters, goes to box. Mahon [?] follows Allen, sits up L. with shove when Musa starts to shake her rug. Booth washes her window.)

(Allen and Taylor beat three measures until Serena starts down stairs[;] as she comes down stairs the count becomes $\frac{2}{4}$ and the pounding stops. On the measure they beat out the Charleston. Thomas pushes vegetable cart across from left to R. singing his wares. After which he comes on and stands by window R2. As Charleston starts police Bell. Both go to forths [sic] and all crowd up to gate to see who it is. When bell sounds Mingo runs off stage into Peter's house.)

POLICE/BELL/MOTOR

(The patrol bell off L. sounds loudly. They go to gate and look to see what it is. Everybody PORGY! Porgy outside the gate. His air is one of mystery, he enters. They part for him and he comes to L. of table R.C. Porgy gives Scipio bundles. Policeman who brought Porgy on exits. Mingo is R. of table. Maria below table. Bruce above table. Serena at foot of steps. Lily Holmes is L. of Porgy. Porgy is L. of table)

APPENDIX B

SYNOPSIS OF *PORGY AND BESS*

ACT 1, SCENE 1: CATFISH ROW

Saturday evening. Jasbo Brown plays the piano. Clara, with child, sings the lullaby **"Summertime."** Her husband, Jake, takes the baby and sings **"A Woman Is A Sometime Thing."** Porgy arrives, then Crown, a stevedore, and Bess, his woman. Crown is drunk. During a craps game, he picks an argument with Robbins and slays him with a cotton hook. Everyone quickly disperses, with Bess going to Porgy's room.

ACT 1, SCENE 2: SERENA'S ROOM

Robbins's body is lying on a table. Mourners, collecting money for the funeral, sing **"Gone, Gone, Gone."** Porgy and Bess enter. Serena refuses Bess's contribution, thinking the money is Crown's. When it is explained that the money is Porgy's, it is accepted. The mourners sing **"Overflow."** A white detective enters and orders that the body be buried the next day. He accuses Peter, an old man, of the murder. Peter, terrified, identifies Crown as the killer. Peter is taken away as a witness until Crown can be found. Serena, Robbins's widow, sings **"My Man's Gone Now."** The undertaker arrives and agrees to bury the body. Bess leads a spiritual: **"Leavin' For The Promise' Lan'."**

ACT 2, SCENE 1: CATFISH ROW

A few weeks later. Jake and the fishermen are repairing their nets: **"It Takes A Long Pull."** Clara warns of September storms. Porgy sings **"I Got Plenty O' Nuttin'."** Maria chases away the dope-peddling Sporting Life: **"Frien's Wid You, Low Life?"** Lawyer Frazier enters looking for Porgy and sells him a "divorce." Mr. Archdale, a white lawyer, chastises Frazier; he assures the community he will put up bail for Peter. A buzzard flies overhead: Porgy's **"Buzzard Song."** People prepare for the picnic on Kittiwah Island. Porgy and Bess, alone, sing **"Bess, You Is My Woman Now."** The **Orphanage Band** enters. Picknickers sing **"Oh, I Can't Sit Down."** Maria (who has accepted Bess) urges Bess to join the group. Maria and Bess depart for the picnic.

ACT 2, SCENE 2: KITTIWAH ISLAND

Sporting Life tells the picknickers **"It Ain't Necessarily So."** They depart by steamboat—but Bess is detained by Crown, who has been hiding from the police on the island. They quarrel: the duet **"What You Want Wid Bess?"** But Bess submits.

ACT 2, SCENE 3: CATFISH ROW

Defying storm warnings, the fishermen take their boats out to sea. Bess, returned from Kittiwah Island, is delirious in Porgy's room. Serena prays: **"Oh, Doctor Jesus."** The Strawberry Woman, the Honey Man, and the Crab Man sing street cries. Bess regains consciousness: **"I Loves You Porgy."** The hurricane bell sounds.

ACT 2, SCENE 4: SERENA'S ROOM

Dawn the following day. The storm rages: **"Oh, De Lawd Shake De Heavens."** Pounding is heard above the din: **"Oh, Dere's Somebody**

Knockin' At De Do'." Crown enters looking for Bess. He drowns the lamenting with **"A Red-Headed Woman."** Clara screams: she sees Jake's boat capsized. She rushes into the storm. Crown rushes after her. Prayer resumes.

ACT 3, SCENE 1: CATFISH ROW

The storm has passed. The community grieves for those lost: **"Clara, Don't You Be Down-Hearted."** Crown enters the empty courtyard and crawls towards Porgy's door. Porgy slays Crown.

ACT 3, SCENE 2:

The white detective and coroner arrive to investigate Crown's murder. They take Porgy away to identify Crown's body. Sporting Life tempts Bess: **"There's A Boat Dat's Leavin' Soon For New York."**

ACT 3, SCENE 3: CATFISH ROW

A week has passed. The community awakes **(Occupational Humor-esque)**. Porgy returns from jail: **"Oh Bess, Oh Where's My Bess?"** He resolves to go to New York to find Bess: **"Oh Lawd, I'm On My Way."**

APPENDIX C

FOUR VERSIONS OF THE ENDING

1. DuBOSE HEYWARD'S NOVELLA *PORGY* (1925)

In the fresh beauty of an early October morning, Porgy returned home. There were few of his friends about, as work was now plentiful, and most of those who could earn a day's wage were up and out. He drove through the entrance, pulled his goat up short, and looked about him.

Serena was seated on her bench with a baby in her arms.

Porgy gave her a long look, and a question commenced to dawn in his eyes. The child turned in her arms, and his suspicions were confirmed. It was his baby—his and Bess's.

Then Serena looked up and saw him. She arose to great confusion, clasped the infant to her ample bosom, and, without a word of greeting, stepped through her doorway. Then, as though struck by an afterthought, she turned, thrust her head back through the opening, and called loudly:

"Oh, Maria! Hyuh Porgy come home."

Then she disappeared and the door slammed shut.

Mystified and filled with alarm, Porgy turned his vehicle toward the cook-shop and arrived at the door just as Maria stepped over the threshold.

She seated herself on the sill and brought her face level with his. Then she looked into his eyes.

What Porgy saw there caused him to call out sharply:

"Where's Bess? Tell me, quick, where's Bess?"

The big negress did not answer, and after a moment her ponderous face commenced to shake.

Porgy beat the side of his wagon with his fist.

"Where, where—" he began, in a voice that was suddenly shrill.

But Maria placed a steadying hand over his frantic one and held it still.

"Dem dutty dogs got she one day w'en I gone out," she said in a low, shaken voice. "She been missin' yuh an' berry low in she min' 'cause she can't fin' out how long yuy is lock up fuh. Dat damn houn' she knock off de warf las' summer fin' she like dat an' git she tuh tek swalluh ob licker. Den half a dozen of de mens gang she, an' mek she drunk."

"But whu she now?" Porgy cried. "I ain't keer ef she wuz drunk. I want she now."

Maria tried to speak, but her voice refused to do her bidding. She covered her face with her hands, and [her] throat worked convulsively.

Porgy clutched her wrist. "Tell me," he commanded. "Tell me, now."

"De mens all carry she away on de ribber boat," she sobbed. "Dey leave word fuh me dat dey goin' tek she all de way tuh Sawannah, an' keep she dey. Den Serena, she tek de chile, an' say she is goin' big um er Christian raisin'."

Deep sobs stopped Maria's voice. For a while she sat there, her face buried in her hands. But Porgy had nothing to say. When she finally raised her head and looked at him, she was surprised at what she saw.

The keen autumn sun flooded boldly through the entrance and bathed the drooping form of the goat, the ridiculous wagon, and the bent figure of the man in hard, satirical radiance. In its revealing light, Maria saw that Porgy was an old man. The early tension that had characterized him, the mellow mood that he had known for one eventful summer, both had gone; and in their place she saw a face that sagged wearily, and the eyes of age lit only by a faint reminiscent glow from suns and moons that had looked into them, and had already dropped down the west.

She looked until she could bear the sight no longer, then she stumbled into her shop and closed the door, leaving Porgy and the goat alone in an irony of morning sunlight.

[end of book]

2. THE PUBLISHED SCRIPT FOR *PORGY*, BY DuBOSE AND DOROTHY HEYWARD (1927)

PORGY

Bess! Ain't yo' dere, Bess? (MARIA comes to her doorway. PORGY turns to her, his eyes wide with alarm.) Where' Bess? (MARIA sits on her doorstep. PORGY turns his goat and drives over to her.) Tell me quick. Where' Bess? (MARIA does not answer.) Where? Where?

MARIA

(trying to put on a bold face.) Ain't we tell y' all along, Porgy, dat 'oman ain't fit fo' yo'."

PORGY (Frantically)

I ain't ask yo' opinion. Where's Bess?

(They all shrink from telling him. Each evades, trying to leave it to the others.)

MARIA

Dat dirty dog Sportin' Life make us all t'ink yo' is lock up fo' a yeah.

PORGY

Won't somebody tell me, where Bess?

SERENA

Bess very low in she min' 'cause she t'ink yo' is gone fo' a yeah. (Pauses, unable to come to the point.)

PORGY

But I home *now.* I want to tell she I is here.

SERENA

She gone back to de happy dus' an' de red eye. She been very drunk two day'.

PORGY

But where she now? I ain't care if she was drunk. I want she now.

LILY

Dat houn' Sportin' Life was foreber hangin' 'round and gettin' she to take more dope.

PORGY (driving again to his own door. Calls.)

Bess! Bess! Won't nobody tell me—

MARIA (following him.)

Ain't we tellin' yo'? Dat houn' Sportin' Life—

PORGY (desperately.)

I ain't ask 'bout Sportin' Life. Where' Bess?

SERENA

She gone, Porgy, An' I done take dis chile to gib um a Christian raisin'—

PORGY

Where she gone?

SERENA

Dat gal ain't neber had Gawd in she heart', an' de debil get um at last.

MARIA

'Tain't de debil. De happy dus' done for um.

PORGY (wildly.)

Yo'—Bess?—Yo' ain't means Bess dead?

SERENA

She worse dan dead.

LILY

Sportin' Life carry she away on de Noo Yo'k boat.

(They are all silent, gazing at PORGY. He, too, is silent for a moment.)

PORGY

Where dat dey take she?

MINGO

Noo Yo'k.

MARIA

Dat's way up Nort'.

PORGY (pointing.)

It dat way?

MARIA

It take two days by de boat. Yo' can't find um.

PORGY

I ain't say I can find um. I say, where it is?

MARIA

Yo' can't go after she. Ain't yo' hear we say yo' can't find um.

ANNIE

Ain't yo' know Noo Yo'k mos' a t'ousand mile' from here?

PORGY

Which way dat?

LILY (pointing.)

Up Nort'—past de Custom house.

(PORGY turns his goat and drives slowly with bowed head toward the gate.)

MARIA

Porgy, I tells yo' it ain't no use!

LILY

Dat great big city. Yo' can't find um dere!

SERENA

Ain't we tells yo'—

(But PORGY is going on toward gate as if he did not hear, and they cease to protest and stand motionless watching him. As PORGY reaches the gate, SCIPIO silently opens it. PORGY drives through and turns to left, as LILY pointed. St. Michael's chimes the quarter hour. The gate clangs shut.)

(Curtain)

3. *PORGY* SCRIPT AS AMENDED IN ROUBEN MAMOULIAN'S HAND (1927)

There are two sources for the following text, both to be found in the Mamoulian Archive at the Library of Congress: a full script with changes in Mamoulian's hand, found with his "Porgy" materials (box 115, folder 7) and a typed script with the changes incorporated, found with his "Porgy and Bess" materials (box 87, folder 1).

[Commencing after Maria says "'Tain't de debil. De happy dus' done for um."]

PORGY

You ain't mean Bess dead.

SERENA

She worse dan dead—she gone to Noo Yawk.

PORGY

Gone? Where dat?

MARIA

Noo Yawk.

PORGY

I hear yo say Noo Yawk—where dat?

MINGO

Mos' a thousand miles from here.

MARIA

It take two days by de boat. You can't find 'um.

PORGY

Which way Noo Yawk?

MARIA

Dat's way up Nort'.

PORGY

It dat way? (Points left.)

LILY (Points right.)

Up nort'—past de custom house.

PORGY

Bring m' goat.

MARIA

What you wants wid yo' goat. Yo bes' not go any place.

PORGY

Bring m' goat!

SERENA

You bes' stay wid yo' frien', Porgy—a little rest it make you feel better.

PORGY

Won't nobody bring my goat. (It is brought.)

MARIA

Aint we tell you, you cant find um.

SERENA

For Lawd's sake, Porgy, where yo' goin'?

PORGY

Aint you say Bess gone to Noo Yawk. Dats where I goin'. I gots to be wid Bess. I gonna find her. I'm on my way.

MARIA starts to sing softly.

LILY

Porgy. Porgy.

MINGO

Don't go Porgy.

LILY

You best stay wid us.

PORGY raises his hands—prays silently and repeats "I'm on my way"—then the others realize there is a spiritual to fit the occasion and all start singing as he crosses to goat cart, exits off Right.

SERENA

    May the good Lord be wid you.

    (Singing [by all] continues.)

    I'm on my way to heavenly land
    Oh Lord, I'm on my way
    I'm on my way
    To heavenly land
    I'm on my way
    To heavenly land
    I'm on my way
    To heavenly land
    O, Lord, I'm on my way!

    I'm on my way to the heavenly land, Oh lord, I'm on my way
    I'm on my way
    Oh lord, I'm on my way
    Oh Brother, come with me
    Oh Sister, come with me.

               (Curtain.)

4. *PORGY AND BESS* (1935) BY GEORGE GERSHWIN (MUSIC), DuBOSE HEYWARD (LIBRETTO), AND HEYWARD WITH IRA GERSHWIN (LYRICS)

PORGY:

    Maria, Maria, where's Bess,
    Tell me quick, where's Bess, tell me quick
    Where's Bess? Where is Bess? Oh, Bess!

MARIA

    Ain' we tell you all along, Porgy,
    Dat woman ain' fit fo' you?

PORGY

    I ain' axin' yo' opinion,

[TRIO: PORGY, MARIA, SERENA:]

    Oh, Bess, oh where's my Bess,

    Won't somebody tell me where (etc.)

                •   •   •

LILY

    Bess is gone. An' Serena take dis chile to give 'im a Christian raisin'.

PORGY

    You ain' mean Bess dead?

SERENA

    She worse than dead, Porgy.

    She gave herself to de debbil, but she still

    Livin', an' she gone far away.

PORGY

    Alive, Bess is alive!

    Where Bess gone?

MINGO

    New York.

PORGY

    I hear you say New York. Where dat?

MINGO

    A thousand mile from here.

PORGY

    Which way New York?

MARIA

    It's way up North pas' de custom house.

PORGY

Bring my goat!

MARIA

What you want wid goat, Porgy?
You bes' not go any place.

PORGY

Bring my goat!

SERENA

You better stay wid yo' frien', Porgy, you'll be happy here.

PORGY

Won't nobody bring my goat?

MARIA

Ain't we tell you, you can't find her, Porgy?

SERENA

For Gawd's sake, Porgy, where you goin'?

ALL

Where you goin' Porgy?

PORGY

Ain't you say Bess gone to New York? Dat's
Where I goin',
I got to be wid Bess. Gawd help me to
Fin' her.

(Mingo leads goat and cart over, Porgy holds up arms and is helped into cart)

I'm on my way.

(Cart is led off)

Oh Lawd, I'm on my way.

PORGY and ALL

I'm on my way to a Heav'nly Lan',
I'll ride dat long, long road.
If You are there to guide my han'.
Oh Lawd, I'm on my way.
I'm on my way to a heav'nly Lan'.
Oh Lawd, it's a long, long way,
But You'll be there to take my han'.

(Curtain)

NOTES

EPIGRAPHS

Mamoulian quoted by Bennett Oberstein in 1973 interview, Rouben Mamoulian Archive, Library of Congress (LOC), box 154, folder 5. Mamoulian quoted in William Becvar in 1973 interview, "The Stage and Film Career of Rouben Mamoulian," diss., University of Kansas (1975), p. 69. Gershwin in *New York Times*, Oct. 20, 1935.

PROLOGUE: MAMOULIAN, GERSHWIN, AND CULTURAL FLUIDITY

1. Sondheim in *New York Times*, Aug. 10, 2011. Shirley in conversation with the author.
2. Copland in Carol Oja and Judith Tick, eds., *Aaron Copland and His World* (2005), p. 404. Downes in *New York Times*, July 12, 1937. Rosenfeld in the *New Republic*, Jan. 4, 1933. Charles Schwartz in *New Grove*.
3. Joseph Horowitz, *Classical Music in American: A History* (2005), p. 462.
4. Larry Starr, *George Gershwin* (2011), pp. 159–160.
5. Starr, p. 154.
6. Mark Spergel, *Reinventing Reality: The Art and Life of Rouben Mamoulian* (1993), p. 9.
7. Spergel, p. 21.
8. Mamoulian house: William Becvar interview with Mamoulian (March 20, 1973), Rouben Mamoulian Archive, Library of Congress (LOC), box 154, folder 4. Student days: Columbia University oral history (1958) (hereafter, Columbia), pp. 4–5, in LOC, box 153. Stanislavski "greatest man": Becvar, p. 7, LOC, box 154, folder 4.
9. Historian is Mel Gordon, quoted in Spergel, p. 33. Diary and article: LOC, box 199, folder 8.
10. *Deluge* review quoted in Spergel, p. 33. Also see *Evgeny Vakhtangov*, compiled and edited with commentary by L. D. Vendrovskaya and G. P. Kaptereva (All-Russian Theater Society, Moscow, 1984) and Ruben Simonov's *With Vakhtangov* (State

Publishing House *Iskusstvo*, Moscow, 1959). (I am grateful to Solomon Volkov for sharing these books with me, and to my wife, Agnes, for translating pertinent passages into English.)

11. Spergel, pp. 20, 24.
12. Columbia, p. 16, in LOC, box 153.
13. For instance: Tim Carter's *Oklahoma!: The Making of an American Musical* (2007) makes scant mention of Mamoulian's creative contributions to the show. Even the booklet for Decca's 2006 *Porgy and Bess* recording, re-creating the 1935 Theatre Guild production, barely mentions Mamoulian.
14. *New York Times*, Feb. 11, 1934. Radio talk, Oct. 16, 1935: LOC, box 161, folder 8. *Cleopatra*: David Robinson, "Painting the Leaves Black," *Sight and Sound* 30, no. 3 (Summer 1961). *Los Angeles Times*, April 5, 1970.

CHAPTER 1: ENTER *PORGY*

1. DuBose Heyward, *Porgy* (1925), p. 1. (My page numbers refer to the Bantam paperback edition.)
2. For background: James M. Hutchisson, *DuBose Heyward: A Charleston Gentleman and the World of "Porgy and Bess"* (2000).
3. Heyward, pp. 32–33.
4. Heyward, p. 147.
5. Heyward, pp. 27, 3, 108, 59, 131, 107, 82–85.
6. Heyward, pp. 41, 25, 133, 24.
7. Hutchisson, p. 52.
8. Hutchisson, pp. 49, 54, 55, 61, 62. "Beautiful and enriching": Howard Pollack, *George Gershwin: His Life and Work* (2006), p. 571.
9. Heyward, p. 47.
10. "He was torn": Hollis Alpert, *The Life and Times of "Porgy and Bess"* (1990), p. 45. "Good forerunner": Bennett Oberstein, "The Broadway Directing Career of Rouben Mamoulian," diss., Indiana University (1977), p. 35.
11. Previously, "Deep River" was a lesser-known spiritual; the touring Jubilee Singers rendered a relatively upbeat version much different from Burleigh's. Being for solo voice rather than choral, Burleigh's spiritual arrangements were a novelty. As in the case of "Deep River," they were sometimes as much compositions as transcriptions. Burleigh's a cappella version of "Deep River" for male chorus (1917) makes explicit his debt to Dvořák's Largo: it begins with a chord procession echoing the chordal opening of Dvořák's famous slow movement.
12. *New York Herald*, May 21, 1893.
13. Alpert, pp. 48, 51.
14. Spergel, p. 56.
15. Spergel, p. 57.
16. Oberstein, p. 26.

17. "A good idea": Columbia, p. 51 in Rouben Mamoulian Archive, Library of Congress, box 153. Bennett: Hutchisson, p. 81.
18. "I am . . . a Southerner": Oberstein, p. 40. "Southern Negroes": Spergel, p. 60. "My favorite idea": Columbia, p. 51.
19. Al Jolson would later appear as *Porgy* in a short radio adaptation.
20. Oberstein, p. 41.
21. Ella Madison: Ruth W. Sedgwick, "Two Adventures in Direction," *Stage*, Oct. 1935. Ball: Oberstein, p. 45.
22. Hutchisson, p. 82.
23. Spergel, pp. 65–66.
24. Columbia, p. 52.
25. Theresa Helburn, *A Wayward Quest* (1960), p. 193. Barnes in Spergel, p. 64. Moeller in Columbia, p. 56.
26. Alpert, p. 60. Hutchisson, pp. 83–84. Columbia, p. 57.
27. Woollcott, *New York World*, Oct. 11, 1927. *New Republic*, Oct. 26, 1927. *New York American*, Oct. 11, 1927. *New York Times*, Oct. 11, 1917.
28. *Billboard*, Oct. 22, 1927. *Herald Tribune*, Dec. 11, 1927. *New York Times*, Oct. 16, 1927. *New Republic*, Oct. 26, 1927. *Daily Eagle*, Oct. 23, 1927. *Theatre Arts Monthly*, Dec. 1927. Hammond in Alpert, p. 67.
29. Woollcott in *New York World*, April 28, 1928. Brown in *New York Post*, Sept. 16, 1929. James Weldon Johnson, *Black Manhattan* (1968), pp. 211–212. *New Age*, Oct. 15, 1927. Reinhardt in Spergel, p. 67.
30. A decade later, James M. Hutchisson, in his biography of DuBose (2000), compressed Alpert's four sentences into two.
31. Oberstein, p. 39. Alpert, p. 55. Mamoulian in Columbia, pp. 50–51.
32. A clean typescript of the final, revised *Porgy* script may be found among Mamoulian's *Porgy and Bess* materials in the Mamoulian Archive of the Library of Congress, box 87, folder 1.
33. In Gershwin's opera, he sings, "Oh, little stars, little stars, roll, roll, roll me some light."
34. Mamoulian interpolates two further reprises of the same tune as sung by Bess and Porgy (act 2, scene 1), and by Mingo (act 2, scene 3).
35. Mamoulian's "Symphony of Noises" script—an insert to the annotated typescript of the entire play—names eighteen individuals, plus "four small boys from band."
36. Columbia, p. 55.
37. Heyward, p. 38.
38. Heyward, pp. 2, 45, 56.
39. Spergel, p. 63.
40. Christine Edwards, *The Stanislavsky Heritage* (1965), pp. 230–231.
41. Spergel, p. 67.
42. Alpert, p. 68. Pollack, p. 573.

CHAPTER 2: EXPERIMENTS IN MUSICAL THEATER

1. Deems Taylor, *Of Men and Music* (1937), p. 203, quoted in Joseph Horowitz, *Classical Music in America: A History* (2005), p. 374.
2. Horowitz, pp. 131–132.
3. Horowitz, p. 147.
4. Horowitz. p. 145.
5. Paul Horgan, "How Dr. Faustus Came to Rochester," *Harper's*, April 1936.
6. Paul Horgan, "Rouben Mamoulian in the Rochester Renaissance," in Horgan, *A Certain Climate* (1988).
7. Ruth Glenn Rosing, *Val Rosing: Musical Genius* (1993), p. 79.
8. Vincent Lenti, *For the Enrichment of Community Life: George Eastman and the Founding of the Eastman School of Music* (2004), pp. 125, 127.
9. *Rochester Democrat and Chronicle*, Nov. 26, 1923.
10. Horgan, *A Certain Climate*, p. 202.
11. Horgan, *A Certain Climate*, p. 206.
12. Nicolas Slonimsky, *Perfect Pitch* (1988), p. 86. Horgan, *A Certain Climate*, p. 208.
13. Slonimsky, p. 84. Rouben Mamoulian, "Exciting the Imagination of the Picture Audience," *Exhibitors Trade Review*, Jan. 16, 1926, in Rouben Mamoulian Archive, Library of Congress (LOC), box 180, folder 6.
14. Horgan, *A Certain Climate*, p. 209.
15. Clippings, LOC, boxes 103, 180, 181.
16. Horgan, "Dr. Faustus," *Musical America*, Jan. 25, 1925.
17. Clippings, LOC, box 101.
18. Horgan, *A Certain Climate*, pp. 216–220.
19. Now in LOC.
20. Clippings, LOC, box 161, folder 6.
21. LOC, box 121, folder 6.
22. Clippings, LOC, box 180.
23. Clipping, LOC, box 121. Luening in Mark Spergel, *Reinventing Reality: The Art and Life of Rouben Mamoulian* (1993), p. 51, and Otto Leuning, *The Odyssey of an American Composer* (1957), p. 272. Horgan, *A Certain Climate*, p. 218.
24. Spergel, p. 53.
25. *Los Angeles Times*, Sept. 1, 1963.
26. Spergel, p. 135.
27. LOC, box 139, folder 10.
28. LOC, box 72, folder 8.
29. Paramount clippings files: LOC, box 78. *New York Telegraph*, Aug. 8, 1932. *New York Times*, Aug. 9, 1932. *Cleveland Plain Dealer*, Sept. 7, 1932. *London Evening Standard*, Nov. 9, 10, 1932. *Times* of London, Nov. 18, 1932. *Daily Telegraph*, Nov. 21, 1932. *New Statesman*, Nov. 28, 1932. *Cinématographie Française*, July 9, 1921.

CHAPTER 3: *PORGY AND BESS*

1. Howard Pollack, *George Gershwin: His Life and Work* (2006), p. 8.
2. Pollack, p. 176.
3. Maxie Rosenzweig in Isaac Goldberg, *George Gershwin* (1958), p. 58. "The great musical influence," in Pollack, p. 25.
4. Pollack, p. 147.
5. Irving Berlin in Pollack, p. 48. Gershwin in Merle Armitage, ed., *George Gershwin* (1938), p. 227.
6. Pollack, p. 125.
7. *New York Herald Tribune*, Dec. 27, 1926. *New York Times*, Dec. 27, 1926. Rosenfeld in *The Dial*, April 1927. Thomson in *Modern Music*, Nov.-Dec. 1935. Winthrop Sargeant, *Geniuses, Goddesses, and People* (1949), p. 109.
8. Pollack, p. 567.
9. DuBose Heyward, "Porgy and Bess Return on Wings of Song," *Stage*, Oct. 1935.
10. A topic treated at length by Larry Starr in his *George Gershwin* (2011), chapter 5.
11. Pollack, p. 567.
12. "Flattered" in Pollack, p. 574. Munsell in James Hutchisson, *DuBose Heyward: A Charleston Gentleman and the World of "Porgy and Bess"* (2000), p. 153. Helburn in Rouben Mamoulian Archive, Library of Congress (LOC), box 199, folder 9. Gershwin in Pollack, p. 592. Munsell in LOC, box 116.
13. Mamoulian in Armitage, pp. 47–57. Woollcott in Joseph Horowitz, *Classical Music in America: A History* (2005), p. 463. Ira in Pollack, p. 20.
14. Armitage, p. 49.
15. Mark Spergel, *Reinventing Reality: The Art and Life of Rouben Mamoulian* (1993), p. 60.
16. As Wayne Shirley (editor of a forthcoming critical edition of *Porgy and Bess*) has shown, the published vocal score and the full orchestra score differ in only minor details. The Theatre Guild production is documented by a variety of scores, none of them published. See Charles Hamm, "The Theatre Guild Production of *Porgy and Bess*," *Journal of the American Musicological Society* 40, no. 3 (Autumn 1987). My references in the present chapter to Mamoulian's cuts and additions refer to the vocal score with changes in Mamoulian's hand, copies of which may be found at both the Library of Congress (Mamoulian Archive) and the New York Public Library.
17. Booklet for *Porgy and Bess* recording, Decca B0007431-02 (2006).
18. Wayne Shirley, "The 'Theatre Guild Version' of *Porgy and Bess*," unpublished paper (2009).
19. Shirley.
20. Cited by Shirley, "The 'Theatre Guild Version'."
21. Gershwin's act 2 hurricane is in two parts. It stops to accommodate a scene change from the Catfish Row courtyard (scene 3) to Serena's room (scene 4). It then resumes with "Oh, Dr. Jesus." Mamoulian's score shows that he considered

musically eliding these two scenes: though the curtain would fall (two before 226—sixteen measures earlier than in Heyward's libretto), the orchestra would continue playing until the curtain rose on "Oh, de Lawd Shake de Heavens." But the New York orchestral parts tell a different story. There was a continuous hurricane (including a reprise, to give the stagehands more time) with the curtain down. The cadential E major chord ending scene 3—at one point deleted by Mamoulian—was nevertheless retained; however briefly, the music came to a full stop.

22. The possible harmonic organization of this scene has been differently assessed by Charles Hamm ("The Theatre Guild production of *Porgy and Bess*," *Journal of the American Musicological Society* 40, no. 3 [Autumn 1987]), and Larry Starr ("Toward a Reevaluation of Gershwin's *Porgy and Bess*," *American Music* 2, no. 2 [1984]).

23. Duncan quoted in Robert Wyatt and John A. Johnson, eds., *The George Gershwin Reader* (2004), p. 223. I am indebted to Miles Kreuger for sharing with me his rare recording of the "Magic Key" broadcast (which may also be heard at the Library of Congress).

24. Duncan in Armitage, p. 59, and in Wyatt and Johnson, p. 223. Brown in Wyatt and Johnson, p. 231. Nazimova: Mamoulian, *Porgy and Bess* scrapbook, LOC, oversize box 24.

25. *Theatre Arts Monthly*, Nov. 1935. *Stage*, Oct. 1935.

26. Duncan said in 1990: "You know, the Porgys these days don't always make the grade. I'm going to say this to you and I know it's ungracious of me, but I think I owe it to posterity at this time to make this statement. It seems that the Porgys that I've heard really don't know who Porgy is. They've not gone into the depth of who the character is; they don't know the man himself. And when they sing 'I Got Plenty o' Nuttin'' they think it's a buffoon song or a blackface 'step-and-fetch-it' song. It's not that at all. It is very deep philosophy and I got it from the composer himself. It is making fun of very wealthy white people. I got this from George Gershwin's own mouth when he said to me, 'Todd, you're not singing what we're after. This is a bitter song and you have to sing it with tongue-in-cheek; you have to sing it smiling all the time. Because what you're doing is making fun of us. You're making fun of people who make money and to whom power and position is very important.'" Wyatt and Johnson, p. 224.

27. Hamm, p. 512.

28. *Boston Herald*, Oct. 1, 1935. *Boston Traveler*, Oct. 1, 1935. *Christian Science Monitor*, Oct. 1, 1935. See also *New York Herald Tribune*, Oct. 1, 1935.

29. *Boston Evening American*, Oct. 1, 1935. *Billboard*, Oct. 2, 1935. *Variety*, Oct. 2, 1935.

30. Mamoulian's memory, in later life, that all the cuts preceded the Boston run, cannot be correct. Also, there were cuts made after the New York opening.

31. Duncan in Armitage, p. 62. Gershwin in Pollack, p. 602. Duncan in Wyatt and Johnson, p. 198.

32. Armitage, p. 52.

33. Duncan and Swift in Pollack, p. 602. Gershwin in LOC scrapbook. *New York Times*, Oct. 20, 1935. Ira in LOC scrapbook.

34. DuBose Heyward, *Jasbo Brown and Selected Poems* (1931), p. 9.

35. "While the chorus sing [*sic*] primitive pentatonic Da-doo-das, Jazzbo [*sic*] introduces the tawdry sophistication of Tin Pan Alley chromatics; the two worlds of the folk community and of New York are . . . juxtaposed," writes Wilfrid Mellers in *Music in a New Found Land* (1964), p. 394.

36. Mamoulian in Bennett Oberstein, "The Broadway Directing Career of Rouben Mamoulan," diss., Indiana University (1977), p. 186. Brown in Wyatt and Johnson, p. 233. Linchpin: see Mellers, p. 402. Some half a dozen other "Mamoulian cuts," if less instantly conspicuous, are relatively prominent. The deletion of Maria's denunciation of Sporting Life ("I hate yo' struttin' style") and the picnic jubilation "I Ain't Got No Shame" shorten Gershwin's profuse 90-minute act 2 (acts 1 and 3 of the vocal score last approximately 60 and 45 minutes). An abridgment of the trio "Oh Bess, O Where's My Bess" spares Porgy a high F at the end of the evening. (According to Duncan, this last cut was for Gershwin the cruelest of all—an understandable opinion.) Several Mamoulian cuts eliminate strophic repetition. We have already encountered two examples: trimming "Leavin' for the Promise' Land" and "A Red-Headed Woman," Mamoulian secures a more consolidated forward thrust. He also cuts verses from the mourning chorus for the storm victims (act 3, scene 1), the Honey Man's Call (act 2, scene 3), and "Oh, de Sun Goin' to Rise" (act 2, scene 4). Where Gershwin is prolix—the act 1 craps game; Crown's hurricane scene harangue, taunting Peter and Serena; the act 3 fight between Porgy and Crown—Mamoulian snips and tucks with positive results. (Gershwin's storm music would have been similarly curtailed had it not become a means of covering a time-consuming scene change.) Deleted and unmissed are Mr. Archdale's ultimatum to Lawyer Frazier ("this divorce mill must close") and a chunk of the Detective's act 3 interrogation of Serena and Porgy.

37. Hamm, pp. 514–526.

38. Pollack, p. 602.

39. According to the *Playbill* for the show.

40. In early 1938, Merle Armitage toured *Porgy and Bess* in California in a production codirected by Mamoulian.

41. A survey of more than three dozen New York reviews does not support Howard Pollack's generalization that "the reviews parted ways most, perhaps, over Mamoulian's direction. Some found it brilliant and inspired—and a welcome change from the wooden stagings at the Met—while others thought it fussy and mechanical." See Pollack, p. 606.

42. All reviews Oct. 11, 1935, except *Stage* magazine, Oct. 1935.

43. *The Nation*, Oct. 30, 1935. *New Republic*, Oct. 30, 1935.

44. *New York Times*, Oct. 11, 1935.

45. *New York Herald Tribune*, Oct. 1, 1935.

46. Paul Rosenfeld, *Discoveries of a Music Critic* (1936), pp. 264–272.

47. Johnson in *Opportunity* 14, no. 1 (Jan. 1936). Pollack, pp. 167, 607.

48. Virgil Thomson, "George Gershwin," *Modern Music*, Nov.–Dec. 1935.

49. No subsequent writer has surpassed Henderson's characterization of the polyvalent slow movement: "It is an idealized slave song made to fit the impressive quiet of night on the prairie. When the star of empire took its way over those mighty Western plains blood and sweat and agony and bleaching human bones marked its course. Something of this awful buried sorrow of the prairie must have forced itself upon Dr. Dvorak's mind when he saw the plains after reading 'The Famine' [i.e., Minnehaha's death, in Longfellow's *The Song of Hiawatha*]." *New York Times*, Dec. 17, 1935.

50. *New York Times*, Dec. 17, 1893.

51. Addressing "Gershwin's use of leitmotivs and motivic development as sources of unity and continuity," Starr explored treatments of rhythmic, harmonic, and melodic aspects of Porgy's theme. In a subsequent book (2011), Starr stressed the dramatic and musical integration of "Broadway" and "opera" in the ostensible "melting pot" of Gershwin styles. Even in "My Man's Gone Now," where Gershwin is most operatic, Starr wrote, the "venerable old Broadway AABA" form is in play; even where Gershwin is most lighthearted, as in "I Got Plenty O' Nuttin'," the rapid expansion of harmonic horizons leads to expressive realms unknown in all previous "banjo songs." And, celebrating one of the opera's most criticized features, Starr called Gershwin's recitatives "remarkably diverse and imaginative," "little jewels of melody . . . on virtually every page of the score."

52. "Thrilled" in Pollack, p. 145. Christopher Reynolds, "*Porgy and Bess*: An American *Wozzeck*," *Journal of the Society for American Music* 1, no. 1 (Feb. 2007).

53. Pollack, p. 800.

54. "Bastards" in 1973 interview cited in Oberstein, p. 47. Duncan, Elzy, Bubbles, Brown, Harvey in LOC scrapbook. Jessye (Dec. 13, 1935) in LOC, box 116, folder 5.

55. Mamoulian in Oberstein, p. 229. Telegrams and Duncan letter in LOC scrapbook.

56. *New York Times*, July 12, 1937.

57. Heifetz in album note by Greg Gormick, "*Porgy and Bess*—Early Recordings," Naxos 8.110219-20. Leonard Stein, ed., *Style and Idea* (1975), p. 477. Pollack, p. 134.

58. Oberstein, p. 198.

59. Pollack, pp. 11, 205. "Cantorial" in Horowitz, p. 467.

60. Armitage, p. 56.

61. I am indebted to Mark Spergel for sharing this essay with me—and to Agnes Horowitz and Olga Verterich for translating it.

62. William Becvar, "The Stage and Film Career of Rouben Mamoulian," diss., University of Kansas (1975), p. 69.

63. Rosenfeld, p. 269.

CHAPTER 4: *PORGY AND BESS* AND HOLLYWOOD

1. Ira quote in Larry Starr, *George Gershwin* (2011), p. 154. Howard Pollack, *George Gershwin: His Life and Work* (2006), p. 667.
2. Pollack, p. 667.
3. The entire score, as Howard Pollack observes, shows Gershwin mastering the latest popular swing styles directly in the wake of *Porgy and Bess* (Pollack, p. 672).
4. It successfully resurfaced as a novelty piece titled *Promenade*.
5. Pollack, pp. 673, 674, 675.
6. Levant, Gershwin, and Zorina in Pollack, pp. 686–687.
7. Mark Spergel, *Reinventing Reality: The Art and Life of Rouben Mamoulian* (1993), p. 173.
8. Andrew Sarris, *Hollywood Voices: Interviews with Film Directors* (1971), p. 60.
9. Joseph Horowitz, *Artists in Exile: How Refugees from Twentieth-Century War and Revolution Transformed the American Performing Arts* (2008), p. 360.
10. Mark N. Grant, *The Rise and Fall of the Broadway Musical* (2004), p. 238. Roberts in Horowitz, *Artists in Exile*, p. 360. Buloff in Bennett Oberstein, "The Broadway Directing Career of Rouben Mamoulian," diss., Indiana University (1977), p. 251. *Theatre Arts*, Oct. 1935.
11. Molnár in Horowitz, *Artists in Exile*, p. 360. Grant, p. 242.
12. Mamoulian and his wife remained cordially in touch with Richard and Dorothy Rodgers until Richard died in 1979. In fact, Mamoulian was expected to direct Helen Hayes in *Happy Birthday*, a 1946 Rodgers and Hammerstein production. "There is no doubt in my mind that you can handle this piece more skillfully and successfully than any other director in the business," Rodgers wrote to Mamoulian on January 23, 1946. (Rouben Mamoulian Archive, Library of Congress [LOC], box 154.)
13. Spergel, pp. 188–210.
14. Richard Rodgers, *Musical Stages: An Autobiography* (1975), p. 223.
15. Spergel, p. 232.
16. Spergel, p. 232.
17. In 1933, Tibbett had galvanized Metropolitan Opera audiences singing *The Emperor Jones* in blackface. In 1953, well past his prime, he was scheduled to sing *Porgy and Bess* onstage in the Robert Breen production, but canceled because of "food poisoning." (See Pollack, p. 620.)
18. Brown in Robert Wyatt and John Andrew Johnson, *The George Gershwin Reader* (2004), p. 229. Warfield, *Pittsburgh Courier*, and Hicks in Pollack, pp. 617 and 621.
19. Pollack, p. 648.
20. Poitier, in conversation with the author (Sept. 20, 2011), stressed that he discovered himself nominated to play Porgy through no initiative of his own. (A friend with whom I shared this exchange memorably quipped that casting Poitier as Porgy "was like casting Barack Obama as Sporting Life.") Of the film itself, Poitier said:

"I don't talk about it. I've dismissed it. I did it, I didn't want to do it. I did not want to be stopped in my tracks."

21. Interview with the author, Sept. 12, 2011.
22. LOC, boxes 84, 85, 86.
23. Spergel, p. 225. *Los Angeles Evening Mirror News*, July 2, 1958.
24. LOC, box 87, folder 3.
25. LOC, box 87, folder 3.
26. LOC, box 87.
27. Spergel, p. 223.
28. Spergel, pp. 223–224.
29. Mamoulian probably exaggerated his role in persuading Poitier and Dandridge to undertake *Porgy and Bess*. A variety of documents confirm that both Goldwyn and Mamoulian met with Poitier during the casting process. But Poitier (in a Sept. 20, 2011, interview with the author) does not remember any significant interactions with Mamoulian. Mamoulian's other claims, in his letter to the Guild, are supportable. Previn (in a Sept. 12, 2011, interview with the author) does not remember which "compressions" of Gershwin's score were his own, which Mamoulian's. That Previn congratulated Mamoulian for his work on the score is true; the claim that Previn denied having worked with Mamoulian on the recording is obviously false. Previn recalls that Preminger discarded the recordings undertaken by Mamoulian; he started over. But the surviving evidence is conflicting. It seems unlikely that the recordings for Mamoulian were wholly (or even mostly) discarded. For Preminger's allegations, see LOC, box 87.
30. LOC, box 87.
31. Previn interview with the author, Sept. 12, 2011. A. Scott Berg, *Goldwyn: A Biography* (1989), p. 486.
32. *Variety*, May 27, 1959.
33. Previn interview.
34. Goldwyn's film singularly failed to credit the singers dubbing Porgy, Bess, Serena, and Clara. The cover of the original cast recording, on Columbia Records, showed only three names: "Porgy," "Bess," and "Goldwyn." Preminger complained loudly that he was insufficiently acknowledged as the film's director.
35. *New York Times*, July 6, 1959. *Washington Post*, Oct. 15, 1959. *Time*, July 6, 1959. *Ebony*, Oct. 1959. UPI, July 26, 1959.
36. Not composed by André Previn, according to André Previn (Previn interview).
37. Previn: "Sidney told me he was 'tone-deaf.' I said 'C'mon.' So I sat down at the piano and played two notes, one at the top of the keyboard, one at the bottom. 'Now which note is higher?' I asked Poitier. 'It's your job to tell me,' he answered." (Previn interview).
38. Previn interview.
39. I am indebted to Mark Spergel for sharing with me various late Mamoulian jottings and writings, including this poem.

40. Hovsepian, Kreuger, and Osheen Keshishian interviewed by the author, Nov. 14, 2011.

41. The filmed interview is a bonus feature on the Kino Video DVD (2003) of Mamoulian's *Applause*.

42. Richard Crawford, "It Ain't Necessarily Soul: Gershwin's *Porgy and Bess* as a Symbol," *Anuario Interamericano de Investigación Musical* 8 (1972). Friedrich in Pollack, p. 626.

43. Mamoulian saw it and complained: "They put in all the recitatives which I had cut, the Buzzard Song. . . . the [Jasbo Brown] piano music." Miles Kreuger, ed., program for Gershwin tribute at Wilshire Theatre, Beverly Hills, March 21 and 22, 2009.

44. For the author's *Times Literary Supplement* review ("*Porgy and Bess* Writ Small"): http://www.artsjournal.com/uq/2012/02/porgy-and-bess-writ-small.html.

45. Wilfrid Mellers, *Music in a New Found Land* (1964), p. 413. Crawford, p. 32.

46. At the same time, Todd Duncan said of O'Brien's production, "Every single move is just right. It is so Negro." In Pollack, p. 629.

47. LOC, box 36.

48. Bing must have meant *Rosalinda*, which played on Broadway from 1942 to 1944.

49. LOC, box 36.

50. May 15 letter, Metropolitan Opera Archives, LOC, box 36.

51. LOC, box 124.

52. Letter from Frederick Koch, Aug. 14, 1966, LOC, box 125.

53. LOC, box 204.

54. LOC, box 125.

55. Bizet's act 2 entr'acte—a perky soldier's march with staccato accompaniment—is positioned in between José's arrest ending act 1 (he has just permitted Carmen to escape) and the Gypsies of Lillas Pastia's inn igniting act 2. Mamoulian applies the march to a military prison corridor. José is being led to a cell. "The sharp clicking of military heels and the jangle of spurs"—Mamoulian's response to Bizet's snare drum accompaniment—"is echoed by the stone walls." Antonio, a corporal, banters: "Two months in jail for a Gypsy! Men are fools, fools! . . . You know what Dolores did to me last year?" "Corporal, I am not interested," José responds. Antonio throws his arms up and walks away. The orchestra's bassoons and pizzicato strings chortle in response. Mamoulian repositions the act 3 entr'acte so that it directly precedes the act 4 entr'acte—creating a substantial playground for pantomime. Micaela has just told José—now an outlaw rebuffed and disgraced—that his mother is dying. In the distance, Escamillo sings his song, boasting of conquests to come. Bizet here proceeds to the bullring and act 4. Mamoulian proceeds to a small country house "mellowed by time and poverty." The act 3 entr'acte, repositioned, now accompanies an episode new to *Carmen*: José visits his dying mother. To the strains of Bizet's exquisite flute and harp interlude, the mother expires in the arms of her son. The stomping act 4 entr'acte shat-

ters the mood. We see Carmen's room. Immune to José, she is excitedly dressing for the bullfight. A poster of Escamillo, on the wall, dissolves to Escamillo's apartment. He is donning his matador's wardrobe. Dissolve to a bull pen and its restless occupant, to the crowds entering the arena. Dissolve to José on the street, pale and feverish. The ebullient entr'acte now becomes bitterly ironic. Bizet, in his opera, sets the fatal confrontation of José and Carmen outside the arena. Mamoulian, in his film, cuts repeatedly to the pageantry inside: the procession of toreadors, banderilleros, and picadors, the crowd's surging enthusiasm, Escamillo's mastery of cape and sword. Outside the arena, José plunges his knife into Carmen's breast. In Bizet, the crowd, leaving the arena, enters and stares mutely; the orchestra pounds its cadence; the curtain falls. This terse conclusion is difficult to stage convincingly: it is over the moment it begins. And so Mamoulian expands the last page of the score. He has Escamillo rush into view to a reprise of the Toreador Song. Then the fate theme returns fortissimo. The orchestra cadences softly.

56. Kreuger interview.
57. LOC, box 158, folder 7.
58. Spergel, p. 15.
59. Spergel, pp. 240–243.
60. In a late Jotting, looking back, Mamoulian called *Applause* an "underground" film.
61. LOC, box 140, folder 2.
62. Leonard Stein, ed., *Style and Idea: Selected Writings of Arnold Schoenberg* (1975), p. 476. Mamoulian in LOC, box 116, folder 5.
63. Joseph Horowitz, *Understanding Toscanini: How He Became an American Culture-God and Helped Create a New Audience for New Music* (1987), pp. 189–196.
64. *Partisan Review*, Spring 1960.
65. Horowitz, *Understanding Toscanini*, pp. 206–210.

PERMISSIONS

―――― ∿ ――――

TEXT CREDITS

PHOTOGRAPH CREDITS

INDEX

ABOUT THE AUTHOR

———— ᨆ ————

JOSEPH HOROWITZ was born in New York City in 1948. He is the author of nine previous books, including (for W. W. Norton) *Classical Music in America: A History* (2005), an *Economist* best book of the year. His book-in-progress is a historical novel about Anton Seidl and American Wagnerism in the late Gilded Age. From 1992 to 1997 he served as artistic advisor and then executive director of the Brooklyn Philharmonic Orchestra, resident orchestra of the Brooklyn Academy of Music, and there pioneered in juxtaposing orchestral repertoire with folk and vernacular sources, engaging gamelan orchestras, flamenco dancers and singers, and Russian and Hungarian folk artists. He has subsequently served as an artistic advisor to various American orchestras, most regularly the Pacific Symphony. He has also cofounded, with the conductor Angel Gil-Ordóñez, PostClassical Ensemble, a chamber orchestra in Washington, D.C. For the NEH he has directed a National Education Project and a Teacher-Training Institute, both dealing with "Dvořák and America," and "Music Unwound," a national consortium of orchestras engaged in contextualized thematic programming as a new template for the field. He has taught at CUNY, Colorado College, the Eastman School, the New England Conservatory, the Manhattan School of Music, and Mannes College. He regularly contributes articles and reviews to the *Times Literary Supplement* (UK); other publications for which he has written include *American Music, The New Grove Dictionary of Music and Musicians, The New Grove Dictionary of Opera*, the *Musical Quarterly*, the *New York Review of Books*, and *Nineteenth-Century Music*. He is the author of "Classical Music" for both the *Oxford Encyclopedia of American History* and the *Encyclopedia of New York State*. His website is www.josephhorowitz.com. His blog is www.artsjournal.com/uq.